Overfitting and Heuristics
in Philosophy

THE RUTGERS LECTURES IN PHILOSOPHY

Dean Zimmerman, series editor

School of Arts and Sciences

Published in the series

Vagueness: A Global Approach
Kit Fine

*Freedom of Speech and Expression:
Its History, Its Value, Its Good Use, and Its Misuse*
Richard Sorabji

Propositions: Ontology and Logic
Robert Stalnaker

Overfitting and Heuristics in Philosophy
Timothy Williamson

Overfitting and Heuristics in Philosophy

TIMOTHY WILLIAMSON

Oxford University Press is a department of the University of Oxford. It furthers the University's objective of excellence in research, scholarship, and education by publishing worldwide. Oxford is a registered trade mark of Oxford University Press in the UK and certain other countries.

Published in the United States of America by Oxford University Press
198 Madison Avenue, New York, NY 10016, United States of America.

© Oxford University Press 2024

All rights reserved. No part of this publication may be reproduced, stored in a retrieval system, or transmitted, in any form or by any means, without the prior permission in writing of Oxford University Press, or as expressly permitted by law, by license, or under terms agreed with the appropriate reproduction rights organization. Inquiries concerning reproduction outside the scope of the above should be sent to the Rights Department, Oxford University Press, at the address above.

You must not circulate this work in any other form
and you must impose this same condition on any acquirer.

CIP data is on file at the Library of Congress
ISBN 978–0–19–777921–7

DOI: 10.1093/oso/9780197779217.001.0001

The manufacturer's authorised representative in the EU for product safety is Oxford University Press España S.A. of El Parque Empresarial San Fernando de Henares, Avenida de Castilla, 2 – 28830 Madrid (www.oup.es/en or product.safety@oup.com). OUP España S.A. also acts as importer into Spain of products made by the manufacturer.

Contents

Series Foreword   vii
Preface   ix

1. Heuristics   1
   1.1 Counterexamples   1
   1.2 What are heuristics?   2
   1.3 The persistence heuristic   7
   1.4 The suppositional heuristic for conditionals   16
   1.5 Disquotation and heuristics for belief ascription   27
   1.6 The weighing heuristic for reasons   39
   1.7 Implications for philosophical methodology   43

2. Overfitting and Degrees of Freedom   51
   2.1 Error-fragility   51
   2.2 Data fitting   56
   2.3 Overfitting in philosophical analysis   63
   2.4 Overfitting in semantics   73
   2.5 Overfitting in logic   84
   2.6 Overfitting in philosophical model-building   94
   2.7 Summing up   103

3. Case Study: Hyperintensionalism   105
   3.1 Two revolutions?   105
   3.2 Extensional, intensional, hyperintensional   111
   3.3 Hyperintensional semantics: impossible worlds   118
   3.4 Hyperintensional semantics: truthmakers   129
   3.5 Hyperintensional semantics: Russellian propositions   135
   3.6 The 'why?' heuristic   145

4. Frege Puzzles   159
   4.1 Representational hyperintensionality   159
   4.2 The Fregean consensus   161

4.3	The failure of the Fregean consensus	162
4.4	Frege puzzles and synonymy	166
4.5	Frege puzzles from the inside	174
4.6	The necessary a posteriori and the contingent a priori	177
4.7	Heuristics for belief ascription	181
4.8	Heuristics for knowledge ascription	192
4.9	Evidence	202
4.10	Probability	211
4.11	Epistemic and doxastic logic	222
4.12	Drawing the threads together	225
5.	Intensional Metametaphysics	230
5.1	Semantic challenges to metaphysics	230
5.2	The coarse-grained challenge to metaphysics	234
5.3	Generalizing the problem	237
5.4	The metalinguistic strategy	244
5.5	Reconceiving the problem	248
5.6	In brief	255

Bibliography   257
Index   271

Series Foreword

The Rutgers Lectures in Philosophy were established by Larry Temkin when he was chair of the department, and the inaugural lectures were given in 2016 by Kit Fine. Larry's plan was simple and has proven successful: the lecture series would bring some of the best philosophers in the world to Rutgers for an extended visit. While here, each lecturer would give three talks as well as informally exchange ideas with faculty, graduate students, and undergraduates. With the expert editorial assistance of Oxford University Press, each philosopher's lectures would appear as a monograph in an elegant series of volumes.

The faculty of philosophy at Rutgers remain grateful to Larry for designing a vehicle for philosophical engagement that continues to enrich our department; to Peter Ohlin of Oxford University Press for coming up with the idea of a published Rutgers lecture series, working out the details, and overseeing production of the books; and to the dean's office of the School of Arts and Sciences for steadfast support. We are especially grateful to Timothy Williamson for coming to Rutgers and introducing us to the exciting ideas found in these pages.

Karen Bennett and Dean Zimmerman
New Brunswick, New Jersey
January 2024

Preface

Although the occasion for this book was recent, it came as a welcome opportunity to explain and explore the confluence of two lines of thought about philosophical methodology on which I had been brooding separately for much longer. They correspond to the two words conjoined in the title, 'overfitting' and 'heuristics'.

In April 2020 I received an email from Larry Temkin with an invitation to give the Rutgers Lectures in Philosophy once COVID-19 permitted. I was delighted to accept, and finally gave the three lectures at Rutgers in September 2022. They grew into the first three chapters of this book.

The two earlier lines of thought developed thus:

Overfitting. As an undergraduate at Oxford in the mid-1970s, studying mathematics and philosophy, I remember feeling disgust at the ugly, messy, *ad hoc* complications of the analyses many contemporary philosophers seemed content with. They contrasted sharply with the elegant, powerful, well-motivated definitions central to logic and mathematics. I knew how unlikely one was to make significant progress if one started from bad definitions. In a space of abstract structures, a sense of form functions as a compass; without it one wanders, lost. My paradigm of a philosopher guided by a strong aesthetic sensibility has always been Plato; in his own metaphor, he understood the need to cut at the joints.

I wrote my DPhil thesis on approximation to the truth (1976–80), inspired by Karl Popper's failed conception of verisimilitude. Of my philosophical contemporaries at Oxford, I was closest to the late Peter Lipton, whose DPhil thesis on inference to the best explanation later became a classic book on the topic (Lipton 1991). Loveliness (his preferred term) as a criterion for a good explanation was a familiar theme in our conversations. Already then, what is now called a broadly abductive methodology struck me as the only viable approach to philosophical theorizing, despite the opposition of my final supervisor, Michael Dummett. In my book on vagueness (Williamson 1994), the case for an epistemicist theory is fundamentally abductive. Alternatives to classical logic and bivalent semantics are not dismissed as ultimately nonsensical; they are just inferior theories, judged by normal scientific standards. In *Knowledge and Its Limits* (Williamson 2000), I treat attempts to analyse knowledge, causation, meaning, and so on in more basic terms like Ptolemaic astronomy, to which new epicycles must continually be added to fix up anomalies. To invoke Imre Lakatos's useful category, many philosophers seemed unable to recognize a degenerating research programme when they saw one.

Oddly, the first edition of *The Philosophy of Philosophy* (Williamson 2007) mentions abductive methods only in passing. The reason was not any temporary loss of confidence in them but simply that my main concern was to correct more basic misconceptions about philosophical questions and evidence in philosophy. Once the book was published and I had to answer frequently asked questions about my positive view of philosophical methodology, I found myself giving centre stage to abduction and soon wished I had discussed it properly in the book, rather than leaving it to do its work offstage. I later started to fill the gap with articles on abductive theory comparison in philosophy (Williamson 2016c, reprinted in the second edition of *The Philosophy of Philosophy*) and in logic (Williamson 2017b). In particular, classical logic is unrivalled in its combination of simplicity, strength, and fit with evidence.

Around that time, inspired by a seminal paper by Malcolm Forster and Elliott Sober (1994), I started connecting overcomplication as an abductive vice in philosophical theories with overfitting as a recognized pathology in the natural and social sciences, where it prototypically manifests as profligacy with degrees of freedom in fitting quantitative data: at each stage, an equation with many parameters closely fits the data so far but makes bad predictions about new data, and so is replaced by a new equation with even more parameters that closely fits the old and new data so far, and so on. Of course, the data in philosophy are rarely quantitative, so the specific mathematical results that Forster and Sober use to justify tight limits on degrees of freedom are not relevant to philosophy. Nevertheless, one can recognize a similar pattern in philosophical programmes of analysis, with accepted verdicts on real or hypothetical cases as the data and proposed analyses of the target term in place of equations. At each stage, a complicated analysis fits the accepted verdicts on the cases so far, but makes bad predictions about new cases, and so is replaced by a new, even more complicated analysis that fits the accepted verdicts on the old and new cases so far, and so on.

As a reality check, I have taken to asking scientists whom I find myself sitting next to at a meal whether overfitting is a problem in their research area. In my experience, they are all familiar with overfitting, both the word and the pathology, and can get quite worked up denouncing the practice. Their understanding of it is informal, not narrowly mathematical: they see overfitting as a lazy-minded way of describing a data set without gaining theoretical insight into what is really going on. Of course, on an informal understanding of overfitting, one cannot expect an algorithm for determining what counts and what does not. It takes experience and good judgment to determine in a particular case how many degrees of freedom are too many, how much complication is too much. So understood, overfitting in philosophy is possible, and indeed actual. It is therefore cause for concern how many philosophers have never even heard of overfitting and how few are on the alert for it as a danger in philosophical theorizing. One aim of this book is to do some consciousness-raising.

There is a gap in the story so far. The main reason why overfitting in natural and social science leads to bad predictions is that it is too respectful of occasional erroneous data points, which are almost certain to arise in large data sets, if only through random noise. Such errors are then built into an overfitted equation. To complete the analogy with overfitting in natural and social science, we need to understand how errors can arise in philosophers' accepted case judgments. Such judgments are sometimes even assigned a quasi-definitional status. In *The Philosophy of Philosophy*, my focus was on showing that accepted verdicts on hypothetical cases in philosophy are in effect just ordinary judgments of counterfactual conditionals and can be known in the same ordinary ways: appeals to conceptual truth, philosophical intuition and so on are obscurantist and miss the point. Although such an anti-exceptionalist account supports the generic expectation that accepted case judgments in philosophy will be subject in principle to ordinary human error, it does not supply details. Will the errors be just occasional random noise, or are they more systematic? How big is the problem?

The most high-profile attempt to show that accepted case judgments in philosophy are unreliable has been the 'negative program' of experimental philosophy, which tried to show that judgments on given cases vary with factors irrelevant to their truth, such as ethnicity, gender, and the order of the questions, using the methods of social psychology. However, in recent years, the negative program—though not experimental philosophy itself—has largely run out of steam. Many of its signature results turned out not to be repeatable, once the experiments were done with proper controls. In other cases, experiments were poorly designed because subjects were asked questions involving words used as technical terms in philosophy. Indeed, there is increasing evidence that many of the crucial case judgments are more like human universals. Meanwhile, general epistemological arguments for the negative program implicitly supported more general forms of scepticism inimical to science, contrary to their proponents' intentions. This book does not discuss the negative program in detail; the first edition of *The Philosophy of Philosophy* contains an initial critique of it, the 2021 edition supplies more specific and extensive objections, and I prefer not to repeat myself.

However, the negative program is not the only threat to the reliability of accepted case judgments. The second line of thought leading to this book concerns a potential source of error in case judgments even when they are humanly universal.

Heuristics. In *The Philosophy of Philosophy*, another role for our ordinary capacity to know counterfactual conditionals is in explaining our knowledge of metaphysical modality—necessity, contingency, possibility, impossibility. In a standard combined logic for counterfactual conditionals and modal operators, something is necessary if and only if its negation counterfactually implies a contradiction, and similar equivalences hold for the other modal operators. Thus, if your cognitive system has the power to handle counterfactual conditionals, it also has the power to handle modal operators. This does not require it to *define* the latter in terms of the former; it just needs to handle them alike.

The equivalences are validated by standard semantic accounts of modal operators and counterfactual conditionals in a framework of possible worlds. They can also be derived by standard modal logic from two plausible and more general linking principles: first, whatever is necessarily implied is counterfactually implied; second, no possibility counterfactually implies an impossibility. So far, everything fits nicely together. Integral to this picture is the *vacuous truth of counterpossibles*: any counterfactual conditional with an impossible antecedent is true. That follows from the first linking principle by standard modal logic, for an impossibility necessarily implies anything. Semantically, no world is a counter-instance to a counterfactual conditional whose antecedent is false at every world.

Around 2004, in the run-up to *The Philosophy of Philosophy*, I started presenting this material in talks on the epistemology of modality. One feature of the reactions slightly took me aback: the vehemence with which many able philosophers rejected the vacuous truth of counterpossibles, on the basis of what they took to be decisive counterexamples, obviously false counterpossibles. The alleged counterexamples themselves did not surprise me. *Of course*, pre-reflectively, some counterpossibles—such as 'If there were a largest prime, it would make no difference to mathematics'—struck me (and still strike me) as repugnant. What I found naïve or frivolous was the confidence with which carefully developed, elegant and powerful logical and semantic theories were thrown out on the basis of such uncritically accepted first impressions. It only got worse when cumbersome, feeble, and unexplanatory alternatives such as semantic frameworks of impossible worlds were invoked as substitutes to vindicate whatever the first impressions happened to be. In teaching logic to clever students, one spends much of one's time explaining how plausible-sounding objections to standard theorems are subtly mistaken. In present terminology, I regard 'counterexamples' to the vacuous truth of counterpossibles as clear cases of overfitting.

Still, an explanatory task remains. *Why* do the 'counterexamples' seem so compelling? It is surely not just a brute psychological fact. I noticed two features of typical alleged examples of false counterpossibles. First, they are rejected on the basis of what seems to be very shallow cognitive processing: the judgment is immediate, and the antecedent's impossibility plays no apparent role. After all, they are presented as *obvious* counterexamples. Second, the opposite counterpossible is found obviously *true*, where opposite counterfactuals have the same antecedent and mutually contradictory consequents, as in 'If p were true, q would be true' and 'If p were true, q would be false'. For example, we accept the counterpossible 'If there were a largest prime, it would make a difference to mathematics' without needing to consider whether its antecedent is impossible or just contingently false. We just think how much actual mathematics involves the infinity of primes. This suggests the hypothesis that we treat opposite counterfactuals as mutually inconsistent, so, having accepted one, we immediately reject the other.

Opponents of the vacuous truth of counterpossibles might respond that we treat opposite counterfactuals as mutually inconsistent because they *are* mutually inconsistent; so two opposite counterpossibles cannot both be true. However, the principle does not fit our practice in full generality. For, on the equally obvious-seeming principle that a conjunction counterfactually implies its conjuncts, we accept both 'If the Russell set were a member of itself and not a member of itself, it would be a member of itself' and 'If the Russell set were a member of itself and not a member of itself, it would be not a member of itself', which are opposite counterfactuals. The mutual inconsistency of opposite counterfactuals is also hard to reconcile with their natural use to articulate arguments by *reductio ad absurdum*, when we refute the hypothesis h by proving (for some q) *both* 'If h were true, q would be true' *and* 'If h were true, q would be false'.

I therefore proposed treating the mutual inconsistency of opposite counterfactuals as a *heuristic* in the psychologists' sense: a cognitive shortcut, reliable in most but not all cases. I generalized it to the mutual inconsistency of counterfactuals with the same antecedent and *contrary* consequents, which need not be contradictory, such as 'If Maria were in Europe, she would be in Italy' and 'If Maria were in Europe, she would be in Spain'. We often rely on heuristics without realizing that we are doing so, for example, when they are built into our unconscious perceptual processing. I argued that apparent examples of false counterpossibles are artefacts of our unconscious reliance on the heuristic for mutual inconsistency of counterfactuals. It fails *only* for counterpossibles; since few counterfactuals are counterpossibles, it is quite reliable. Those who take themselves to be refuting the vacuous truth of counterpossibles have been suckered by their own heuristics (Williamson 2017c, 2018b).

However, postulating one heuristic for handling the special case of counterfactuals with the same antecedent and contrary consequents left me in an unstable position. The heuristic leads you, having accepted one counterfactual, to reject other counterfactuals related to it in the special way, but it does not lead you to accept any counterfactual in the first place. It is useful only if you already have some *other* way of cognitively assessing counterfactuals and accepting or rejecting them. But if you have that other way, why do you need the heuristic for the special case?

Fortunately, the special heuristic hinted towards a much broader generalization. For simplicity, take the analogous case for plain conditionals, without 'would'. Compare 'If A, C' and 'If A, C^*', where C and C^* are contraries. Suppose A. On that supposition, we have C and C^*, an inconsistency. By the analogous special heuristic for plain conditionals, we project that inconsistency conditional on A onto an unconditional inconsistency between the corresponding conditionals with antecedent A. The general rule is to project an assessment of $C_1, \ldots, C_n$ on the supposition A onto the same assessment outright of the conditionals 'If A, C_1', ..., 'If A, C_n'. In particular, for $n = 1$, 'If A, C' is assessed outright as C is assessed on the supposition A. Thus, we accept 'If A, C' outright when we accept C on the supposition A, and we reject 'If A, C' outright when we reject C on the supposition A.

A similar pattern applies to counterfactual conditionals, with a slightly different style of assessment appropriate to counterfactual suppositions, which are more 'distanced' from reality. From this general heuristic, one can then recover the original principle that opposite counterfactuals are mutually inconsistent as a special case.

This large step of generalization is not meant as a compelling argument. It just explains how natural it was for me to reach the hypothesis of a simple, general, supposition-based heuristic for assessing conditionals. The hard work was then to show in detail how postulating such a heuristic explains our assessment of conditionals. I did that work in my book *Suppose and Tell: The Semantics and*

Heuristics of Conditionals (Williamson 2020a). Once I had the central idea, I wrote the book quickly, because everything fell into place much more smoothly and neatly than I had anticipated.

The suppositional heuristic was by no means a completely new idea. It is closely related to a seminal suggestion by Frank Ramsey about how we assess conditionals, known as the 'Ramsey test'. It is also reminiscent of the attractive, much-discussed, but problematic idea that the probability of a conditional should be the conditional probability of its consequent on its antecedent. More generally, it explains the central role of *imagination* in our assessment of conditionals, because the natural human way to develop the consequences of a supposition is by a reality-constrained exercise of the imagination. Indeed, that is arguably the main cognitive function of the imagination (Williamson 2016e). In turn, much of the cognitive value of using conditional words like 'if' is that they enable us to extract, articulate, and communicate information embedded in our experientially informed ways of developing suppositions, which are 'offline' analogues of our capacities for updating our expectations about the future 'online'.

Attempts to build such ideas about conditionals directly into their semantics had led to disaster, as shown by various impossibility theorems proved by David Lewis and others. In brief, the unqualified suppositional test is *inconsistent* in various ways, both in itself and with uncontentious background knowledge. From my perspective, those results showed, not that the ideas should be abandoned but that their plausibility comes from their match to the *heuristics*, not to the semantics, of conditionals. An inconsistent test can give correct results most of the time, but it cannot be *valid*.

Since the basic cognitive role of the imaginative assessment of conditionals makes it likely to be a human universal, it constitutes a potential source of error in our case judgments of conditionals which the usual methods of experimental philosophy would not pick up.

In postulating a general heuristic for conditionals, I have encountered far more resistance from semanticists in both philosophy and linguistics than I have from psychologists and psychologically informed philosophers. The latter groups' reaction seems to be: 'Of course we rely on heuristics in assessing conditionals, just as we do in other cognitive tasks—how else would we do it? The question is *which* heuristics we use.' By contrast, semanticists are more likely to question the need for an intermediate level of heuristics between the semantics and our assessments of particular conditionals in particular contexts. It is as if the semantic evaluation of the conditional in the context is transparent to competent speakers and hearers, cognitively effortless; they can read off its semantic status directly. Although it would be uncharitable to accuse semanticists of really believing that, I often find them reluctant to admit that the cognitive task might be hard enough to require heuristics. They seem understandably afraid that admitting the role of heuristics risks losing them their data, since common native speaker assessments of sample sentences will no longer be reliable. But such fears are overpessimistic. The natural sciences have operated for centuries with less than fully reliable data and have found ways to manage the risks. Aversion to overfitting is one of those ways. Significantly, contemporary semantics shows increasing signs of overfitting, with very complicated semantic clauses for common words (such as 'if'), and little sense that adding new parameters of semantic evaluation might have a cost in degrees of freedom. I have even seen simplicity as a criterion of theory choice incredulously rejected as quite alien to semantics. In *Suppose and Tell*, I argue that the 'paradoxes' of material implication and even more apparently decisive counterexamples to the simplest semantics for 'if', as a material conditional, are just artefacts of the suppositional heuristic, and that the material interpretation makes the best overall sense of our total practice of using conditionals, for example, to store and communicate information.

When writing the conditionals book, I naturally wondered what role heuristics might be playing in other philosophical problems.

Unsurprisingly, my thoughts turned to the problem of vagueness. I saw how the tolerance principles for vague terms which serve as major premises in sorites paradoxes can be understood as artefacts of a labour-saving heuristic. That some philosophers classify them as 'analytic' or 'conceptual connections' just indicates the poverty of the received list of options for general principles. It needs to be expanded with 'heuristic' as another option. To emphasize its generality, I added a few pages on tolerance principles as heuristics to *Suppose and Tell*. I even showed how to estimate their reliability in some cases: although tolerance principles generate paradoxes, in almost all instances they are truth-preserving. Subsequently, I realized that tolerance principles are just special cases of a much more general heuristic which is neither specific to vague terms nor merely labour-saving, but is instead practically unavoidable, as I explain below (chapter 1.3).

Other candidates for philosophically significant heuristics are also mentioned in the conditionals book, such as disquotational principles for truth and falsity: in continual use but responsible for the Liar and other semantic paradoxes.

Around the 1970s, the default front cover design for books of analytic philosophy showed a paradoxical image by the artist M. C. Escher. Philosophical paradoxes were analogized to visual illusions. Fallible heuristics built into our visual systems generate visual illusions; fallible heuristics built into our more general cognitive systems generate philosophical paradoxes. This book expands the project of tracing the role of heuristics in producing both genuine and illusory knowledge.

In deciding what to lecture on at Rutgers, I also had in mind a specific application of the general ideas about overfitting and heuristics:

Hyperintensionality. Studying philosophy at Oxford in the 1970s, I grew up in an environment where familiarity was assumed with the modal-metaphysical theorizing of Saul Kripke, David Lewis, and many others, even though such theorizing was regarded as suspect by still-influential figures of an older generation such as Michael Dummett and Donald Davidson. Of all these thinkers, Kripke impressed me most. He was unquestionably the best logician, and also, despite his day-to-day unworldliness, the philosopher most in touch with common sense realism. Even for those of my generation with different philosophical loyalties, 'Naming and Necessity' (at first the article version, Kripke 1972) was a central text in metaphysics, philosophical logic, the philosophy of language, and to some extent the philosophy of mind.

Older critiques of the Kripkean modal approach usually accused it of manufacturing illusory metaphysical distinctions, for instance, between the necessary and the a priori, or the essential and the accidental: in short, of making reality *too subtle*. By contrast, newer critiques of the approach increasingly accused it of neglecting more fine-grained metaphysical distinctions: in short, of making reality *not subtle enough*. For example, the possible worlds apparatus was well suited to defining relations of *supervenience* between families of properties, so one could claim that mental properties supervened on physical properties. By the 1980s, a commonly heard complaint in discussions of the mind-body problem was that the modal nature of supervenience made it unsuitable for capturing the sense in which, it was alleged, physical properties *determine* mental properties whereas mental properties do not determine physical properties; the challenge was to clarify the nature of such asymmetric determination. We were also uneasily aware of Elliott Sober's causal argument that some necessarily co-extensive properties are distinct (Sober 1982). Those were straws in a wind blowing towards what is now called *hyperintensional* metaphysics.

I first became aware of hyperintensional metaphysics as a systematic trend in 1992, when Kit Fine presented an early version of his seminal paper 'Essence and Modality' (Fine 1994) to a discussion group in Oxford, arguing for a non-modal conception of essence which distinguished between the necessarily co-extensive properties of being Socrates and being a member of the singleton set {Socrates}. I felt the power of Fine's examples. As his work developed, I also felt suspicious of the proliferating distinctions. They were not exactly unmotivated, but their motivation felt rather flimsy. In present terms, there was a whiff of overfitting. However, since I was working on other topics, mainly in epistemology, I could take a wait-and-see attitude, content to judge hyperintensional metaphysics by its explanatory fruits. A new research programme, ably pursued, deserves time and space to demonstrate its potential.

As the years passed, and hyperintensional metaphysics spread more widely, my scepticism increased. Instead of deriving many phenomena from a few simple laws, it seemed to derive a few phenomena from many complex laws. Still I did not engage with it, though in *Modal Logic as Metaphysics* (Williamson 2013a) I said, rather peremptorily, that only representational matters are hyperintensional. Finally, once my thoughts on overfitting and heuristics were sufficiently developed, I felt in a position to give a proper methodological critique of hyperintensional metaphysics. I could propose a psychologically plausible heuristic to explain data points of the kind typically presented as decisive counterexamples to merely intensional metaphysics, and why the heuristic is unreliable in such cases. I could also point to many signs of overfitting in the semantic frameworks used to make sense of hyperintensional theorizing.

Admittedly, I had previously assumed a hyperintensional treatment of representational phenomena, such as ascriptions of propositional attitudes. I had long rejected the Fregean distinction between sense and reference, because it is so ill-suited to the needs of natural language semantics, and, even in an individualistic setting, interposing a level of sense between the level of expressions and the level of reference does not pay its way in explanatory rewards. For many years, I envisaged a framework of Russellian structured propositions—complexes of the objects, properties, and relations they are about—as a reasonable compromise, with an unspecified fix for Russell-Myhill paradoxes. Robert Stalnaker's austerely intensionalist treatment of propositional attitudes as relations to sets of possible worlds seemed hopelessly coarse-grained, and his metalinguistic strategy for handling non-contingent discourse broke down. However, I realized that my preferred strategy for tracking cognitive significance in Frege cases of unrecognized co-reference—by relativizing attitudes to guises of propositions—in principle works just as well for intensional propositions as for structured ones. I gradually came to the conclusion that the huge extra complexity of a framework for structured propositions is not adequately compensated by the opportunity to do without guises in some but not all Frege cases. A better bargain is the simplicity of intensional content—which shares a common framework with both probabilistic approaches and epistemic and doxastic logic—combined with a willingness to relativize to guises (to which we are independently committed anyway) whenever we need to distinguish between different forms in which the same content can recur. A rough analogy: sometimes we can just make calculations about point masses; sometimes we must acknowledge that planets are more complicated than that.

This book is organized into five chapters:

Chapter 1, 'Heuristics', grew out of the first Rutgers lecture. It first discusses the nature of heuristics. It then describes several general heuristics and explains both why they are useful and how their limitations generate philosophical paradoxes. It concludes by assessing the implications for philosophical methodology of our unreflective reliance on such heuristics, arguing that they require a more sophisticated attitude to our data but do not justify scepticism. After all, fallible heuristics are built into our sensory systems and sometimes generate perceptual illusions, but that does not mean that scientists should stop using sense perception.

Chapter 2, 'Overfitting and Degrees of Freedom', grew out of the second Rutgers lecture. It first discusses the nature of overfitting, why it is a pathology, and why natural and social scientists emphasize the need for limiting degrees of freedom. It then describes apparent cases of overfitting in philosophy, especially in semantics, logic, philosophical analysis, and philosophical model-building, and discusses why philosophers may have stayed unaware of the danger. It emphasizes the need for philosophers' practice to be better informed by reflective awareness of abductive methodological constraints.

Chapter 3, 'Case Study: Hyperintensionalism', grew out of the third Rutgers lecture. It first discusses the nature of the distinctions between extensionalism, intensionalism, and hyperintensionalism, and how they map onto developments in the history of analytic philosophy. It then considers three frameworks for hyperintensional semantics, involving impossible worlds, truthmakers, and Russellian structured propositions, respectively, explaining their problems and in particular the extent to which they exhibit overfitting. Finally, a natural new heuristic is postulated to explain the case judgments underpinning typical 'counterexamples' to intensionalism. The heuristic is shown to generate errors in cases closely related to the alleged counterexamples, which are therefore not probative.

The final section adapts and develops some material from my lecture to celebrate the 25th anniversary of the journal *Disputatio*, delivered online to an audience in Lisbon in October 2021 and published as 'Degrees of freedom: is good philosophy bad science?', *Disputatio*, 13, 61 (2021): 73–94.

Chapter 4, 'Frege Puzzles', does not correspond to any of the Rutgers lectures but is included because it fills out my account of apparent hyperintensionality by discussing propositional attitude ascriptions. In particular, it shows how Kripke's article 'A Puzzle about Belief' (Kripke 1979) can be read against his intentions as pointing towards a fallible heuristic for ascribing belief and its absence. This leads to a discussion of heuristics for ascribing other attitudes and shows how Frege puzzles can be understood as manifesting the fallibility of those heuristics.

Much of the chapter uses material from my previously published article 'Epistemological consequences of Frege puzzles', *Philosophical Topics*, 49 (2021): 287–319, though with elimination of overlaps and significant revision. I have also added a section on heuristics for knowledge ascription, based on a section of my chapter 'Where did it come from? Where will it go?' in Arturs Logins and Jacques Vollet (eds.), *Putting Knowledge to Work: New Directions for Knowledge-First Epistemology* (Oxford: Oxford University Press, forthcoming), and modified the conclusions accordingly. Parts of section 4.10 and all of sections 4.11–12 are new.

Chapter 5, 'Intensional Metametaphysics', also does not correspond to any of the Rutgers lectures but is included because it fills out my account of apparent hyperintensionality in inquiries into non-contingent matters, mainly metaphysics, but logic and mathematics too. It argues that attempts to reinterpret such inquiries because they do not admit of non-trivial, substantive truths rest on a misdiagnosis of the problem and an underestimation of its generality. The underlying issue is not necessary truth but necessary equivalence, irrespective of the modal status of the equivalent propositions. It is just another manifestation of the coarse-grained consequences of intensionalism, and must be handled in the usual way. Metalinguistic reinterpretations of the relevant sentences do not work, but relativization to linguistic guises does. One should not conclude anything special about metaphysics, logic, or mathematics.

Most of the chapter uses material from my previous published article 'Metametaphysics and semantics', *Metaphilosophy*, 53: 2-3 (2022): 162–175, though with elimination of overlaps and significant revision.

Acknowledgments

First of all, I thank the Department of Philosophy at Rutgers, for the invitation, and all the hospitality and stimulus provided over the week of my enjoyable stay in New Brunswick. Those most involved in setting up, organizing, and running the events were Larry Temkin, Karen Bennett, and Dean Zimmerman. Unsurprisingly, the book has gained much from all the valuable constructive questions and comments from numerous members of the audiences at the lectures and participants in other discussions at Rutgers, formal and informal.

I thank Peter Ohlin of Oxford University Press (New York) for being such a supportive and efficient editor, a pleasure to deal with.

My wife Ana Mladenović Williamson kept the show on the road as always throughout the writing of this book.

In the period from writing rough drafts of the Rutgers lectures in August 2022 to submitting the final version of the book to Oxford University Press in October 2023, I have presented parts of the material at numerous events. Two of the most extensive presentations, in several sessions, both in the first half of 2023, were to a class at Yale University and a class at the University of Oxford. I also gave talks on parts of the material at a conference in Glasgow of the British Society for the Theory of Knowledge, a workshop at Bochum University on 'Experimental Philosophy and the Method of Cases', and a meeting of the student philosophy society at the University of Italian Switzerland, Lugano (all in 2022), a session of the American Philosophical Association Pacific Division Meeting in San Francisco on 'Modality, Essence, and Ground', three separate events at the London School of Economics (a symposium on Anna Mahtani's fine book *Objects of Credence*, a workshop, and a meeting of the student philosophy society), a conference at University of St Andrews on 'Analysis: History and Metaphilosophy', a LOGOS Anniversary Conference at the University of Barcelona, and a workshop on 'Higher-Order Metaphysics' at the University of

Oxford (all in 2023). I thank participants in all those events who helped improve the book in one way or another—disentangling the causal chains would be an impossible task.

I have also been extremely lucky in the philosophers who have read versions of all or part of the material and given me excellent feedback on it. The three referees for Oxford University Press provided comments of exactly the kind that are most *really* helpful at a comparatively late stage of the writing process; having agreed to waive their anonymity, they are Cian Dorr, John Hawthorne, and Brian Weatherson. At earlier stages, Jennifer Nagel, Mariona Miyata-Sturm, Daniel Kodsi, Alexander Roberts, and Benjamin Brast-McKie volunteered exceptionally detailed and perceptive written comments on the material in the first three chapters. In being given reactions of this quality from so many people, I feel that I am experiencing the philosophical community at its best.

Chapters 4 and 5 also inherit earlier acknowledgements from their article ancestors, which can be found in the footnotes to them.

In early October 2023, shortly before submitting the finalized manuscript to Oxford University Press, I gave it a last try-out in a week-long pre-read seminar with faculty and graduate students at the University of Costa Rica in San José, organized by Lorenzo Boccafogli. We did a chapter a day, with several hours of lively, focused discussion on each. The sessions led me to add several passages of further clarification and argument. I write these words in Playa Chiquita, Costa Rica, to an accompaniment of Caribbean forest sounds.

1
Heuristics

1.1 Counterexamples

Counterexamples keep theorists honest. It is easy to regard counterexamples as the epistemological gold standard, as in Karl Popper's falsificationism. But just as there is fool's gold as well as genuine gold, so there are fool's counterexamples as well as genuine counterexamples. And just as all of us can be fooled if we trust our first impressions of apparent gold, so all of us can be fooled if we trust our first impressions of apparent counterexamples.

To check whether something is genuine gold, you can ask to have it tested at your nearest assay office. To check whether something is a genuine counterexample to a philosophical generalization, you can ask to have it tested at your nearest philosophy department, though somehow that sounds less reassuring. You may be disappointed to find that the philosophers' tests hardly go deeper than their first impressions.

Of course, if your local philosophy department is slightly old-fashioned, it may claim to possess a philosopher's stone, which turns base metals into pure gold. The likely mechanism is to reclassify the proffered counterexample as an *analytic* or *conceptual* truth, built into the use of the relevant terms. But that will be unsatisfying if the source of the case judgment in question is also the source of other case judgments inconsistent with it. They cannot *all* be pure gold.

In this book, I will argue that many alleged examples and counterexamples in philosophy are the products of *heuristics*, which can produce mutually inconsistent case judgments, so we are indeed in the envisaged predicament. The philosophical questions are not usually *about* the heuristics, and we needn't use the heuristics in *asking* the questions. But we do rely on the heuristics to generate the data on whose basis we *answer* the questions. The trouble is that we tend to rely on those outputs uncritically, treating them as data that our theories must fit. When some of the outputs are false, we are liable to dismiss true theories erroneously, as falsified by those counterexamples. The apparent counterexamples may be all too convincing.

The situation is not all bad. If a heuristic produces mutually inconsistent outputs, *no* theory will be consistent with all of them together. False theories as well as true ones will appear falsified. Moreover, we may be able to identify what heuristics produced the outputs, and consequently to understand their strengths and weaknesses. That may enable us to handle our data in a more sophisticated and critical way, as other sciences have learnt to do. The occurrence of heuristic-induced errors is not a generic justification for scepticism. Our capacities for knowledge are hard to extricate from our propensities to error. The same cognitive systems enable us, in good cases, to learn how things are, yet, in bad cases, make us misjudge how they are: no risk, no gain. This interdependence of strength and weakness is crucial to the operation of the heuristics integral to so much cognition—human, animal, and artificial.

1.2 What are heuristics?

Roughly speaking, a heuristic is a rule of thumb for solving problems of some type. The application of the rule may be automatic or deliberate; it may be conscious, unconscious, or somewhere in between. Even if it involves conscious activity, one may or may not know what rule one is applying, and one may or may not think of it as a heuristic. Even on reflection, it may not be obvious to us when we are using a heuristic, still less what heuristic it is.

The function of a heuristic is to provide a way of solving problems of a given type that is fast, easy, efficient, and reliable enough to be useful. The way must be feasible in real time. It can be reliable enough without being *perfectly* reliable. Reliability here is equated with the probability that the way provides a *correct* solution, where the standard of correctness is built into the specification of the problem. For example, sniffing food to check whether it smells bad is a heuristic for determining whether it is still good to eat. Since food can go bad without smelling bad, it is not a fully reliable test, but it is quicker, more convenient, and less expensive than having the food tested in a laboratory. It is more reliable for some foods than for others.

Heuristics are often described as *shortcuts*. That is roughly right, but we should not assume that there is also a long way round, slower but safer. Sometimes such an alternative is available; sometimes there is none.

Psychologists have studied many heuristics intensively. Sometimes they characterize heuristics negatively, as 'cheap and dirty', in the tradition of Daniel Kahneman (Kahneman, Slovic, and Tversky 1982), sometimes more positively, as 'fast and frugal', in the tradition of Gerd Gigerenzer (Gigerenzer, Hertwig, and Pachur 2011). At worst, heuristic-based cognition is regarded as a form of *irrationality*, at best, as a form of *bounded rationality*. Presumably, some heuristics are better than others, at least for a given purpose under given conditions. We might be better off avoiding *some* heuristics, but the nature of human cognition—perhaps of finite cognition in general—precludes our avoiding them *all*.

Heuristics, as understood here, can be culturally acquired, or even idiosyncratic. For example, medical experts—communally or individually—develop heuristics for interpreting X-rays. But many important heuristics are virtually universal to humans. For example, visual illusions are probably by-products of such heuristics built into the visual systems of humans and other animals (Fleming 2012, Gigerenzer 2021). The heuristics responsible for such illusions are topics for psychological investigation. When heuristics are virtually universal, they may be innately hardwired, or at least the natural outcome of innate domain-general principles and learning mechanisms. Either way, evolutionary adaptiveness will often play a large role in explaining how we have come to use such heuristics. Still, in principle, checking on Google could become a culturally transmitted virtually universal heuristic, whether or not it is evolutionarily adaptive.

One heuristic that often involves conscious thought is *take-the-best* (Gigerenzer and Goldstein 1996). It is a way to choose between two alternatives for some purpose, given various epistemic cues ranked by 'validity' (how well they indicate optimality for that purpose). Take-the-best tells you simply to follow the highest-ranked cue that discriminates between the alternatives—as opposed, for instance, to somehow constructing and comparing weighted averages over all the cues. Thus, one might simply decide to shop at the nearest supermarket, without having taken into account price, range, or quality of goods. Of course, even when one consciously applies the heuristic, one rarely thinks of oneself explicitly *as* applying take-the-best.

Often, there is a slower but more accurate alternative to using a given heuristic. For instance, our visual systems routinely treat colour contours as a guide to the shapes of three-dimensional material things. Camouflage succeeds in misleading observers about those shapes by exploiting their reliance on that heuristic. In principle, we can correct such mistakes, for example, by using our sense of touch, though that alternative may be unfeasible in the circumstances, as in time of war. Still, heuristics are in principle, and often in practice, *defeasible*.

Sometimes no more reliable alternative is available. With take-the-best, one might expect to do better when time permits by consciously 'weighing up all the pros and cons'. But that may be over-optimistic. One may have only the faintest idea how to individuate the relevant considerations, what relative weights to assign them, and how to measure performance on one dimension against performance on another. When I try to take a decision by weighing up all the pros and cons, the result is only to make me vividly aware how open the process is to manipulation in favour of whichever alternative I independently prefer. Indeed, experimental studies suggest that take-the-best is surprisingly reliable, compared to more elaborate methods available to the subjects at the time, where the correct answer is known to the experimenter by some method unavailable to the subjects at the time (Gigerenzer and Goldstein 1996). When many complex ramifications of different kinds really must be taken into account in making a difficult decision, my preferred method is to procrastinate until one morning I wake up knowing what I'm going to do. Conscious reflection passes the buck to unconscious processes, which may do a better job of integrating information from many sources (on the limits of reflection, see Kornblith 2012). In retrospect, that method has served me fairly well. Many other people seem to do likewise.[1]

When we rely on a heuristic without thinking of it as such, and with no conception of a more reliable way of solving the problem, we may mistakenly regard the heuristic's output as *indefeasible*. For lack of an alternative category to put it in, a philosopher may even call it an 'intuition', an 'analytic truth', a 'conceptual connection', or whatever. That illustrates the poverty of the philosophically current taxonomy and is all the more reason to make room for the category of heuristics in philosophers' working vocabulary.

In discussing heuristics, I have not specified whether being a heuristic entails being less than perfectly reliable, or being above some moderate level of reliability, or whatever. More generally, I will

---

[1] According to Daniel Rothschild, 'heuristics in the psychology literature (such as those posited by Kahnemann and Tversky, including the famous conjunction fallacy) can be overruled by slower, more careful reasoning' (2023: 214). This is of course true in principle. However, take-the-best is a heuristic in the psychology literature that may be hard to overrule, because it is far from obvious to agents that the slower, more careful reasoning involved in reflectively weighing up the pros and cons or the like is more reliable than take-the-best itself.

not stipulate a precise definition for the word 'heuristic'. No such definition is needed for present purposes, and at this early stage of inquiry, picking one might even be harmful, by cutting across, instead of along, a cognitive joint. We have a range of more or less paradigm cases of heuristics, as already indicated, and by classifying something as a heuristic we draw attention to its similarities to such cases. For present purposes, that is what matters. Heuristics are *typically* moderately reliable, but perhaps some perfectly reliable or hopelessly unreliable methods play a very similar psychological role in our lives to paradigm heuristics.

Just as heuristics built into the human visual system produce visual illusions in special circumstances, so heuristics built into the human cognitive system may more generally have the capacity to produce philosophical *paradoxes*, which can be properly diagnosed only once we identify the heuristics at work. Such heuristics may be very general, but even much more specific heuristics may play a role in generating philosophical paradoxes: for example, heuristics for attributing beliefs to people on the basis of what they say, and heuristics for individuating physical objects on the basis of visual perception.

Naturally, postulating a new heuristic does not come free. For the postulate to be initially plausible, the candidate heuristic should be simple, quick, efficient, and useful. In particular, the problem it solves should crop up often enough to make a solution dedicated to that problem worth our storing it up for future use. Postulating a heuristic is especially plausible when it would be strange if we *didn't* use something like that heuristic.

Philosophers may be tempted to postulate that what we *really* use is not the first-proposed crude heuristic but some complex refinement of it, constructed by adding exception-clauses, restrictions, and qualifications, to rule out counter-instances and so enhance its reliability. One should resist that temptation, for the 'refined' heuristic is likely to be psychologically unrealistic, since it increases computational times and costs of application, typically for a comparatively small gain in reliability, and perhaps even a loss in generality. Those increases will be drastic if they require conscious reflection, which is very slow by neural standards, and liable to create a bottleneck in processing. In the midst of action, a prompt, moderately reliable answer usually does better than a very reliable answer when it is too late, or than no answer at all. When over-reflective creatures pause to reflect, they risk being eaten, or at least beaten to scarce resources, by their less reflective predators or competitors. Even in modern life, indecision can lead to disaster. Of course, philosophers may use the refined heuristic themselves in their consciously controlled theorizing, but they should not attribute it to ordinary pre-reflective human cognition.

In general, what heuristic we use, if any, under given circumstances is a psychological question, open to experimental test. Evolution does not guarantee that our actual heuristics will be the optimally efficient ones. In this chapter, however, the concern will not be with such experimental work, though the need for it in the long run is obvious. The aim here is to clarify our initial theoretical understanding of the potential relevance of specific heuristics to philosophy, rather than to engage 'blind' with the psychological literature. We need to develop theoretical hypotheses properly before we test them, to know what we are looking for.

In the next four sections, I will explain and discuss some plausible candidates for heuristics on which we may be relying, knowingly or unknowingly, when we wrestle with some philosophical problems. In such cases, we risk getting suckered by our own heuristics.

1.3 The persistence heuristic

Here is a short vignette:

Mary was in London when a man wolf-whistled at her. She took a step towards the man, then slapped him.

To check whether a subject has properly understood the vignette, a psychologist might ask this comprehension question:

Where was Mary when she slapped the man?

A natural answer, which the psychologist would presumably accept, is:

She was in London when she slapped him.

However, the vignette only specifies that Mary was in London *when he wolf-whistled at her*. It adds that she took a step towards him before slapping him. Thus, the natural answer in effect assumes that if someone is in London, and takes a step, then they are still in London. But that assumption is not universally correct, for people occasionally walk out of London. In comprehending the vignette, one automatically updates the initial information 'Mary was in London' to the slightly later time when she slapped him, because the change involved in taking a step forward is treated as 'too small to matter'. That treatment is the default, but it is defeasible: if you had previously been told that Mary lived right on the edge of London, or that she had seven-league boots, you might have been wary about updating her supposed location in that way.

The example illustrates a very general cognitive tendency. For instance: you learn today from a trustworthy source that Emomali Rahmon is the president of Tajikistan. Tomorrow, someone asks you 'Who is the president of Tajikistan?' It would be natural for you to answer (complacently): 'Emomali Rahmon'. To answer 'Well, Emomali Rahmon was the president yesterday' would be unnatural and pedantic, even though you know that presidents can die or resign in a day; no president is forever. One day is treated as too small a change to matter.

Of course, we have some sense of such information having a use-by date; if you are asked twenty years from now 'Who is the president of Tajikistan?', having heard nothing about Tajik politics in the meanwhile, you may answer 'It used to be Emomali Rahmon'.

To stamp each piece of present-tense information with an expiry date for its validity as it goes into memory would involve significant expenditure of time and energy, for questionable benefits—inefficient, and probably infeasible. Naturally, most memories fade away, at different rates, but that does not mean that the timetable for their doing so has to be written into their content.

What we treat as too small to matter is sensitive to our vague, general sense of realistic timescales for different states and activities: 'He is thin' or 'He is asleep', 'She is writing a novel' or 'She is writing an email'. How all this works is a topic for detailed psychological investigation. For present purposes, what counts is the general form of the phenomenon, not the specifics of its implementation.

When we update information in present-tense form, we often do so by *retaining* the present tense, even though such *present-tense updating* involves going beyond our original information. Much of what we describe as factual 'memory' is the result of present-tense updating ('Do you remember who is the president of Tajikistan?'). By contrast, *past-tense updating* sticks closer to the original content rather than the original form of the information, by putting it in past-tense form, with reference to the time when it was strictly expressed in present-tense form ('Emomali Rahmon was president of Tajikistan on 15th October 2022' or 'The last I heard, Emomali Rahmon was president of Tajikistan'), as we might do when we regard change as plausibly imminent. Past-tense updating is more appropriate for episodic memory of particular events. If one cannot date the event, one may simply use a memory demonstrative such as 'then' or 'that time we were in Barcelona' or 'when I was pick-pocketed'.

Although present-tense updating is not always truth-preserving, it is *usually* truth-preserving. Almost every step that starts in London ends in London; almost every president of a country yesterday is its president today, and so on. Moreover, there is no feasible alternative to present-tense updating, however much sceptics may complain about its fallibility. No one can be constantly rechecking everything. Indeed, even computer data bases use present-tense updating perforce. Once someone's address has been entered into a data base, it cannot be checked every day, let alone every second, to test whether it is still their current address.

Predictive processing models of perception may also rely on present-tense updating. For example, Andy Clark writes about the perception of a moving object against a stable background: 'most of the background information for the present frame can be assumed to be the same as the previous frame' (2016: 26). Without such assumptions, the task of prediction could easily become intractably complex.

Present-tense updating does not reflect some peculiarity of the human brain, but instead far more general features of the problem of information-gathering and retention. Artificial intelligence will have to do present-tense updating, just as natural intelligence does. For example, much of the data on which an AI system was trained up will sooner or later go out of date.

One advantage of present-tense updating over past-tense updating is that the questions to which the former gives direct answers tend to be of more practical significance than the questions to which the latter gives direct answers. For instance, if you want to get food and drink, it is usually more helpful to know where food and drink are *now* than to know where they were *yesterday*. Creatures without episodic memory, as some non-human animals are alleged to be, may well be unable to do past-tense updating; for many of their purposes, present-tense updating will suffice. Even for humans, although we can sometimes make inferences from the outputs of past-tense updating to the information we need for decision-making—from where food and drink were yesterday to where they are now—conscious inference is psychologically costly. In the heat of action, it is more useful to have the required information already available directly—at one's fingertips—than to spend time and attention inferring it. That consideration favours present-tense updating.

The underlying heuristic is more general than the phrase 'present-tense updating' may suggest. The heuristic provides much of our understanding of physical things as persisting through change over time. Seeing a tree, I think 'This tree is here', using 'this tree' and 'there' as perceptual demonstratives. The next day, somewhere else, I remember the tree as so located, thinking 'That tree is there'—not just 'That tree *was* there'—using 'that tree' and 'there' as memory demonstratives anaphorically linked respectively to the original perception, even if I am sure that it lost some leaves over the intervening windy day. I unreflectively treat such changes as too small to matter to the tree's identity. The same underlying principle applies modally as well as temporally, to variation across counterfactual possibilities as well as to variation across times: just as we allow that this ship will soon have another plank in place of this rotten one, we allow that it *could have been originally made* with another plank instead of this one with which it was originally made: a difference of one plank is too small to matter.

The underlying heuristic can be summed up in the generic slogan 'Small changes don't matter'. We may call it the *persistence heuristic*. It plays a major if largely passive role in solving the problem of adapting what we know or believe to new situations as efficiently as possible.

In the slogan 'Small changes don't matter', 'changes' should be understood loosely, even metaphorically. In particular, for present purposes, zero change counts as the smallest change. By the heuristic, things persist when they remain unchanged. Furthermore, the difference from one possibility to a counterfactual alternative, or from one object to a similar object, also counts as a change for these purposes, as will be illustrated below.

Examples of the persistence heuristic and its inhibitors are easily multiplied. Normally, one need not keep rechecking someone's scalp to retain knowledge that they are not bald, even though they lose a few hairs every day. But if you tell me that John, though not yet bald, is rapidly going bald, I may keep glancing at his scalp. If you have borrowed a book, you need not keep asking yourself whether you still have that book every time you dislodge a few molecules off a page with your fingers. But if the book is a priceless, crumbling medieval manuscript, you may worry more about its survival. 'I wish this table had been made slightly longer' is much less likely than 'I wish this table had been made ten times longer' to prompt the default-breaking thought 'Would that still have been this table?' The persistence heuristic explains such patterns, obviating the need to postulate more elaborate forms of proto-metaphysical thinking.

Of course, experience and testimony can modify our sense of what counts as a small change for a specific kind of object, and so raise or lower the threshold for inhibiting the persistence heuristic. But tweaks in how we implement the heuristic do not replace it by something else.

We also use the persistence heuristic to transfer information about one thing to another. I pick an apple from a tree and bite it. The apple tastes sour. I expect it to taste sour at the next bite too, and I expect another similar-looking apple from the same tree to taste sour also. With respect to taste, the difference between the two apples is treated as too small to matter. That is a primitive form of induction.

We use the persistence heuristic *offline* as well as *online*. We use it online when we update on new evidence, perhaps received from sense perception or from testimony. We use the heuristic offline when we adapt what we know or believe to a hypothetical supposition. For example, in deciding whether to eat that other similar-looking apple, I suppose 'I eat that apple', and develop its consequences in imagination; as a result, I may decide *not* to eat that apple. You may have been carrying out such offline processing, using your imagination, when reading this chapter, as you considered the various hypothetical cases presented above.

Naturally, what counts as a small change depends on what we are talking about—the table, the house, the city, the country, the planet. A noticeable difference in taste between two bites of the same apple may surprise us more than between two bites of different apples from the same tree. Differential standards for smallness surely have to be calibrated by experience. But most of this happens offstage, without troubling consciousness.

The persistence heuristic is a crucial labour-saving device. Without it, cognition would be continually restarting from scratch. That would be hopelessly inefficient. The heuristic's utility is manifest. As already emphasized, it is defeasible. Persistence is only the default, and we can often identify its failures. When a large change is in the offing, or we know or strongly suspect that a boundary is nearby, the operation of the heuristic is inhibited. But normally we need not actively exclude such defeating conditions, for that would undermine the heuristic's utility, which is exactly to avoid such testing. We rely on persistence unless something sets off a mental alarm.

One corollary of the persistence heuristic's inhibiting conditions is that the heuristic is more easily inhibited for precise terms than for vague ones. For a precise term, we are more clearly aware of its boundaries and where they lie. Our awareness of their proximity sounds an alarm; the heuristic's operation is inhibited. By contrast, for a vague term, we have no such clear awareness of its boundaries, and usually no alarm is sounded; the heuristic's operation is not inhibited—though we may feel growing unease as we slide down a slippery slope. But the heuristic itself is applicable equally to precise and vague terms. For example, in the vignette about Mary and the wolf-whistler, the heuristic delivers the verdict that she is still in London after taking a step, irrespective of whether one envisages the boundaries associated with the name 'London' as vaguely or precisely defined. When one reads the vignette, that question does not naturally arise. Checking whether the terms in play are vague or precise is no part of the persistence heuristic: such checking would use up valuable time and energy for no commensurate benefit. The heuristic itself applies equally in vague and precise cases, but is more liable to be psychologically defeated in the latter than in the former because the boundary is psychologically salient.

In cases of vagueness, the shortage of defeaters for the persistence heuristic makes it prone to *sorites paradoxes*, since it can be applied iteratively—which rarely happens under normal conditions. Many small differences add up to a large difference. Correspondingly, the heuristic validates *tolerance principles* such as 'If n grains make a heap, $n-1$ grains make a heap' for arbitrary 'n' or 'If x looks red and y is visually indiscriminable from x then y looks red too'. One assesses the principle by supposing the antecedent 'n grains make a heap' or 'x looks red and y is visually indiscriminable from x' and applying the heuristic under that supposition to verify the consequent '$n-1$ grains make a heap' or 'y looks red'. Informally, one imagines a heap, imagines one grain being removed, or something looking red, and something else where one can see no difference in colour, and uses the heuristic offline in the imagination to confirm that what remains is still a heap or that the second thing looks red too. There is no psychologically salient boundary for 'heap' or 'looks red' to inhibit the heuristic's operation. We have experienced no relevant analogue of taking a second bite of an apple and suddenly tasting something rotten to make us cautious. By default, the tolerance principle is accepted. Notoriously, it suffices to generate the sorites paradox, which drives one from an obviously true starting-point such as 'Ten thousand grains make a heap' to an obviously false conclusion such as 'One grain makes a heap', or from 'This looks red' said of a prototype of red to 'This looks red' said of a prototype of yellow. The tolerance principle only needs to fail at one step out of many in the sorites series for the sorites argument to be unsound. Our instinctive reliance on the highly but not perfectly reliable persistence heuristic helps explain why we are cognitively vulnerable to paradoxes of this form, why we find them so hard to resist.[2]

---

[2] The phrase 'tolerance principle' goes back to Wright 1976. Williamson 2020: 63–7 treats tolerance principles as heuristics, though not with the generality of the persistence heuristic, in relation to sorites paradoxes, and provides numerical estimates of their reliability in some cases. Williamson 2023b (a review essay on Dorr, Hawthorne, and Yli-Vakkuri 2021) makes the generalization to the persistence heuristic. The latter

Some philosophers have got the impression that tolerance principles for vague expressions are somehow 'analytic' or 'semantic', or that they are 'conceptual connections' built into the corresponding concepts, thereby rendering those concepts defective.[3] That is a misunderstanding of the principles' status, perhaps resulting from the absence of 'heuristic' from the traditional philosopher's impoverished menu of options. Tolerance principles for vague expressions are no more 'analytic' than are the analogous tolerance principles for precise expressions; they are all applications of the same heuristic. The difference is just that some of them are psychologically more easily inhibited than others. Since our susceptibility to sorites paradoxes simply results from our reliance on the persistence heuristic in epistemically non-ideal conditions, it motivates no revision of classical logic or bivalent semantics. Much of the literature on vagueness exhibits one of the harms done by the 'linguistic turn': the tendency to seek linguistic solutions for epistemic problems.

exchange contributes to a debate about whether the S4 axiom (that what is possibly possible is possible) holds for metaphysical possibility, despite apparent examples of series of cases where each case entails the possibility of the next, but the first case does not entail the possibility of the last because the difference between neighbouring cases (for instance, in the original constitution of a given artefact) is 'small enough' but the difference between the first case and the last is 'too large'. Salmón 1989 argues that the cases are genuine counterexamples to S4, Williamson 1990 that the underlying motivation for his premises is soritical, and Salmón 1993 that the motivation is not soritical. Dorr, Hawthorne, and Yli-Vakkuri 2021 argue for a metasemantic approach on which a tolerance principle for constitution as uttered in a given possible world expresses a true proposition, but which proposition it expresses is contingent, while the corresponding necessitated tolerance principle expresses a false proposition. They defend the unnecessitated tolerance principle by non-soritical, epistemological considerations. Williamson 2023b responds that the pre-theoretic appeal of the tolerance appeal extends to the necessitated tolerance principle, because it does not depend on thinking of the cases as actual, and is best explained as deriving from the persistence heuristic. Similarly, the appeal of the crucial premises in Salmón's anti-S4 reasoning is easily explained as deriving from the persistence heuristic. When an independently attested heuristic validates an assumption, explaining the latter's pre-theoretic appeal in some other way is typically ill-motivated. Incidentally, although the persistence heuristic does not figure in the case for an epistemicist account of vagueness in Williamson 1994, our reliance on it supports my approach there.

[3] See Eklund 2002 for an account of how principles can be 'analytic' without being true.

1.4 The suppositional heuristic for conditionals

The persistence heuristic is general-purpose. For contrast, we now consider a heuristic primarily for the assessment of conditionals, expressed by sentences of forms such as 'If A, C', although it can also be applied to the assessment of generic generalizations, as explained below (see Williamson 2020, henceforth 'S&T', for a book-length discussion of the heuristic). Arguably, it is humans' primary way of assessing conditionals, though not our only one. It is not a new discovery: for example, it is closely related to the Ramsey Test, originally described by Frank Ramsey, which uses a form of hypothetical updating. But its role has been misunderstood, because its heuristic status went unrecognized.

Here is Ramsey's concise description, in a footnote (1929: 143, with change of lettering):

If two people are arguing 'If A will C?' and are both in doubt as to A, they are adding A hypothetically to their stock of knowledge and arguing on that basis about C.

A simple, schematic version of the suppositional heuristic is this:

Assess 'If A, C' outright as you assess 'C' on the supposition 'A'.

We can see how this works with some examples. Mary has bought a ticket in a lottery. The prize is a million pounds. Here are three conditionals about it:

(1)   If Mary's ticket wins, she will get lots of money.
(2)   If Mary's ticket wins, it will lose.
(3)   If Mary's ticket wins, she will buy a new house.

To assess (1)-(3), we first suppose their shared antecedent, 'Mary's ticket wins', and then assess their consequents on that supposition.

Since the prize is lots of money, we accept (1)'s consequent 'She will get lots of money' on the supposition of (1)'s antecedent 'Mary's ticket wins'. Using the suppositional heuristic, we therefore accept (1) outright.

Since Mary's ticket winning is inconsistent with its losing, we reject (2)'s consequent 'It will lose' on the supposition of (2)'s antecedent 'Mary's ticket wins'. Using the suppositional heuristic, we therefore reject (2) outright.

Since we have no idea of Mary's priorities, we suspend judgment on (3)'s consequent 'She will buy a new house' on the supposition of (3)'s antecedent 'Mary's ticket wins'. Using the suppositional heuristic, we therefore suspend outright judgment on (3).

These predictions fit natural reactions to (1)-(3). Similarly, as we learn more about Mary's priorities, her buying a new house will look more or less likely conditional on her ticket's winning, and (3) will come to seem correspondingly more or less likely outright. There is extensive evidence that speakers' assessments tend to conform to the suppositional heuristic (Evans and Over 2004, Douven 2016, S&T).

Often, we need to assess conditionals not outright but on a further set of background suppositions, Γ. Strictly speaking, that was already happening with our assessments of (1)-(3), since 'Mary has bought a ticket in a lottery' and 'The prize is a million pounds' really played the role of background suppositions; we did not believe them outright. For these purposes, we need a more general version of the suppositional heuristic:

Assess 'If A, C' on the suppositions Γ as you assess 'C' on the suppositions $\Gamma \cup \{\text{'A'}\}$.

The original, simpler version corresponds to the special case where Γ is the empty set. In more complex reasoning, we often find ourselves making suppositions within suppositions. For example, when we are devising a strategy with multiple choice-points as we confront different contingencies at different stages, we need to consider a tree of branching possibilities. In constructing or following a tricky mathematical proof, one typically has to make hypotheses in the scope of hypotheses already made. Without the generalized suppositional hypothesis, one would be stymied in one's natural attempts to assess conditionals in such situations, but that does not happen. In effect, in the outright version of the heuristic, the final verdict on the conditional itself is online, whereas the generalized version extends the heuristic to offline cases too.

How does such hypothetical thinking help us? Many of our dispositions to form expectations have been calibrated by experience, our own or our ancestors', and so encode information about the world so experienced. We may need to apply such information to a prospective new situation, in advance of encountering it. Is it a danger to be avoided or an opportunity to be sought? How can we prepare ourselves to encounter it? We imaginatively suppose that the situation obtains, and use our expectation-forming dispositions 'offline' to assess what it may be like and what it may lead to. We can then store such information in the convenient form of a declarative sentence, as a conditional: 'If the situation obtains, such-and-such will happen'. Such reality-oriented cognitive uses of the imagination are plausibly central to its evolutionary function (Williamson 2016e). In short, the suppositional heuristic enables us to use connections implicit in our cognitive system to make them explicit in a conditional.

One advantage of suppositional thinking is that it is often feasible when truth-functional thinking is not, because we cannot assess the antecedent or consequent separately. I may know that *if* John drops the vase, it will smash, even though I have no idea how likely he is to drop the vase, and so no idea how likely it is to survive. This is an epistemological point, not a semantic one. It does not show that 'if' is not truth-functional. After all, we may verify the truth-functional disjunction 'Either he will not drop the vase or it will smash' or falsify the truth-functional conjunction 'He will drop the vase and it will not smash' by supposing 'He drops the vase' and on that basis verifying 'It will smash'. Just as we can verify a disjunction without verifying either disjunct, and we can falsify a conjunction without falsifying either conjunct, we can verify a conditional without either falsifying its antecedent or verifying its consequent. But conditionals *invite* hypothetical thinking in a way that disjunctions and conjunctions do not; conditionals as it were *ask* to be so assessed. To put it another way, hypothetical thinking feels like a *direct* way of assessing a conditional, but an *indirect* way of assessing a conjunction or disjunction. That difference manifests the suppositional heuristic's naturalness for conditionals.

The suppositional heuristic can also be applied to generic generalizations, such as 'Tigers are striped', which we do not treat as refuted by an occasional albino tiger. For 'Ns are F' can be paraphrased as 'If it's an N, it's F' ('If it's a tiger, it's striped'), where 'it' is treated as if it referred to an arbitrarily chosen item. One assesses 'It's striped' on the supposition 'It's a tiger', which gives the appropriate result. Even when the generic is not expressed in conditional form, the suppositional heuristic is still applicable (S&T: 142–6). Much of humans' general knowledge is most naturally expressed in such generics.

Of course, many of our general biases and prejudices are also most naturally expressed in generics. But that is not the suppositional heuristic's fault, for it prompts one to accept 'Ns are F' only if one *already* has the bias or prejudice, disposing one to accept 'It's F' on the supposition 'It's an N'. What the heuristic does is to enable one to make one's implicit bias or prejudice explicit in a conditional or a generic generalization. The heuristic can hardly be expected to do *better* than the underlying cognitive dispositions—its role is to use them, not to filter the good ones from the bad. Although well-intentioned proposals have occasionally been made to ban the utterance of generics, the likely effect of such a ban would be to force the biases and prejudices underground, while doing the same to most of ordinary humans' general knowledge of the natural and social world, very little of which consists in exceptionless universal generalizations.

Despite all its virtues and benefits, the suppositional heuristic is *inconsistent*, both in itself and with uncontroversial background knowledge. This can be shown in various ways.

One route to inconsistency goes via graded attitudes. Let Prob(X | Y) be the probability (in any relevant sense) of X conditional on Y, and A * C formalize 'If A, C'. Applying the simple version of the suppositional heuristic gives the equation Prob(A * C) = Prob(C | A), the identification of the probability of the conditional with the corresponding conditional probability, as proposed by various authors (Jeffrey 1964, Ellis 1969, Stalnaker 1970). For Prob(A * C) is the probabilistic assessment of 'If A, C', while the conditional probability Prob(C | A) is the probabilistic assessment of C on the supposition A, that is, with all but the A-possibilities excluded. The same connection holds for the generalized version of the suppositional heuristic. Let B be the conjunction of the background suppositions. Then applying the generalized heuristic to assignments of probability results in the equation Prob(A * C | B) = Prob(C | A ∧ B), which is in effect the previous equation conditionalized on B. This is the generalized version of the identification of the probability of a conditional with the corresponding conditional probability. For Prob(A * C | B) is the probabilistic assessment of 'If A, C' on the supposition B, while Prob(C | A ∧ B) is the probabilistic assessment of C on the suppositions A and B. The generalized equation feels very natural, thanks to the suppositional heuristic, but a version of an argument originally devised by David Lewis shows the equation to imply that no three mutually exclusive possibilities have nonzero probability (Lewis 1976, S&T: 42–3). That is an absurdly restrictive constraint: when a die is thrown, there are six mutually exclusive outcomes, each with probability 1/6. Attempts to find a loophole in Lewis's argument all founder when applied to the corresponding argument for the generalized suppositional heuristic; it is simply a mathematical result.

Much ingenuity has been spent on finding subtle restrictions or complications of the equation to get around Lewis's result. For a heuristic, that is exactly the wrong reaction. The heuristic's utility depends on its unrestricted simplicity. No subtle restrictions or complications are baked in. Of course, philosophers can seek consistent semantic approximations to the generalized probabilistic identity, but the identity is just one manifestation of a more general heuristic, which has non-probabilistic manifestations too. Treating the probabilistic case in isolation is arbitrary.

Another proof of the heuristic's inconsistency does not even require the assumption of three mutually exclusive possibilities. It is worth sketching to give an idea of what is going on (S&T: 37–42 presents the proof in more detail).

First, we apply the generalized heuristic to assessments of *deductive entailment*. This is like the special case of the probabilistic equation for probability 1, the principle that $\text{Prob}(A * C \mid B) = 1$ if and only if $\text{Prob}(C \mid B \wedge A) = 1$, but without the mathematical complications that arise for probabilities conditional on a hypothesis whose probability is 0 (when the standard ratio definition of the conditional probability, $\text{Prob}(X \mid Y)$ as $\text{Prob}(X)/\text{Prob}(X \wedge Y)$, involves division by 0). The result can be formalized as the equivalence of $\Gamma \vdash A * C$ with $\Gamma \cup \{A\} \vdash C$, where $\vdash$ is interpreted as deductive entailment. That equivalence amounts to the combined rules for a standard conditional in a standard system of natural deduction: the implication from $\Gamma \vdash A * C$ to $\Gamma \cup \{A\} \vdash C$ is in effect modus ponens (the conditional elimination rule), while the implication from $\Gamma \cup \{A\} \vdash C$ to $\Gamma \vdash A * C$ is just conditional proof (the conditional introduction rule). These rules can be shown to make * equivalent to the material (truth-functional) conditional. So far so good, at least for friends of the material reading of 'if'.

The trouble is that we can also apply the generalized heuristic to assessments of *deductive incompatibility*. This is like the special case of the probabilistic equation for probability 0, the principle that $\text{Prob}(A * C \mid B) = 0$ if and only if $\text{Prob}(C \mid A \wedge B) = 0$, but again without the complications arising for probabilities conditional on a hypothesis of probability 0. The result can be formalized as the equivalence of $\Gamma \vdash^\neg A * C$ with $\Gamma \cup \{A\} \vdash^\neg C$, where $\vdash^\neg$ is interpreted as deductive incompatibility. Since being deductively incompatible with something is equivalent to deductively entailing its negation, in effect $\Gamma \vdash \neg(A * C)$ is equivalent to $\Gamma \cup \{A\} \vdash \neg C$. That can be shown to make $\neg(A * C)$ equivalent to the negated conjunction $\neg(A \wedge C)$, which in turn makes * equivalent to *conjunction*. But * cannot be simultaneously equivalent to *both* the material conditional *and* conjunction, since any material conditional with a false antecedent is true, whereas any conjunction with a false conjunct is false. In brief, two legitimate special cases of the heuristic force mutually incompatible readings on natural language conditionals.

Human reliance on the inconsistent suppositional heuristic in assessing conditionals helps explain why their semantics has puzzled logicians for over two millennia, on and off. The issue was so controversial in Alexandria during the third century BCE that the poet Callimachus wrote, 'Even the crows on the roof-tops are cawing about which conditionals are true' (Mates 1949: 234). Although some applications of the heuristic require the material reading, using the heuristic we reject (2) above ('If Mary's ticket wins, it will lose'), even though it is almost certainly true on the material reading, since its antecedent is almost certainly false. More generally, when A is highly improbable or C highly probable, and therefore the material conditional A → C is also highly probable, C can still be highly improbable conditional on A, so by applying the suppositional heuristic one judges 'If A, C' highly improbable. In effect, the suppositional heuristic is responsible for the 'paradoxes' of material implication. Since the heuristic is inconsistent, it will generate apparent counterexamples to *any* proposed interpretation of a natural language conditional.

How can the suppositional heuristic be useful, given its inconsistency? How has it survived the pressures of evolution? The answer is much less straightforward than for the persistence heuristic.

An illuminating case to start with is the practice of mathematical proof. Mathematicians write their proofs in a framework of natural language, afforced with lots of mathematical notation and diagrams, not in some purely formal language—as one can see by glancing at the pages of mathematical journals. In particular, mathematicians reason with natural language conditionals such as 'if'; they receive no special training in how to use them mathematically, no special explanations or warnings. Nevertheless, to a good approximation, their reasoning with 'if' fits standard natural deduction rules for the material conditional—modus ponens and conditional proof—just as in the special case of the heuristic for deductive entailment above. That is why, as often noted, 'if' can be seamlessly read in mathematical texts as a material conditional.

Still, since mathematics seems to press our deductive capacity to the utmost, why does the inconsistency between applying the heuristic to deductive entailment and applying it to deductive incompatibility never surface in mathematics? For example, let A be an implicitly inconsistent mathematical hypothesis. Since A deductively entails any mathematical conclusion C, one can use the heuristic to establish 'If A, C' outright. Since C is also deductively incompatible with A, one can also use the heuristic to refute 'If A, C' outright. That would make mathematics itself inconsistent. Obviously, no such paradox arises in mathematical practice. The reason is that refutability is simply identified with provability of the negation, rather than being treated as an independent form of assessment. In effect, mathematical proofs work with acceptance as the only operative mode of assessment. Near enough the *only* way an unembedded sentence occurs in a mathematical proof is as proved from—deductively entailed by—the set of relevant suppositions. In limit cases, that set is either empty or just the singleton of the sentence itself (in the speech act of supposing it). To that extent, the standard logical framework of mathematical proof is just like that of a natural deduction system. In such a setting, a material reading of 'if' is the only one to validate the suppositional heuristic.

The primacy of acceptance over rejection in mathematical practice may be rooted in a more general pattern of human thought: to register rejection of 'A' by accepting 'Not A', replacing a negative attitude to a positive sentence by a positive attitude to its negation. 'Not A' may then in turn be fleshed out in more positive terms (on the psychology of negation, see Kaup, Zwaan, and Lüdtke 2007). If the default attitude to a sentence occurring in inner speech is acceptance, this would tend to avoid mental clutter, by reducing the need for special attitude-markers. Such a cognitive tendency would be efficient for both outright attitudes and attitudes under suppositions. It would set one up to apply the suppositional heuristic to acceptance, for which it gives good results. That would help explain why the heuristic's inconsistency causes so little trouble in practice, in mathematics or elsewhere, without any special training. Although it would not strictly resolve the inconsistencies lurking in the heuristic, especially as applied to probabilistic assessments, it would help limit the damage.

The effect of the suppositional heuristic is also modified by the generic practice of accepting conditionals preserved by memory or communicated by testimony, without reapplying the suppositional test in the new epistemic context. For example, when I assess the opposite conditionals 'If A, C' and 'If A, not C' by the suppositional heuristic, I do not accept both, because I do not accept both the contradictories 'C' and 'Not C' on the supposition 'A' (when 'A' is consistent). But sometimes I may rationally accept 'If A, C' from one trustworthy source while also accepting 'If A, not C' from another trustworthy source; I then conclude 'Not A'. Perhaps each trustworthy source has direct access to information to which neither I nor the other trustworthy source has direct access, and both trustworthy sources used the suppositional heuristic.[4]

---

[4] S&T: 89–102 discusses such cases in detail. Incidentally, the centrepiece of Daniel Rothschild's critique of S&T is a lengthy argument against that account of conditional testimony (Rothschild 2023: 221–6). At the decisive point, he plausibly claims that 'direct expressions of conditional probabilities might behave as strangely as assertions of conditionals', and concludes 'these cases do not provide a good reason to pull apart conditionals from expressions of conditional probabilities' (Rothschild 2023: 226). But one obvious reason why direct expressions of conditional probabilities might behave as strangely as assertions of conditionals in the relevant cases (where they are made by

Once one takes into account the overall practice of using conditionals to encode and transfer information, one can argue that the information stably associated with a conditional is simply that of the material reading, outside mathematics as well as inside. The point is not obvious, for the suppositional heuristic often grossly underestimates the probability of a conditional on its material reading. For example, the heuristic assigns probability zero to the conditional (1) above, 'If Mary's ticket wins, it will lose', since the consequent is inconsistent with the antecedent and so has probability zero conditional on the latter. That fits the strong unreflective impression that the conditional is idiotic, and the strong unreflective inclination, when asked 'What is the chance that if Mary's ticket wins, it will lose?', to answer 'None'. But the material reading makes the conditional almost certainly true, since its antecedent is almost certainly false, and a material conditional with a false antecedent is true. In isolation, such cases look like decisive counterexamples to the material reading of 'if'. But that attitude is no longer adequate once one realizes that the unreflective judgments are the outputs of an inconsistent heuristic. In those circumstances, we cannot rely on the standard methodology of requiring a semantics for the conditional to vindicate all normal patterns of speakers' unreflective judgments.

a trusted expert) is that, confronted with the authoritative but forbiddingly technical-sounding claim 'My conditional probability for C on A is very high', a natural way to extract something useful from it about the relation of A to C is to think something like 'That's just his way of communicating that if A then C'. How we should directly update our conditional probabilities on information about two experts' conditional probabilities is quite unobvious, even to probabilistic epistemologists. Pre-theoretically, we are much more used to working with conditionals than with explicit conditional probabilities. Similarly, when an expert meteorologist says 'The probability on my current evidence that it will rain is very high', we may cut to the chase and treat him as having said (with professional caution) that it will rain, though we are under no illusion that the literal truth-conditions are the same. Comparisons with explicit statements about probabilities pose no threat to the argument of S&T. Significantly, Rothschild rejects my appeal to heuristics without providing any alternative account to explain how language users ascertain whether sentences' truth-conditions obtain in specific hypothetical cases. This follows a more general practice in semantics of treating the application of semantics to hypothetical cases as in effect epistemically transparent to language users.

We may have to be content with a less direct connection between semantics and heuristics. For example, when we treat the conditional probability Prob(C | A) as an estimate of the probability of the conditional on its material reading, Prob(A → C), it is often too low, but never too high: in that sense, the heuristic may make us trust too little, but will not make us trust too much. More demanding truth-conditions for the conditional lose that advantage, by sometimes making the heuristic overestimate its probability; less demanding truth-conditions make the conditional unnecessarily uninformative, given the heuristic. Thus the material truth-conditions make conditionals as informative as they can be, compatibly with preventing the heuristic from overestimating their probability. Such a useful connection between the heuristic and the truth-conditions provides further confirmation of the overall picture (S&T: 103–10).

Being too cautious with conditionals may be less costly than not being cautious enough. After all, on the present view, the point of conditionals is not to provide access to a special kind of information but rather to provide a special kind of access to information. For example, on the material reading, 'If Mary's ticket wins, it will lose' has the same truth-condition as 'Mary's ticket will either lose or not win'; although we cannot access the high probability of that condition's obtaining via the suppositional heuristic, we can access it via the known high probability of Mary's ticket losing. As already noted, suppositional thinking comes into its own with conditionals like 'If the vase is dropped, it will break'. Even though it has the same truth condition as 'The vase will either break or not be dropped', we may be unable to access the high probability of the condition's obtaining via the separate probabilities of the disjuncts, because we have no idea how to estimate the latter probabilities. Instead, we can apply the suppositional heuristic, since we can access the high probability of the vase's breaking conditional on its being dropped, through an imaginative exercise constrained by our background knowledge.

The suppositional heuristic's limitations are a small price to pay for its distinctive benefits.[5]

1.5 Disquotation and heuristics for belief ascription

Here is an elementary speech exchange between two children:

JOHN: I'm taller than you.
JANET: That's not true! I'm taller than you.

We might articulate Janet's underlying thought process as an inner monologue like this:

JANET: John said 'I'm taller than you'. He said that he's taller than me. But I'm taller than him, so he's not taller than me. So what he said is not true.

---

[5] Care is needed in applying the suppositional heuristic to conditionals involving descriptions of cognitive status. For example, 'If Elvis lives, it is surprising that he lives' has a true reading, whereas 'It is surprising that if Elvis lives, he lives' has no true reading. This may look like a case where we are unwilling to apply the heuristic. But that is a confusion. The heuristic tells us to assess 'If A, C' as surprising just when we assess C as surprising on the supposition A: in particular, to assess 'If Elvis lives, he lives' as surprising just when we assess 'He lives' as surprising on the supposition 'Elvis lives'. Naturally, we assess 'If Elvis lives, he lives' as unsurprising, and 'He lives' as unsurprising on the supposition 'Elvis lives'. As usual, the latter involves an *ex post* assessment of 'He lives', already informed by the supposition, not an *ex ante* uninformed assessment. We can record our assessment by saying truly 'If Elvis lives, it is not surprising that he lives', with 'surprising' read *ex post*, in a context already informed by the antecedent. That the same sentence can also read as false with 'surprising' understood *ex ante* is irrelevant. The point comes out clearly when one uses the parenthetical 'surprisingly' in place of the sentential operator 'it is surprising that': there is little difference between 'If Elvis lives, surprisingly he lives' and 'Surprisingly, if Elvis lives, he lives'; in both, the primary propositional content is trivially true, while the secondary parenthetical comment on its cognitive status is obviously false. Of course, we accept 'If Elvis lives, it is surprising that he lives' read *ex ante*, but that just corresponds to accepting 'It is surprising that he lives' read *ex ante* on the supposition 'Elvis lives', again in line with the suppositional heuristic. Similar points apply to explicitly probabilistic operators such as 'the probability is less than 1% that', where one must be careful to distinguish between prior and posterior probabilities.

In passing from the internal direct speech report 'John said "I'm taller than you"' to the internal indirect speech report 'He said that he's taller than me', Janet unreflectively replaces John's pronouns 'I' (first-person) and 'you' (second-person) by her 'he' (third-person) and 'me' (first-person); she also replaces the name 'John' by 'he'. In passing from the thought 'I'm taller than him' to the speech addressed to John, 'I'm taller than you', she unreflectively replaces the third-person pronoun 'him' by the second-person pronoun 'you'. All these effortless replacements are to preserve reference and conversational appropriateness—though Janet's use in inner speech of the third-person rather than the second-person in referring to John suggests that she is keeping her psychological distance from him. By contrast, the words 'taller than' are preserved verbatim from the direct speech report to the indirect speech report, as is the present tense of the verb from 'I'm' (= 'I am') to 'he's' (= 'he is') rather than 'he was', in effect a case of the persistence heuristic, since the speech reports themselves are past tense ('said', not 'says').

In arriving at the indirect speech report, Janet's default is to repeat John's words (homophonic disquotation), while fluently adjusting to the context-sensitivity of pronouns. Reasonably enough, she does not even consider the possibility that John means something different by 'taller' from what she means. Counterfactually, if John had a notorious habit of using words as if they meant the opposite of what they in fact do, her knowledge of his bad habit might have inhibited the default's operation, and she might have reacted differently. Homophonic disquotation is the standard *heuristic* for indirect speech reports, both in speech and in verbalized thought, but it is modified more or less automatically in familiar cases of context-sensitivity, and it can also be modified more reflectively in light of special circumstances. Homophonic disquotation, suitably modified, can also be extended to *refusals* to say: for example, someone who refuses to say 'Abortion is wrong' may be reported as refusing to say that abortion is wrong.

We often need the indirect speech report in order to assess others' statements. For instance, Janet obviously cannot just assess the sentence type 'I'm taller than you', since she addresses that very sentence back to John in rejecting his use of it. Rather, she assesses *what John said*. In doing so, her implicit reasoning is something like this:

(1) John said that he's taller than me

(2) What John said = that he's taller than me

(3) He's not taller than me

(4) That he's taller than me is true if and only if he's taller than me

(5) What John said is true if and only if he's taller than me

(6) What John said is not true

Here (1) is just the indirect speech report, which (2) reworks in a context where nothing else John said is relevant. Line (3) states something Janet knows or believes about John's height compared to hers. Line (4) is just an instance of a standard logical schema for propositional truth, which does not involve disquotation, since 'that' is not a device for quotation:

(T) That P is true if and only if P

Principles not unlike (T) can already be found in Plato's *Sophist* and Aristotle's *Metaphysics*. Line (5) follows from (2) and (4) by the logic of identity (Leibniz's law), since (2) licenses substituting 'what John said' for 'that he's taller than me' in (4). The conclusion (6) follows from (3) and (5) by modus tollens for the biconditional (using its left-to-right direction), a standard principle of propositional logic.

Plato and Aristotle pair their principles about truth with corresponding principles about falsity not unlike (F):

(F) That P is false if and only if not-P

The instance of (F) corresponding to (4) is (4*):

(4*)   That he's taller than me is false if and only if he's not taller than me

Just as Janet can derive (5) from (2) and (4), she can derive (5*) from (2) and (4*):

(5*)   What John said is false if and only if he's not taller than me

The conclusion (6*) follows from (3) and (5*) by modus ponens for the biconditional (using its right-to-left direction), another standard principle of propositional logic:

(6*)   What John said is false

Unless Janet suspects that John is insincere, she may well conclude that what he *thinks*, as well as what he *said*, is false, and not true. She may go straight from the indirect speech report 'He said that he's taller than me' to the belief ascription 'He thinks that he's taller than me' ('think' is the usual term in ordinary English where philosophers say 'believe'; they are near-synonyms in this context). In effect, Janet uses what someone *says* as a heuristic for what they *believe*. The default assumption is *sincerity*: if someone says that P, they believe that P. Call that the *sincerity heuristic*.

What about the converse principle, a default assumption of *non-reticence*, that if someone believes that P, they say that P (when the question arises)? If they say that not-P, by the default assumption of sincerity, they believe that not-P, and so do not also believe that P, unless they are inconsistent. But if they say neither that P nor that not-P, can we assume by default that they have no belief either way? Obviously not, when the question whether P did not even arise in the conversation. But if they positively *refuse* to say that P, when the question does arise, a reasonable default assumption is that they lack the belief that P. As usual, the default can be inhibited: for instance, when the matter is confidential, or the speaker did not understand the question, or was unable to speak. Call that the *non-reticence heuristic*.

One can get from a *direct* speech report to a belief ascription by first applying the (suitably modified) homophonic disquotation heuristic and then applying the sincerity heuristic to the result. This can lead to Frege puzzles about co-referential terms such as 'Hesperus' and 'Phosphorus'.

For example, imagine this speech:

NN: Some people confuse Mike Brearley, the former captain of the England cricket team, with J. M. Brearley, the former lecturer at Newcastle University. They are not the same person. J. M. Brearley was once a professional philosopher. Mike Brearley was never a professional philosopher.

NN is mistaken. Mike Brearley, the former captain of the England cricket team, *is* J. M. Brearley, the former lecturer in philosophy at Newcastle University.

Imagine Brearley overhearing NN's speech.

When NN says 'J. M. Brearley was once a professional philosopher', Brearley can use the homophonic disquotational heuristic to make the indirect speech report 'NN said that J. M. Brearley was once a professional philosopher', but normal conversational standards for the use of pronouns *also* allow him to report 'NN said that I was once a professional philosopher'. Since NN's sincerity is not in question, Brearley then applies the sincerity heuristic to infer 'NN believes that I was once a professional philosopher'.

When NN says 'Mike Brearley was never a professional philosopher', Brearley can use the same heuristic to report 'NN said that Mike Brearley was never a professional philosopher', but normal conversational standards for the use of pronouns *also* allow him to report 'NN said that I was never a professional philosopher'. By the sincerity heuristic again, Brearley infers 'NN believes that I was never a professional philosopher'.

Putting the pieces together, Brearley ends up concluding 'NN believes both that I was never a professional philosopher and that I was once a professional philosopher', thereby accusing NN of having mutually contradictory beliefs. Yet NN may be a leading classical logician, with a militant aversion to inconsistency.

In that respect, the threatened contradiction is in NN's beliefs. But contradiction also threatens Brearley's own beliefs, by the non-reticence heuristic. For NN is far from reticent, and he clearly refuses to say 'Mike Brearley was once a professional philosopher'. Thus, by the homophonic disquotational heuristic, Brearley can report 'NN refuses to say that Mike Brearley was once a professional philosopher', but normal conversational standards for the use of pronouns *also* allow him to report 'NN refuses to say that I was once a professional philosopher'. Brearley then applies the non-reticence heuristic to conclude 'NN does not believe that I was once a professional philosopher'. But, as seen above, Brearley has already concluded 'NN believes that I was once a professional philosopher'. The threatened contradiction is now in Brearley's own beliefs (about NN's beliefs), not just in NN's beliefs.

Of course, there is a long history of trying all sorts of ingenious strategies to resolve the inconsistencies, from Frege's distinction between sense and reference to contemporary contextualist accounts of the implicit constraints on the guises or modes of presentation of the relevant objects under which the subject must conceive them in taking the putative attitude, for the attitude ascription to count as true. But when Janet complains to a friend 'John thinks that he's taller than me', she does not seem to be implying that, in so doing, John thinks of her in some way relevantly similar to the way in which she thinks of herself, or anything of the kind; the issue of the guise under which John thinks of her seems not to arise at all. Naturally, one can imagine deviant cases where John thinks of her in some surprisingly convoluted way, but most things we say can be true in surprising ways. Rather than assume that some elaborate semantic apparatus is needed to explain the puzzle cases, we should explore the hypothesis that they are just predictable outcomes of our fallible heuristics for attitude ascriptions, as the Brearley example illustrates. That may be the right moral to draw from Saul Kripke's article 'A Puzzle about Belief' (1979), even though it is probably not the one he intended—what he seems to treat as an incoherence in the very concept of belief may be better understood as manifesting the inevitable limits of some of our ordinary, useful heuristics for ascribing belief (see chapter 4 for more discussion).

The sincerity and non-reticence heuristics are obviously specific to belief and do not generalize in any straightforward way to other propositional attitudes, such as hope, fear, and intention. One would expect the human capacity for what psychologists call 'mindreading' to comprise heuristics for many different such attitudes. Furthermore, the sincerity and non-reticence heuristics are specifically based on *speech* behaviour. Yet we also apply our mindreading capacity to ascribe propositional attitudes, including beliefs, to pre-linguistic and non-linguistic creatures, such as very young children and non-human animals, often thereby explaining their behaviour much better than we could if we refrained from ascribing such attitudes to them. We may therefore need other mindreading heuristics to operate on non-linguistic behaviour.

How far can all these mindreading heuristics be unified? After all, linguistic and non-linguistic behaviour are not totally independent of each other, and propositional attitudes are interrelated in various ways: hopes and fears are connected to beliefs about the probabilities of good and bad outcomes, and intentions to beliefs about what one will do. To what extent different mindreading heuristics can all be understood as applications of one more general mindreading heuristic is an open question.

One should not assume that the default is always *not* to ascribe an attitude, in the absence of positive behavioural evidence—such as speech—for ascribing it. In particular, for the central attitude of *knowledge*, the default may be the other way round, to ascribe knowledge of truths unless there is some specific reason not to. For the most efficient cognitive policy may be to treat the world as by default open to view for all potential knowers, and then track specific obstacles to cognitive access. Metaphorically, if each of us carries around a mental map of the world in our head, I don't want to carry around mental maps of everyone else's mental maps, and so on ad infinitum. It would be easier just to carry around one mental map, mark on it where others are, and make further requisite adjustments on that basis in more or less systematic ways, or at worst ad hoc, rather than treating other minds as by default blank slates. With such an open-world heuristic, we will ascribe plenty of knowledge to creatures who exhibit no speech-like behaviour at all (Williamson forthcoming-b, section 8). Given that knowledge is treated as entailing belief, we will ascribe plenty of beliefs to them too—at least when the occasion arises, since there is most point in attributing belief when we are not willing to attribute knowledge. Thus several more or less independent heuristics or sub-heuristics can combine, or even compete, in ascribing the presence or absence of the same attitude to the same subject at the same time. The result is not 'conceptual incoherence' but just what one might expect when several methods or sources of evidence are available for answering the same question.

We have seen how homophonic disquotational principles for the ascription of belief generate paradoxes of belief. Notoriously, and for related reasons, homophonic disquotational principles for the ascription of truth and falsity generate Liar-like semantic paradoxes. From the present perspective, such paradoxes are evidence that an underlying heuristic is at work. Although (T) and (F) are not strictly disquotational themselves, they are still associated with versions of the Liar paradox.

For example, I say 'What I'm saying is not true'. The corresponding first-person present-tense indirect speech report is (7) (which I can think rather than say):

(7) I'm saying that what I'm saying is not true

In a context where nothing else I say is relevant, I can rework (7) as (8), just as Janet could rework her indirect speech report (1) as (2) above:

(8) What I'm saying = that what I'm saying is not true

The relevant instance of (T) is (9):

(9) That what I'm saying is not true is true if and only if what I'm saying is not true

Just as Janet could derive (5) from (2) and (4) above by the logic of identity, so I can derive (10) from (8) and (9), substituting 'what I'm saying' for 'that what I'm saying is not true' in (9):

(10) What I'm saying is true if and only if what I'm saying is not true

But (10) is a contradiction, since it is of the form 'P if and only if not-P', and so cannot be true, given classical logic.

In the analogous paradox for (F), I say 'What I'm saying is false'. The relevant indirect speech report is (7*):

(7*) I'm saying that what I'm saying is false

In a context where nothing else I say is relevant, I can rework (7*) as (8*):

(8*) What I'm saying = that what I'm saying is false

The relevant instance of (F) is (9*):

(9*) That what I'm saying is false is false if and only if what I'm saying is not false

In the same way as before, I can derive (10*) from (8*) and (9*), substituting 'what I'm saying' for 'that what I'm saying is false' in (9*):

(10*) What I'm saying is false if and only if what I'm saying is not false

But (10*) is another contradiction, since it too is of the form 'P if and only if not-P'.

These paradoxes have been taken to warrant revision of classical logic, in particular by accepting some instances of 'P if and only if not-P'. From the present perspective, such drastic reactions look methodologically perverse. There is a far more obvious suspect: the homophonic disquotational heuristic for speech reports. We already know that it is only a heuristic, as the elementary case of pronouns and other indexicals makes clear. With the indirect speech reports (7) and (7*), the problem is not with the personal pronoun 'I'. Rather, the natural explanation is that in uttering the sentence 'What I'm saying is not true' or 'What I'm saying is false' in the envisaged contexts, I fail altogether to say that something is the case. No positive indirect speech report at all is appropriate. Such failures may be initially surprising, but they violate no law of logic. Since (7) and (7*) are to be rejected, the paradoxical arguments do not even get started.

A natural objection is that the underlying problem does not really depend on indirect speech reports, because it still manifests in direct speech reports such as (7D) and (7*D):

(7D) I'm uttering 'What I'm uttering is not true'

(7*D) I'm uttering 'What I'm uttering is false'

Here 'utter' is used in place of 'say' to indicate that a relation to sentences rather than to propositions is in play. What is uttered is a sentence. So understood, (7D) and (7*D) are much harder to deny than (7) and (7*). Where no other utterances are relevant, we then have the required equations:

(8D)   What I'm uttering = 'What I'm uttering is not true'

(8*D) What I'm uttering = 'What I'm uttering is false'

Since the problem now concerns the truth or falsity of sentences, it requires appropriately modified analogues of (T) and (F). The closest analogues are these familiar disquotational schemata:

(TD)   'P' is true if and only if P

(FD)   'P' is false if and only if not-P

The paradoxical arguments can then proceed much as before, with quotation marks in place of 'that' and 'utter' in place of 'say'.

However, a reason for restricting homophonic disquotational indirect speech is also a reason for restricting (TD) and (FD). To put it schematically, when in uttering 'P' you fail to say that P, you cannot be expected to have said something that is true if and only if P, or false if and only if not-P. For instance, when you utter the sentence 'I'm hungry', you do not say that *I'm* hungry, so I do not expect the sentence as uttered by you to be true if and only if *I'm* hungry, or false if and only if *I'm* not hungry. More generally, (TD) and (FD) should be restricted to contexts where the homophonic disquotational schema (D) also holds:

(D)   In uttering 'P', one says that P.

A gloss is needed, for an actor can utter a declarative sentence on stage without asserting that anything is the case, and so in a sense without really saying that anything is the case. For purposes of disquotation, we can understand 'say' more liberally than that. Such non-assertive utterances will form another case where the sincerity heuristic for belief ascription is inhibited.

Of course, when you utter 'I'm hungry', you say something that is true if and only if *you* are hungry, and false if and only if *you* are not hungry, for you say that *you* are hungry. Thus, the proper generalizations are something like these non-homophonic principles (where *s* is a sentence):

(TG)   In contexts where, in uttering *s*, one says that P, *s* is true if and only if P

(FG)   In contexts where, in uttering *s*, one says that P, *s* is false if and only if not-P.

From (TG) and (FG), one can recover the homophonic principles (TD) and (FD) respectively for contexts where (D) holds. The paradoxes are resolved because one cannot recover the relevant instances of (TD) and (FD) in the relevant contexts, since (D) fails there (see Williamson 1998 and Andjelković and Williamson 2000 for some relevant discussion). For the sentential as well as the propositional versions of the paradoxes, the culprit is the homophonic disquotational heuristic for indirect reported speech. A similar diagnosis applies to versions of the paradoxes for thought rather than speech.

Although the specific problems for disquotation differ between Frege puzzles and semantic paradoxes, they both manifest its rough-and-ready character. Naturally, much remains to be explored about exactly where and why homophonic disquotational speech breaks down. In particular, we need to understand better the mechanisms of its failure in semantic paradoxes, which may also help explain its failures elsewhere. Since we already have decisive independent evidence that homophonic disquotation has merely heuristic status, postulating failures in unrelated principles—such as those of elementary propositional logic—is gratuitous and methodologically wrong-headed.

1.6 The weighing heuristic for reasons

Talk of 'reasons' is central to much contemporary debate in metaethics and, more generally, metanormativity. It promises to unify the practical with the theoretical: there are both reasons for action and reasons for belief. The term 'reasons' is assumed to be intellectually perspicuous enough to serve in the most abstract reasoning, yet also securely enough rooted in pre-philosophical normative thought and talk to ground what we say in concrete cases. There is even a research programme with the slogan 'Reasons first', which proclaims that the category of reasons is explanatorily fundamental (Schroeder 2021).

The use of the word 'reasons' in the plural is a reminder that we need some way of thinking and talking about *combining reasons*, on pain of being left at a loss when more than one reason bears on our decision. For example, in a group debate on whether or not to take a certain course of action, each side may present various considerations for and against taking that course, and the group faces the challenge of combining those considerations and resolving them into a decision one way or the other. As a single individual, one may carry out a similar process in one's own head.

We do indeed have such a way of combining reasons, for we often speak of 'weighing reasons', 'adding up' or 'balancing' the 'pros and cons', the 'reasons for' and the 'reasons against', and of reasons that 'outweigh' other reasons. The metaphor is of a pair of scales, with reasons-for going into one pan, reasons-against into the other, and the decision for or against depending on which pan goes down, which up. The metaphor is not inert. It structures our thinking about what to do or what is the case, when we think about more than one reason. *Without* this organizing metaphor, our thought about reasons would be in danger of impotence.

The metaphor of weighing reasons is in effect an *additive* model. If you put two lumps of metal into a pan, the added weight is the sum of the weight of one lump and the weight of the other. Likewise, two reasons-for add up to a weightier case-for than either reason-for by itself.

Such an additive model has costs as well as benefits. For sometimes it gives the wrong result. Here is a simple case. A number labelled 'N' has been chosen from the set {1, 2, 3, 4, 5, 6, 7, 8, 9, 10, 11, 12}, by a random draw. You have to guess whether 'N is even' or 'N is odd'; if you are right, you win $100, if you are wrong, you lose $100. A perfectly trusted and trustworthy informant, X, tells you just 'N is in the set {2, 4, 6, 7}'. X's testimony is a good reason for guessing 'N is even', since its probability on X's testimony is 75%. Another perfectly trusted and trustworthy informant, Y, tells you just 'N is in the set {7, 8, 10, 12}'. By parity of reasoning, Y's testimony is another good reason for guessing 'N is even', since its probability on Y's testimony is again 75%. But X's testimony and Y's testimony together amount to a decisive reason *against* guessing 'N is even', since the conjunction of what you learn from X's testimony and what you learn from Y's testimony entails that N is 7. Thus, two good reasons for doing something can together make a decisive reason against doing it, contrary to the additive model of weighing reasons (see Titelbaum 2019 for more extensive discussion of such cases, Nair 2021 for more examples and non-additive ways of combining reasons, Schroeder 2008: 32–4, 125–6 on adding up reasons, and more generally Kagan 1988 and Lord and Maguire 2016).

Friends of the additive model tend to object to such examples along the following lines. When you have just one of the two testimonies, it is a reason for guessing 'N is even'. But once you have *both* testimonies, each of them is a reason *against* guessing 'N is even', given what else you know. The trouble with such replies is that they effectively abandon the weighing metaphor as a useful way of structuring our thinking about how to combine reasons. If putting a second lump of metal into one pan of the scales may cause both lumps to jump into the other pan, all bets are off. Less metaphorically, such replies on behalf of the weighing model presuppose that we already have some *other* way of thinking about how to combine reasons, so that we can determine the new strength and valence of each reason once it is combined with the other reasons. Of course, in examples with a simple probabilistic structure like that above, we *do* have such an alternative structure, because we can work with conditional probabilities, as the discussion implicitly illustrated. The real work of combining the two testimonies was done in the framework of probability theory, not in the framework of reasons theory (if there is such a thing). A serious defence of the reasons framework must show how to combine reasons *within* that framework, not by abandoning it. Rendering the additive model harmless by rendering it impotent does not constitute such a serious defence.

Friends of the reasons framework can do better by treating the weighing metaphor as a convenient *heuristic* for combining reasons. It assesses the weight of each reason, and which pan it goes into, *separately*, and then combines the results additively. As a result, it will sometimes give the wrong answer, as in the example above. Nevertheless, its friends can plausibly claim, such examples tend to be rather artificial: the additive model may typically give the right answer in realistic cases. In many such cases, any assignment of numerical probabilities would be highly artificial, while the reasons framework is in much less danger of imposing a false precision, and may be psychologically more realistic as a model of human thinking.

In fact, there is *no* exceptionless rule for calculating how much a conjunction supports a conclusion in terms of how much its conjuncts do, since the latter underdetermines the former. To see this, consider a variant case in which X still tells you 'N is in the set {2, 4, 6, 7}' but Y tells you 'N is in the set {2, 4, 6, 9}'. As before, the probability of 'N is even' is 75% on X's testimony and 75% on Y's testimony, but now its probability on the combined testimony is 100%, not 0%. In that sense, the original problem is insoluble. A heuristic is the best we can do.

Failures of the additive model are not just intellectual curiosities. They can have practical consequences. The contested term 'intersectionality' may sometimes be used to get at such practically important failures of the additive model. For example, in an assessment of reasons for compensating someone for discrimination, if the weight of their being a black woman is equated with the sum of the weight of their being black and the weight of their being a woman, then in some circumstances a serious injustice will be done (compare Crenshaw 1989, the seminal text on intersectionality).

Whether the category of reasons is really as useful or as fundamental as proponents of the 'Reasons first' programme like to claim is not a question to be conclusively settled here. Still, one may wonder how fundamental the ideology of weighing reasons really is. After all, the metaphor makes sense only in a society familiar with the mechanism of a balanced scale. Although the technology for weighing and balancing is modest, there may not have been much need of it under evolutionary conditions. In any case, the reasons framework seems much better adapted to the regulation of debate than to tracking perception and memory—the acquisition and retention of the knowledge that should inform the debate. It is a strange child who acquires the category of reasons before they acquire the category of knowledge. Indeed, *having* a reason is arguably a matter of knowing the relevant fact, so that the ideology of reasons has to be explained in terms of knowledge, not the other way round (Hawthorne and Magidor 2018). But even if the category of reasons does not go very deep in the human cognitive system, we still cannot use it properly without heuristics to help us determine the results of combining reasons.

1.7 Implications for philosophical methodology

The last four sections presented various ways in which reliance on unacknowledged heuristics may have distorted our philosophical understanding—in particular, of vagueness, conditionals, belief, truth and falsity, and reasons. Specifically, what look like clear counterexamples to philosophical and logical theories may be the misleading artefacts of fallible heuristics.

This concern should not be confused with the 'negative program' characteristic of the early stages of 'experimental philosophy', which tried to demonstrate by surveys that philosophers' verdicts on hypothetical cases were too sensitive to subjects' ethnicity or gender to be reliable.[6] By contrast, many heuristics like those above are so general and so useful that they may well turn out to be more or less universal features of the human cognitive system and not susceptible to significant variation with ethnicity, gender, social class, or other such factors. Of course, in the long run, the presence or absence of those heuristics in cognition over various human populations can and should be tested experimentally. However, since none of the heuristics at issue is specifically *philosophical*— each of them is targeted on a general class of cognitive challenges that frequently arise in ordinary life—they will be best investigated in the broader setting of cognitive psychology. They do not call for a special experimental branch of philosophy, though naturally frequent two-way interaction between philosophically informed

---

[6] The seminal paper for the negative program was Weinberg, Nichols and Stich 2001, of which Nagel 2012 is an effective critique. For further criticism of the negative program, see Williamson 2011a and 2016d. Many early results of experimental philosophy have turned out not to be repeatable under more rigorous conditions. For instance, after more extensive experimentation, early claims that the Gettier 'intuition' (that the subject of a classic Gettier case lacks knowledge) depends on ethnicity and gender have been replaced by the hypothesis that the Gettier 'intuition' is part of a humanly universal folk epistemology (Machery, Stich, Rose, Chatterjee, Karasawa, Struchiner, Sirker, Usui, and Hashimoto 2017). Most contemporary experimental philosophy is not involved in the negative program. Sytsma and Buckwalter 2016 is a wide-ranging recent survey of experimental philosophy.

psychologists and psychologically informed philosophers is likely to benefit both sides.

How should we react to the discovery that we have been relying on fallible heuristics? Don't panic! After all, sense perception has long been known to rely on heuristics whose limitations result in perceptual illusions, but it would be melodramatic to conclude that we have no perceptual knowledge. Generic sceptical arguments from the occurrence of heuristic-induced errors are no better than generic sceptical arguments from the occurrence of errors of other kinds. Whatever kind of reliability or safety from error knowledge requires, it is local, not global.

We cannot understand all this by treating the heuristic as the major premise of a deductive argument, an unrestricted universal generalization that will inevitably be false and so no basis for knowledge, just as we cannot understand perceptual knowledge by treating it as based on deductions whose major premise is that perception is perfectly reliable. No such premise is in play; it is neither assumed nor needed. Most cognition is not deductive. Like other biological processes, it often functions properly even though it is capable of functioning improperly.

If a heuristic is humanly universal, or nearly so, it is likely to have survived because it is adaptive; in the most straightforward case, a heuristic is adaptive because it tends to give correct results in normal cases. In particular, we should be wary of drawing pessimistic methodological conclusions for philosophy from our reliance on fallible heuristics. The heuristics are not themselves specific to philosophy; they underpin much of our thinking in general. Since our reliance on them does not warrant generic scepticism, assuming it to warrant philosophy-specific scepticism would be arbitrary.

Still, such general reflections do not warrant complacency. We should at least ask what improvements on our current philosophical methodology might make it less vulnerable to heuristic-induced illusions. That is work for the following chapters. It is not easy, for if we are heuristic-using creatures, we are probably creatures who *need* to use heuristics. We can sometimes correct their outputs, but in correcting them we may well rely on other heuristics, or even on other applications of the *same* heuristic. Nevertheless, methodological improvements *are* feasible, and they will call into question some currently fashionable ideas.

The role of sense perception in natural science is a helpful precedent here too. Without sense perception, natural science is simply impossible. Although scientists use artificial aids such as microscopes and telescopes, measuring instruments and computers, at some point or other they must be able to see or hear or touch at least some of the results. To put it crudely: if you are hallucinating, you are in no fit state to do science. Yet human sensory systems are riddled with fallible heuristics. In effect, scientists have learnt how to control their reliance on sense perception in ways that minimize the risks and costs of misperception. Incidentally, they have *not* done it as many epistemological internalists do, by treating subjective perceptual appearances as foundational: such appearances are quite unsuitable to play the role of scientific evidence, since they are not open to inter-subjective checking. Rather, they have applied whatever external controls were needed to resolve specific problems of misperception as they were identified. Something analogous may be possible, and necessary, to control the risk of errors induced by the more abstract heuristics prevalent in philosophy, such as those above.

Before we turn to ways of controlling the risk, its general nature could do with some further clarification. In discussing the *reliability* or *unreliability* of heuristics, one typically presupposes that their outputs are judgments, classifiable as *true* or *false*. The heuristic's degree of reliability may then be identified with the objective probability of true outputs conditional on true inputs. In practice, reliability is often a more complex matter. If the heuristic is inferential, with premise-like inputs, then what counts is truth-*preservation* from inputs to output, rather than just the truth of the output, and the degree of reliability may be identified with the relative frequency of true outputs *given true inputs*. If the heuristic's output is an *estimate* rather than a judgment, it may be assessed on a graded scale of accuracy, rather than on the binary distinction between truth and falsity. One may in turn relativize all such standards of reliability to specified conditions under which the heuristic was applied. And so on. Yet, irrespective of all these complications, reliability is still defined in terms of a standard of truth or accuracy given quite independently of the heuristic itself. More specifically, the heuristic has been assigned no role in determining the *content* of the judgments or estimates which it outputs. That may look like a bad picture when the heuristic is central to our practice of making judgments or estimates with those contents. For example, one might take the disquotational heuristics for ascribing belief and truth and falsity to be at least partially *constitutive* of the meanings of the words 'believe', 'true', and 'false'.

At the opposite extreme, a heuristic—probably not so-described—may be treated as an 'analytic' or 'conceptual' connection, quasi-definitional of the terms at issue. That may induce a philosophical crisis when the heuristic turns out to be inconsistent, at least given uncontroversial background knowledge, as with those above: however important to our lives the practices which involve those terms, they suddenly look 'incoherent'. But, as also emerged in those case studies, once the heuristics are properly identified, they are rarely promising candidates for 'analytic' or 'conceptual' status. Not only are the heuristics inconsistent, given our background knowledge: they fail in straightforward, unpuzzling cases—especially once we strip out the ad hoc apparatus of qualifications added as afterthoughts to disqualify exceptions, with no 'analytic' or 'conceptual' guarantee that no further qualifications will need to be added as further exceptions turn up.

On a better, intermediate alternative, heuristics lack 'analytic' or 'conceptual' status, but still play a role in determining the meanings of the relevant terms. This is at the level of *metasemantics*, the study of the factors on which the semantics of a language as used by a given community supervenes, or at least constitutively depends. At that level, something like a principle of charity operates, to favour interpretations that maximize the attribution of true beliefs or (as I prefer) knowledge to the community, given whatever other constraints on interpretation are operative (Williamson 2007/2021a, chapter 8). The heuristics used by the community or its members belong to the putative supervenience base for the metasemantics. They form a significant part of what has to be interpreted charitably.

Of course, no community or individual is omniscient, or error-free, and something is very wrong with any metasemantic theory that implies otherwise. Inconsistent heuristics merely increase how much ignorance or error must be ascribed. Charitable interpretations still do what they can for a much-used heuristic, making it more rather than less reliable, though not perfectly reliable. For instance, we saw how the material interpretation of 'if' might do that for the suppositional heuristic for assessing conditionals. Despite the persistence heuristic's sorites-susceptibility, it can still exert pressure towards assigning a predicate a *convex* region of the relevant similarity space for its extension. Informally, the convex closure of a shape is the result of filling in all its holes and hollows, and a convex shape is one that is already its own convex closure. More formally, a region is convex just in case any point directly between two points in the region is itself in the region. Violations of convexity tend to multiply counter-instances to persistence without necessity, so persistence militates in favour of convexity. Of course, the convexity constraint falls far short of uniquely determining predicate extensions; typically, the similarity space can be partitioned into convex regions in many different ways. Some of those may be eliminated because they violate other natural constraints (see Gärdenfors 2000 and Douven and Gärdenfors 2020 for more discussion). Still, we have no grounds to expect natural constraints to achieve uniqueness: a residual element of happenstance is likely to remain in the determination of reference.

One general strategy for charitable interpretation is *contextualist*: by varying the assignment of reference to a term with the context in which it is used, the strategy grants itself the flexibility to count more utterances as knowledgeable, or at least true. Contextualist strategies have been applied to all the kinds of case in which heuristics like those above are used: vagueness, conditionals, ascriptions of belief, truth and falsity, and reasons. However, since the heuristics are applicable even within a single context—which contributes to their power and usefulness—contextualism still cannot make them come out perfectly reliable.

Contextualist strategies have their own drawbacks, often overlooked. They do poorly when information in verbal form is transmitted across contexts through memory and testimony, unless agents keep track of the relevant features of all those contexts (Williamson 2005). For example, on some contextualist theories of belief ascriptions, the truth-condition of the sentence 'John believed that Cicero was a Roman orator' varies with which guises John has to have believed the proposition that Cicero was a Roman orator under for the sentence to be true. Believing the proposition under the guise of the sentence 'Tully was a Roman orator' may count in some contexts but not in others (chapter 4 discusses such theories in more detail). Thus, if John loses track of the original set of contextually relevant guises, he in effect loses track of the belief ascription's original truth-conditions, and so is ill-placed to use the stored sentence in a new context, for instance, to pass on information to someone else. Thus, contextualist strategies open up myriads of new error-possibilities for speakers who do not carefully store lots of information about the contexts in which they originally acquired linguistically encoded information. Speakers unaware of such contextualist features of the semantics of their language will be especially liable not to do the hard work of storing all that information.

If we store that information about linguistic contexts in linguistic form, an infinite regress threatens. Even if we do not store the information in linguistic form, we are still in danger of having to back up all semantic memory with episodic memory of contexts, which is psychologically quite implausible.

Of course, obviously context-sensitive terms such as pronouns and demonstratives already do impose burdens of adjustment to changing contexts, which speakers and hearers usually manage to handle, often automatically, but contextualist strategies tend to multiply those burdens drastically, with no serious check on whether the benefits really outweigh the costs. That going contextualist conduces to more charitable interpretation is much less clear than it is normally taken to be. In particular, one should not be too optimistic about the prospects of making heuristics like those above come out much more reliable on a contextualist semantics. For their inconsistency was established with respect to the underlying level of content, whereas contextualism is just a doctrine about the mapping of form to content. For example, in any given context, tolerance principles are false, and the suppositional heuristic is inconsistent. Although contextualists may hope to limit how far the inconsistency is manifested in actual speech situations, that is likely to involve ad hoc complications. If the contextualist can easily model whatever data come in, scientists would tend to regard that as a warning sign of bad science, for reasons explained in the next chapter.

A possible compromise is to have a *default* standard for applying a term, while permitting contextual inhibition of the default. For example, the default comparison class for 'tall' would presumably be all humans, not all basketball players. In the absence of indicators to the contrary, occurrences of the term in testimony or memory would be evaluated according to the default. That would ease the practical difficulties in using a context-sensitive term. By contrast, pronouns and demonstratives have no such default referent. Proposals for a context-sensitive interpretation need to be explicit on whether they are postulating such a default. If they are, the relevant heuristics may still be less than fully reliable on the default reading.

To sum up, the heuristics on which we often rely in philosophy may be very rough indeed. The next chapter will consider some methodological consequences of that conclusion.

For the present, we may console ourselves with one reflection. Although the role of heuristics in our pre-theoretical assessments of examples makes our lives harder methodologically, because our data are less reliable than we thought, it also holds out the prospect that true answers to our theoretical questions may often be much simpler than we thought, because true, simple answers have already been wrongly dismissed on the basis of what are really heuristic-generated fool's counterexamples.

2
Overfitting and Degrees of Freedom

2.1 Error-fragility

On the most naïve reading of Karl Popper's philosophy of science, scientific theories are falsifiable but not verifiable. A scientific theory can be falsified, for it is a universal generalization, to which a particular negative instance, a counterexample, can be observed. But the theory cannot be verified, for however many particular positive instances are observed, they are all jointly consistent with a particular negative instance, which can be observed in the future, so they are all jointly consistent with the theory's negation.

Few contemporary philosophers of science accept that crude picture. By normal scientific standards, the theory of the circulation of blood *has* been verified. Of course, it has not been verified in the sense of having been *conclusively proved by the highest conceivable standard*, but then no scientific theory has ever been falsified either in the corresponding sense of having been *conclusively refuted by the highest conceivable standard*. After all, mistakes in observation are possible, and sometimes actual—through misperception and misinterpretation, incompetence and deceit, and so on. Scientific observation requires skill; things can go wrong. That is why scientists want important experiments to be repeated several times, preferably by different scientists in different laboratories. The reputation of the scientific team performing the experiment matters too—but not all reputations are deserved.

Imagine a scientific community proceeding as if naïve falsificationism were correct. As soon as someone reports an observation inconsistent with a scientific theory, the theory is trashed as refuted for all time, and the community never returns to it. If such a community ever entertains a correct theory, it is in serious danger of sooner or later throwing it out on the basis of a mistaken observation, and never returning to it. In the terminology of Joshua Alexander and Jonathan Weinberg (2014), such a methodology is *error-fragile*. A single error is liable to have catastrophic repercussions.

Even if the community raises its standard for accepting an observation report by demanding repeatability, that does not fully solve the problem of error-fragility. For when an experimental result is repeatable, something could still be wrong: the experimental design itself may be flawed; a crucial systematically interfering factor may have been overlooked, may even be unknown to the whole scientific community, so scientists are not measuring correctly what they think they are measuring. Deriving testable predictions from a scientific theory typically depends on auxiliary hypotheses, too–for instance, about how the experimental apparatus works—so a false prediction may result from falsity in an auxiliary hypothesis rather than falsity in the theory under test, as Pierre Duhem pointed out long ago.

Naïve falsificationism is inadequate in practice, not just in theory. It is a bad methodology, and it is not what scientists do. They rarely treat one observation report as refuting a theory. Even when no specific error has been identified, an apparent counterexample to an accepted theory may be treated as a mere *anomaly*, in something like Thomas Kuhn's sense, in the expectation or hope of resolving it eventually, unless an alternative theory nicely accommodates both the apparent counterexample and the other data (Kuhn 1962).

Of course, mathematics is one area of science where a single counterexample does indeed constitute a decisive refutation—once it has been proved by normal mathematical standards to be a counterexample. Even then, the validity of the proof can be contested, and time may be needed for the mathematical community to reach a consensus. In natural science, the methodological situation is often much messier.

Many contemporary philosophers follow a methodology uncomfortably close to naïve falsificationism. They use thought experiments rather than real-life experiments, but that does not solve the problem of error-fragility. A philosophical theory is put forward, in the form of a necessitated universal generalization. The theory—say, an account of knowledge as justified true belief—implies something about a specific possible case—say, that a Gettier case of a justified true belief deduced from a justified false belief would be a case of knowledge. Pre-theoretically, we judge ('observe') that it would *not* be a case of knowledge. The case is then treated as a counterexample to the theory, which is therefore treated as refuted. In principle, treating our pre-theoretic capacity to judge what would obtain in thought experiments as a source of knowledge is not inherently problematic, just as treating our capacity to observe what obtains in real-life experiments as a source of knowledge is not inherently problematic.[1] But, equally, our pre-theoretic capacity to judge what would obtain in thought experiments is not *infallible*, just as our capacity to observe what obtains in real-life experiments is not infallible. In both natural science and philosophy, our fallibility in classifying examples suffices to make the naïve falsificationist methodology problematic, because it offers no proper means for identifying our errors and correcting them.

The standard methodology for employing thought experiments in philosophy is not maximally naïve, for it does not treat a lone philosopher's verdict on a thought experiment as refuting a philosophical theory. Idiosyncratic errors pose little threat to standard

---

[1] Chapter 6 of Williamson 2007 explains the legitimate role of thought experiments in philosophy as verifying counterfactual conditionals for use as premises in philosophical arguments. Williamson 2021a extends the defence of that account. Chapter 14 of Williamson 2020 streamlines and strengthens the account by replacing the Lewis-Stalnaker semantics for counterfactual conditionals with a simpler semantics on which they express contextually restricted strict conditionals.

philosophical methodology, because the intellectual community will usually not adopt them—unless they are made by a charismatic or powerful figure in an intellectual sub-community with a very deferential culture. Normally, a verdict on a thought experiment will be generally accepted in philosophy only if most of those whose work it affects find it independently persuasive, without collusion. This means that thought experiments in philosophy are in effect required to be repeatable.

One could in principle worry about selection effects, where acceptance into a philosophical sub-community depends on sharing the received verdicts on some key thought experiments. That may indeed happen sometimes. But the overall trend in experimental philosophy over recent years has been to find that professional philosophers' verdicts on most thought experiments match the verdicts of lay people fairly well, once proper controls are in place by the standards of current experimental psychology—for example, to check subjects' comprehension of the hypothetical scenario (Mortensen and Nagel 2016, Knobe 2021). In crude terms, there is increasing evidence that the received verdicts in philosophy on thought experiments are mostly the natural human verdicts, irrespective of ethnicity and gender. Nevertheless, the natural human verdict on a thought experiment is still a human judgment; it is not guaranteed to be *true*.

Chapter 1 explained a potent source of repeatable errors in verdicts on thought experiments: humanly universal heuristics. Such heuristics have limitations and may even be implicitly inconsistent, so no interpretation makes all their deliverances true. The persistence heuristic lures us into false verdicts on sorites series. The suppositional heuristic generates false verdicts on conditionals. Disquotational heuristics do likewise in semantic paradoxes and Frege puzzles. If we take those verdicts at face value, following a naïve falsificationist methodology, we may as a result dismiss as refuted true theories of vagueness, conditionals, truth and falsity, and propositional attitudes. Merely scrutinizing the alleged counterexamples very hard will not solve the problem, especially if the scrutiny itself employs the very heuristic in question. The problem of erroneous data from thought experiments is not just potential; it is actual. Some natural human verdicts on thought experiments are false.

The problem is not confined to philosophy. Semantics as a branch of linguistics employs a similar methodology. Much of its evidence comes from natural human verdicts on sample sentences, envisaged as uttered in hypothetical circumstances. Those verdicts may be mediated by fallible heuristics rather than issuing directly from semantic facts somehow directly available to the speaker. Linguists as well as philosophers are interested in the semantics of vagueness, conditionals, and propositional attitude ascriptions. They face many of the same methodological challenges.

The method of hypothetical cases, applied in a naïve falsificationist spirit, faces the problem of error-fragility in practice, as well as in theory, when verdicts on thought experiments result from humanly universal heuristics of limited reliability. The scientific analogy is not to a poorly executed experiment giving a single false negative, but rather to a repeatable experiment whose design ignores a hidden source of systematic error.

The scientific analogy does not support any proposal to abandon the method of hypothetical cases in philosophy. On the contrary, errors in data from thought experiments should no more motivate philosophers to give up using thought experiments than errors in data from real-life experiments motivate natural scientists to give up using real-life experiments. Instead, what the scientific analogy supports is the search for controls to mitigate the problem by reducing error-fragility. We cannot realistically hope to prevent errors in the data from ever occurring. What we can realistically hope for are methods that will enable us both to prevent such errors from doing too much damage and eventually to identify and correct the errors. In seeking such methods, we should at least consider how the problem of erroneous data is treated in natural science.

To be scrupulous, we should note a terminological subtlety. The analogy between erroneous data from real-life experiments and erroneous data from thought experiments presupposes that verdicts on the latter count as 'data' in the scientific sense. A verdict is like an attempted measurement of the truth-value of a proposition about the hypothetical scenario, somewhat as quantitative data are like attempted measurements of the value of some physical quantity. The term 'data' in this scientific sense is by no means precise. 'Data' are sometimes defined as 'facts', yet the occurrence of errors in data is acknowledged, even though there are no false facts.[2] As I will use the term 'data', some data are indeed false, so data are not facts. Hence data need not be evidence, given that nothing true is inconsistent with the evidence (Williamson 2000: 200-202). For present purposes, we can think of the data as *prima facie* evidence.

Of course, thought experiments are by no means our only source of evidence in philosophy. On my view, anything we know is part of our total available evidence, in philosophy as elsewhere. But for present purposes, we can focus on thought experiments as the relevant source of evidence, in developing the analogy between data in natural science and data in philosophy. In any case, the best test of an analogy is to try it out.

2.2 Data fitting

In considering the error-fragility of a naïve falsificationist methodology, it is natural to focus on the case of a given data point as an apparent counterexample to a given theory. The question is whether one can rely on that data point. One may treat error as conceivable,

---

[2] For quantitative data, 'correct' should be qualified by 'within the specified margin for error'.

though unlikely. But that narrow focus makes the problem look less urgent than it really is. For the overall situation is typically that we have a large body of data, which we are trying to design a theory to fit. Even if each single data point is probably correct, it is often almost certain that the whole data set contains at least one incorrect data point. In natural science, a given data set may include millions of data points. In philosophy, the numbers are obviously much smaller, but a branch such as epistemology has still accumulated scores of thought experiments, any of which may be used to test a given theory. It also has real-life examples, such as chicken-sexers, who can unreflectively but reliably classify chickens on sight as male or female. For simplicity, I will focus on thought experiments. In effect, philosophers are often trying to design a theory to fit such a body of data. Even if one is legitimately optimistic about the reliability of standard verdicts in philosophical thought experiments, it would be very rash to assume that *none* of the standard verdicts is incorrect, either through a heuristic's inherent limitations or for some other reason. In philosophy as well as natural science, a reasonable assumption is that we are trying to design a theory to fit a set of data points not all of which are correct.

We cannot solve the problem simply by resolving to be more careful in coming to our verdicts on thought experiments. Careless errors in thought experiments are usually picked up quite quickly. Many standard thought experiments have been mulled over by the philosophical community for decades. A resolution to take more care would probably make little difference. In any case, if our verdicts are the products of fallible heuristics, taking more care might simply involve applying the heuristic more carefully, when the problem is with the heuristic itself. We cannot realistically expect to make ourselves into error-free thought experimentalists, any more than natural scientists can realistically expect to make themselves into error-free real-life experimentalists.

Instead, we need an error-robust methodology, which enables us to identify and correct our errors after we have made them rather than vainly trying to ensure that we never make them in the first place. More than that, we need to *learn from our mistakes*, by understanding what went wrong and becoming less likely to make such mistakes in the future. We can make progress by considering how curve-fitting works in natural science.

To keep things simple, imagine that we are studying a physical variable y as a function of another physical variable x. The values of x and y in given units are real numbers. We measure the value of y for many different values of x, and graph the results. The aim is to define a mathematical equation (a curve) for y in terms of x that goes as close as possible to the points on the graph. As it turns out, that can be done *perfectly*. Although the number of points to fit may be large, it is still finite, say n. Then one can always find a polynomial equation of degree $n - 1$ that goes exactly through all the data points:[3]

$$y = a_1 x^{n-1} + a_2 x^{n-2} + \ldots + a_{n-1} x + a_n$$

Here the coefficients $a_1, a_2, \ldots, a_{n-1}, a_n$ are real numbers, parameters selected to fit the data. Since the equation is defined by these n independent parameters, the equation (or model) is said to have n *degrees of freedom*—n moving parts, as it were. By hypothesis, some of the data points are incorrect—something went wrong in the process of measurement. Even if there are no systematic errors in the data, there is still random noise. The curve goes through all the data points, irrespective of whether they are correct or incorrect.

What happens when new data points are obtained? Now we have a larger total number of data points, but it is still finite, say $n + k$. Almost certainly, the old curve does not go exactly through the new data points; in other words, the new data falsify the old theory's

---

[3] For simplicity, I assume that the value of y has been measured at most once for any given exact value of x. I also assume that the number of parameters required to fit a polynomial exactly to noisy, partially incorrect data will be the same as the number of data points. These assumptions are typically correct.

predictions. After all, we already know that the equation is incorrect, because it goes exactly through an incorrect data point, and so gives an incorrect value of *y* for that value of *x*. If the old curve went exactly through the new data points, that would be amazingly good luck, unless the errors are very systematic, since the new data points would have to fit in exactly with the old errors. But one can still find a polynomial equation of degree $n + k - 1$ that goes exactly through all the old data points and all the new ones. It will have $n + k$ independent parameters, $b_1, b_2, \ldots, b_{n+k-1}, b_{n+k}$, so the new model will have $n + k$ degrees of freedom. Usually, the new polynomial will behave quite differently from the old one, especially for extreme values of *x*, where the old polynomial's behaviour will be dominated by that of its largest term, $a_1 x^{n-1}$, while the new polynomial's behaviour will be dominated by that of *its* largest term, $b_1 x^{n+k-1}$, which will be quite different. The new curve is also very likely to have more humps and dips than the old one. Although the new curve will coincide with the old one at the *n* original data points, the old curve will typically not be a good approximation to the new one elsewhere.

This process is repeated every time new data come in. The overall result will not be gradual convergence to the correct equation, since the degree of the polynomial always increases. Instead, there may be increasingly wild oscillation. All this involves large failures of prediction at each stage.

The pathology just described is not merely hypothetical. Something like it, in a milder form, is a familiar kind of bad science. Scientists call it 'overfitting' (Forster and Sober 1994). Textbooks of model selection warn against it (see, for example, Burnham and Anderson 2010). Overfitting is well known to result in unstable theorizing and predictive failures.

To some philosophers, the term 'overfitting' may sound like a contradiction in terms. Fitting the data is a good thing; how can one have too much of a good thing? Even granting that one's data set probably contains errors, one might still feel that since it is the best one has to go on, one can do no better than to fit one's theory to it as closely as one can. But bitter scientific experience shows how unlikely that approach is to end well.

For scientists, a key symptom of overfitting is an increase in degrees of freedom. A common platitude is 'With enough degrees of freedom, you can model anything'. To a philosopher, that may sound like welcome flexibility, but it is not intended in that spirit. Rather, the point is that if one has given oneself so much flexibility that one can model anything, then one can smoothly accommodate any errors in one's data, so no difficulty will occur to warn one of a potential error, and one will receive no warning that something is amiss. Not even the most grossly erroneous data point will stick out as anomalous. No data point will be a suspicious outlier, because one's curve will go through them all. A standard form of scientific criticism is that a model has too many degrees of freedom. If increasing the number of degrees of freedom is treated as cost-free, the likely result is unstable theorizing under the influx of new data. Too much flexibility, too much freedom, is a bad thing.

Scientific consensus strongly favours parsimony in degrees of freedom, even at the cost of a looser fit with the data. A large part of the rationale is that allowing oneself less flexibility to fit the data will tend to make incorrect data points show up as outliers, and so let underlying patterns emerge more clearly; the distorting effect of errors in the data is reduced. For example, when scientists use a polynomial, they like its degree to be as low as reasonably possible (linear is best), without totally flattening the data, to minimize the number of coefficients. This is a far more realistic and error-robust strategy than the hopeless aim of trying to be so careful that there are no incorrect data points in need of identification. It is a better strategy for achieving a reasonable level of predictive success.

As Malcolm Forster and Elliott Sober (1994) have argued, the problem of overfitting helps explain and justify scientists' preference for simple theories over complicated ones, for the number of degrees of freedom roughly measures the complexity of a model.

By restricting themselves to comparatively simple theories, they make the data harder to fit, and so reduce the threat of overfitting.

Some philosophers have argued that simplicity is a virtue only in theories at the most fundamental level in physics and metaphysics (Sider 2016, to which Williamson 2016b replies). But that squares neither with scientific practice nor with its theoretical rationale. The threat of overfitting is just as serious in non-fundamental sciences such as geology, biology, and economics, and in non-fundamental branches of physics, as it is in fundamental physics, and biologists, economists, and non-fundamental physicists are just as keen to keep the number of degrees of freedom low. Even detectives prefer simple explanations of the evidence. One of the problems with conspiracy theories is that their complexity rapidly increases as more and more people with varying motives have to be notionally recruited into the conspiracy to explain how it managed to remain secret.

In the latter examples, measuring complexity by the number of degrees of freedom is admittedly a stretch. In truth, the standard definition of degrees of freedom in terms of independent parameters is less rigorous than it may sound. It is right in spirit, and often works in scientific practice, but it is not fully general or precise. After all, Georg Cantor showed that there is a one-one correspondence between the real numbers and the n-tuples of real numbers for any given positive natural number n. Consequently, one can encode any ordered n-tuple of real numbers in a single real number, and thereby encode a model with n real-valued parameters (n degrees of freedom) in a model with just one real-valued parameter (one degree of freedom).

Even if one sticks to functions standardly used in natural science, one can fit all sorts of data with a wave-like sine function specified by just three parameters, for its amplitude, frequency, and phase, by making the frequency high and so the waves close enough together. The match may be perfect even though the data show no overt sign of wave-like behaviour and also perfectly match a simple cubic equation. Absent any background theoretical reason for expecting wave-like behaviour, preferring the sine function would seem scientifically bizarre. Yet cubic equations have four degrees of freedom, which is more than the sine function's three. Thus, the simple criterion of the number of independent parameters in the model is too crude to capture scientific practice exactly. Rather, it is a useful scientific *heuristic*, an imperfectly reliable sign of something subtler.

The vaguer but deeper lesson is that if we make fitting the data too easy, by helping ourselves to such a wide range of options that any supposed data will find a match, we also make ourselves easy victims of the data, because the process will not alert us to any defects or outliers in them. Flexibility has costs as well as benefits. We can still talk of 'too many degrees of freedom', understanding the phrase in that less formal way. Knowing how to recognize when there are too many may be a local matter of enculturation and experience in a given sub-discipline, depending on what is needed to achieve a reasonable level of predictive success in that area.

The informal understanding of 'degrees of freedom' also facilitates generalizations to philosophical methodology, since in philosophy we rarely deal with numerical equations, or fitting quantitative data, or data sets large enough for statistical significance. In most cases, we cannot expect literally to *count* the degrees of freedom in a philosophical theory, since deciding what to count as its 'independent parameters' would involve too many semi-arbitrary choices, though we can come close in more formal areas of philosophy.[4]

---

[4] Recent successes of AI at tasks such as face recognition and text prediction have been taken to mandate a re-evaluation of accepted wisdom about overfitting, since they have been achieved by using almost unlimited numbers of degrees of freedom (Bartlett, Long, Lugosi, and Tsigler 2020, Dar, Muthukumar, and Baraniuk 2021). The programmes are typically trained on vast sets of typically accurate data, and their success is measured by predictive accuracy rather than theoretical understanding. One cannot plausibly argue from such cases that natural scientists have been misguided in their strategy of limiting degrees of freedom. Since philosophical inquiry is much more similar in its aims and methods to scientific inquiry than to face recognition or

2.3 Overfitting in philosophical analysis

Comfort with a succession of increasingly complex theories is easily observed in the still-continuing twentieth-century tradition of providing would-be 'conceptual analyses', or just 'analyses', for philosophically significant terms of ordinary language such as 'know', 'cause', 'mean', and 'free', or for the concepts they are supposed to express. For example, in the case of 'know', one can see the complexity proliferate over a decade by leafing through the pages of Shope (1983); similarly, for the programme of analysing causation in counterfactual terms, following David Hume and David Lewis, see Paul and Hall (2013), and for the programme of analysing meaning in psychological terms, following Paul Grice, see Davis (2002). The adjective in the term 'analytic philosophy' has been closely associated with that tradition of analysis.

Proposed analyses were tested against potential *counterexamples*, mostly drawn from hypothetical cases. Thus, the relevant data were taken to be about hypothetical cases, articulated in roughly the same terms as the analysans (on the right-hand side of the analysis) or the analysandum (on the left-hand side).

---

text prediction, it would be similarly implausible to argue from the successes of AI that philosophers should not be guided by a strategy of limiting degrees of freedom. By training an AI programme on a vast set of data on human answers to questions about a wide range of thought-experimental scenarios, with no restriction on the number of degrees of freedom, one might indeed manage to get the programme to answer questions on further thought-experimental scenarios in a human-like way. But, by itself, that would not advance philosophical understanding of the issues the scenarios were intended to probe: the AI is just doing what humans can already do, perhaps in a slightly different way, perhaps even slightly better. It is not producing an intelligible theory of the philosophical subject matter. The problem is not that the AI can understand phenomena too complex for humans, but that its understanding of them (if we may speak in such terms) is only of the kind that humans already have. Worse, when we have evidence that the data is infected by heuristic-induced errors, it does not tell us which natural human verdicts on the scenarios are *true*, and which *false*. In this respect, the recent successes of AI are not of much direct help to philosophy. However, the field is obviously developing very fast; it may at least prove valuable for testing hypotheses about the workings of human intelligence, and the range of tasks at which AI outdoes human intelligence will presumably broaden.

Since the analysans was supposed to be necessary and sufficient for the analysandum, counterexamples could be to either the alleged necessity or the alleged sufficiency. Notoriously, alternating spirals grew of ever more complex analyses and ever more complex hypothetical counterexamples, each analysis provoking counterexamples and each counterexample inspiring revised analyses. If the counterexample was to the necessity of the analysans for the analysandum, showing the analysans to be too strong, one could weaken it by adding an extra disjunct. If the counterexample was instead to the sufficiency of the analysans, showing it to be too weak, one could strengthen it by adding an extra conjunct. But making the analysans weaker in one place often made it too weak somewhere else, and making it stronger somewhere often made it too strong somewhere else. Conjunctions of disjunctions and disjunctions of conjunctions started to emerge. The whole process was reminiscent of the tradition in Ptolemaic astronomy of adding epicycles whenever a new discrepancy with observation was found.

In retrospect, it is striking how little resistance there was for so long to the ramifying complications. From inside the tradition, it just felt like discovering more and more hidden complexity in ordinary concepts. The analogy with degenerating research programmes in natural science (in the sense of Lakatos 1970) may have been occluded from practitioners by their understanding of themselves as engaged in the a priori conceptual work of analysis, sharply contrasted with the a posteriori empirical work of science. From outside the tradition, it looks like a classic case of overfitting, with the typical symptom of adding ever more terms—here in the form of conjunctions or disjunctions—and the resulting theoretical instability and predictive failures in new cases.

A distinctive aspect of the case was that the postulated complexity was attributed not to the world at large but specifically to the cognitive resources of ordinary people, whose concepts or meanings were supposedly being analysed into more basic terms. As the conceptual structure became ever more complex, to regard it, even metaphorically, as if it were written into lexical entries for the target words in an ordinary person's head became ever less plausible. Yet the complex structure had to be implicit in the ordinary use of the term, and somehow available to a priori reflection, even though normal speakers of the language, presented with the proposed analysis, would typically have great difficulty in so much as comprehending the analysans, and even more in guessing whether or not it corresponded to their use of the analysandum. Unease about the intended cognitive status of analyses found early articulation in the 'paradox of analysis' (Langford 1942): if the analysis is correct, the analysans expresses the same concept as the analysandum, so they differ only verbally, so the analysis is trivial; thus, no analysis is non-trivially correct. The paradox continued to niggle, with no agreed solution, but also without doing much to slow the growth of the analysis industry.

If the complex structure of the analysans is supposed to play some cognitive role in the process of real-time thinking with the analysandum, questions of computational feasibility arise, which were never properly addressed. From an evolutionary perspective, it is hard to understand how the near-ubiquitous use of concepts such as 'know' and 'cause' (or 'make') in ordinary thought could fail to be counter-adaptive if they really had the apparently ad hoc complex structures the analyses attributed to them. Anyone who has tried working out whether such a philosophical analysans applies to a given hypothetical example will have experienced what a tricky and time-consuming task it is, comparable to a lawyer's job of applying a complicated piece of legislation to a given case. The easy fluency with which ordinary folk apply words like 'know' and 'make' in real time would be near-miraculous. On the other hand, if the complex structure of the analysans is *not* supposed to play some cognitive role in the process of real-time thinking with the analysandum, the intended status of the analysis becomes still more mysterious, given that it is supposed to be an analysis of a concept with which we think.

Why should philosophers even *expect* philosophically interesting concepts to have analyses? Analysis is not supposed to be infinite; it is supposed to bottom out somewhere—why not straight away, at least for philosophically interesting concepts, and perhaps for most or all concepts (Fodor 1998)? In early analytic philosophy, the programme of analysis was motivated by much more general assumptions. For example, Bertrand Russell proposed the Principle of Acquaintance: '*Every proposition which we can understand must be composed wholly of constituents with which we are acquainted*'; he called it 'the fundamental epistemological principle in the analysis of propositions containing descriptions' (Russell 1910–11, his italics). Given Russell's extreme empiricist conception of acquaintance, on which we are not acquainted with ordinary material objects, the analysis of almost any proposition is forced to go far below the surface to reach a level of constituents with all of which we can be acquainted. But later analytic philosophers pursued programmes of analysis whose prospects of success were not supported by any such wider vision.

In recent decades, the ideology of 'concepts' and 'conceptual analysis' has come under increasing pressure. Our firmest grip on concepts comes from the words supposed to express them, but then we need an answer to the question: when does a word W used in a context c express the same concept as a word W* used in a context c^*? No really helpful answer is available. Identity in reference is presumably insufficient, since most theorists of concepts agree that 'water' and 'H_2O' can refer to the same stuff without expressing the same concept. One may be told that W in c expresses the same concept as W* in c^* if and only if the condition for understanding W in c is the same as the condition for understanding W* in c^*, but that is unhelpful because the conditions for linguistic understanding are so loose and vague. Alternatively, one may be told that W in c expresses the same concept as W* in c^* if and only if W in c is governed by the same rules as W* in c^*, but that will turn out to be circular because the rules themselves are individuated in terms of their constituent concepts. And so on. Without a workable theory of identity conditions for the concepts words are supposed to express, we lose methodological control of inquiry into the concept expressed by a given word W in a given context c, since we cannot tell which uses of W are irrelevant because they express a different concept. For purposes of this book, we need go no deeper into the disarray of concept theory: not even a theory of concepts in good working order would make the methodological issues of overfitting and heuristics go away.[5]

As enthusiasm for conceptual analysis has waned, and metaphysics has revived in analytic philosophy, many of the philosophers who still seek analyses understand their project as a metaphysical rather than conceptual quest. They seek to analyse causation itself, rather than the concept of causation, or freedom itself, rather than the concept of freedom. Correspondingly, the standard of success for an analysis is just for the analysans to be *metaphysically* necessary and sufficient for the analysandum, rather than *conceptually* necessary and sufficient, and perhaps also for the analysans to be *metaphysically* prior to the analysandum in some sense, rather than *conceptually* prior. The focus has switched from *how* we are thinking to *what* we are thinking about.

In practice, the change has been less radical than it sounds. Objections to a given conceptual analysis were usually cases where the analysans held without the analysandum, or vice versa; since they usually look metaphysically as well as conceptually possible, they also serve as objections to the corresponding metaphysical analysis. Similarly, objections to a given metaphysical analysis are usually cases where one holds without the other; since they usually

---

[5] The status of conceptual analysis is of course closely related to that of the analytic-synthetic distinction, famously attacked by Quine 1951. My critique of analyticity or conceptual truth is developed in Williamson 2007, extended with many replies to objections in Williamson 2021a; it differs from Quine's strategy by not depending on scepticism about semantics. For a nice contrast between extreme optimism and extreme pessimism about the prospects for conceptual analysis, see Jackson 1998 and Fodor 1998.

look conceptually as well as metaphysically possible, they would also serve as objections to the corresponding conceptual analysis. Again, objections to conceptual priority can often be recycled as objections to metaphysical priority, and objections to metaphysical priority can often be recycled as objections to conceptual priority. For such reasons, switching the operative standard from conceptual analysis to metaphysical analysis does little to improve the track record of analysis. The series of analyses do not look convergent; rather, they exhibit the kind of theoretical instability and predictive failures associated with overfitting.

Even if we grant for the sake of argument that everything is somehow metaphysically reducible to an absolutely fundamental level, it does not follow that the reduction of the target phenomena—causation, freedom, knowledge, meaning, whatever—to the fundamental level will be mediated by an initial reduction of them to other phenomena at the highly non-fundamental level characteristic of a philosophical analysans—for instance, for typical analyses of knowledge, at the level of belief, truth, justification, causation, counterfactuals, and the like. The theoretical instability and predictive failures in the programme's track record is evidence that there is no such mediation.

At this point, a friend of philosophical analysis might try to recruit the considerations about heuristics and overfitting to its aid, by arguing that some original, simple analyses may have been right all along, with the apparent counterexamples being mere artefacts of fallible heuristics.

In the case of the original justified true belief analysis of knowledge (JTB), for example, the suggestion would be that knowledge really is simply justified true belief, while the standard negative verdicts in Gettier cases reflect a limitation of a universal human heuristic for ascribing knowledge. Brian Weatherson (2003) makes the related suggestion that the distinction between justified true belief and its absence might cut at a natural joint, thereby making justified true belief a 'reference magnet' that attracts the reference of the word 'know' as we use it, and globally fitting our use well enough despite local failures of fit such as Gettier cases. Such ideas should not be dismissed out of hand.

To be properly developed, rather than remaining just another application of a generic sceptical argument, a heuristic-based defence of JTB would need, first, to specify what the guilty heuristic is; second, to provide independent evidence that we really use such a heuristic; third, to show how the proposed heuristic delivers a negative verdict on Gettier cases; and fourth, to explain why a charitable interpretation of our practice of using 'know' and similar words nevertheless picks out as its referent justified true belief, thereby falsifying our verdicts on Gettier cases, rather than a relation more directly related to the heuristic and absent from Gettier cases, thereby verifying our verdicts. I am not aware of any promising attempt to meet any of those challenges.

The case is worth dwelling on, to see why JTB is *not* an example of a natural, elegant, explanatory hypothesis prematurely dismissed as a result of a glitch in a heuristic. Instead, JTB already shows signs of overfitting; it is an early precedent for the post-Gettier tradition of ad hoc analysis-building.

A defence of the original JTB analysis must employ the original understanding of 'justified', on which justified *false* belief is possible, as Gettier (1963) emphasizes. After all, if only true beliefs can be justified, the truth conjunct in the analysans is redundant, which no defender of JTB intends. Similarly, to understand justification in terms of knowledge would be contrary to the spirit of JTB. Thus, although justified true belief may be necessary and sufficient for knowledge on a more demanding normative understanding of justification, that does not amount to a defence of JTB (for such a more demanding normative conception of justification, see Williamson forthcoming-a).

A different way to assess the plausibility of JTB is by noting that knowledge is a central focus for our ordinary thought and talk about cognitive matters (Williamson 2000, Nagel 2014): is justified true belief a good candidate to play that role? To take one case, our best ordinary understanding of the actions of non-human animals and young children often involves attributing knowledge to them—for example, they need to know where other agents and other relevant things are—but normative questions of justification in the sense of JTB seem out of place and digressive as applied to non-human animals and young children, who are not responsible agents (see also Kornblith 2002). The distinction between knowing and not knowing is much more primitive than the distinction between having and lacking justification for a belief. To see what happens when one starts from the latter distinction rather than the former, we can look at the work of numerous contemporary epistemologists of an internalist bent, who do indeed regard the distinction between having and lacking internal justification for a belief as the right starting-point for epistemology, and such justification as the central epistemic norm. The category of knowledge is typically marginalized in their work, as is the category of justified true belief, which from their perspective looks like an odd hybrid of ill-assorted factors. For they concede that knowledge requires *truth*, a blatantly external factor.

One might also argue on naturalistic grounds against taking justified belief rather than knowledge as basic, because the usual motivation for that preference treats the standpoint of consciousness as privileged, whereas most of the cognitive action is pre-conscious.

Since perceptual knowledge depends on some level of perceptual reliability, as even most internalists concede, we can easily check that *no* internalist standard of justification will make JTB equivalent to knowledge. For internalists typically insist that the external reliability of perception can vary independently of internal phenomenology and justification. On such assumptions, one can easily construct a pair of good and bad cases, identical internally in one's phenomenology, justification, and belief, and externally in the truth-value of a proposition *p* about the environment, although one's perception is reliable only in the good case, so that one knows *p* in the good case but not in the bad case. In such a set-up, JTB automatically fails, for since one knows *p* in the good case, by JTB one has a justified belief in *p* in the good case. Hence, by the internal identity of the two cases, in the bad case too one has a justified belief in *p*, and by hypothesis *p* is still true, so one has a justified true belief in *p*, but one does not know *p*. Thus, JTB fails in the bad case. In other words, the very epistemological outlook that vindicates JTB's order of analysis, by treating justification and belief as more fundamental than knowledge, undermines JTB for other reasons. Consequently, JTB is an ill-motivated theory.

We can also test JTB in a more abstract structural way, by seeing how it plays out in simple models within the formal framework of doxastic logic. The upshot is that although JTB is not a disjunctive analysis in the usual sense, for its analysans is a conjunction, not a disjunction, it has a subtler disjunctive effect. In such a model of JTB, the propositions (modelled as sets of worlds) known at a world *w* are just the disjunctions (unions) of propositions justifiably believed at *w* with the singleton set {*w*}: the disjunction inherits the property of being justifiably believed from the first disjunct and the property of being true from the second disjunct (Williamson 2013b, 2015).[6] The known propositions are just the justifiably believed propositions with one extra pimple; they hardly form a natural class. Although some of the assumptions built into the models may be unrealistic, such as the closure of justifiable belief under single-premise entailment (if *p* entails *q* and *p* is justifiably believed then *q* is justifiably believed), an analysis that behaves so awkwardly under simplifying assumptions is not likely to behave much better when more complications are permitted. Thus, JTB

---

[6] Conjunctive definitions often have such disjunctive effects on what satisfy them. For example, Kripke's examples of the contingent a priori and the necessary a posteriori (Kripke 1980) might prompt a philosopher to think that what really matters is the property of being *both* necessary *and* a priori. But the propositions which are both are just equivalent to disjunctions of any necessary proposition with any a priori proposition; the disjunction inherits necessity from the first disjunct and a priority from the second disjunct.

makes knowledge into a rather artificial, gerrymandered category, not at all a natural candidate for reference, and so unlikely to be meant by the word 'know', since its fit with the use of the word is also poor, as Gettier cases show. JTB is *not* an elegant analysis; it just provides a list of three poorly related bullet points, of the kind which undergraduates like to write down in their notes.

The point of invoking formal models and naturalistic considerations here is not to make thought experiments redundant, but rather to make the rejection of JTB more robust, by basing it on a consilience of different methodologies—traditional, formal, and naturalistic—each pointing to the same conclusion. We have multiple reasons for regarding JTB as a bad theory.

The objections to JTB do not mechanically generalize to other proposed philosophical analyses, but they are suggestive. For example, the formal modelling illustrates how the apparently unifying effect of conjunctive analyses can be more apparent than real, when the conjuncts are not fruitfully related to each other. A conjunction of miscellaneous factors is also a clue to overfitting, since it suggests too many degrees of freedom.

The method of checking theories by calculating how they play out in simplified formal models is capable of being applied far more widely than it currently is in philosophy. It often provides valuable structural information, not least because it displays a theory's consequences over a whole space of propositions, not just one proposition at a time. Most basically, it is a test of the theory's consistency, both in itself and with elementary background constraints. Where such tests are possible, they should be applied. They can save much time and energy wasted on hopeless theories that fail the test.

The programme of philosophical analysis is now most associated with the long-running quest for necessary and sufficient conditions in more basic terms for philosophically central yet non-logical words like 'know', 'mean', 'cause', and 'free'. Overfitting became rife, for philosophers were not taught to minimize degrees of freedom. But, I conjecture, it has not led to the rejection of correct analyses on the basis of misjudged examples, because in these cases there are no correct analyses of the kind sought.

2.4 Overfitting in semantics

The formal semantics of natural languages is pursued in both departments of linguistics and departments of philosophy, with similar methodologies. It makes a fruitful test case for issues about overfitting and degrees of freedom, for several reasons.

First, the formal framework lends itself to counting degrees of freedom. Typically, the semantics is implemented in formal models. Typically, a model assigns semantic values to expressions of the natural language under study relative to various parameters. For simplicity, we can treat the function mapping each sequence of values of those parameters to the semantic value of the expression relative to that sequence as the *meaning* of that expression in the model. The theorist chooses a set of parameters so as to enable the semantics to be *compositional*, in the sense that, in any model, the meaning of a complex expression is determined as a function of the meanings of its simpler constituent expressions and how they are put together. That helps explain how users of the language can understand newly encountered sentences composed of previously encountered words.

As a first approximation, we can equate the number of parameters in the formal framework with the number of degrees of freedom of a model. Really, the situation is more complicated, because a model must assign a meaning separately to each atomic expression of the language—roughly speaking, to each word—so each atomic expression adds another degree of freedom to the model. However, since rival formal frameworks tend to agree that each atomic expression must be assigned its own meaning, and on which expressions are atomic, we can assume that all these degrees of freedom cancel each other out when formal frameworks are compared, leaving only differences between the parameter sets themselves, that is, between the sets of all meanings available in a given framework.[7]

The formal semantics of natural languages lends itself to discussion of overfitting in another respect too: it is strongly data-driven. A typical driver for theory change is that someone identifies examples in some natural language which the old framework seems unable to handle (a background methodological assumption is operative: that the formal framework should be *universal*: suitable for all human natural languages). The examples are typically in the form of sample sentences, often with native speaker judgments as to whether they could be correctly uttered in given hypothetical circumstances. In effect, the data are verdicts on elementary thought experiments. One or two data points of that kind may be taken to motivate a revision of the formal framework.

The formal semantics of natural languages also provides a good test case for accounts of overfitting because, historically, some highly successful revisions of a formal semantic framework *have* indeed taken the form of adding a new parameter, increasing the number of degrees of freedom. For instance, Saul Kripke revolutionized the semantics of modal logic in the period 1959–63 by enhancing models with a new parameter for a 'possible world', in what is sometimes described as the start of the 'intensional revolution'. This development is worth describing in some detail.

Before Kripke's innovation, there were *extensional* models for non-modal predicate logic. Each non-modal model provides a set of individuals to be the domain of quantification, an extension

---

[7] Some semantic theories posit complex logical forms for syntactically simple expressions, such as 'cause to die' for 'kill', but the choice of logical form for a given such expression itself constitutes at least one degree of freedom. A further complication is that a formal framework may treat some atomic expressions (such as 'is', 'not', 'or', 'and', 'if', 'some', and 'all') as 'logical constants' with a fixed interpretation, so models need not assign them meanings separately. Formal frameworks can differ from each other in which atomic expressions they treat as logical constants. However, most atomic expressions of a natural language are not plausibly treated as logical. In practice, the whole situation is often much messier than indicated in the text—which is typical of model-building. I have aimed to provide a reasonable first approximation.

over the domain for each atomic predicate of the formal object-language, and a referent in the domain for each individual constant. The truth-value of each formula of the object-language in the model is then defined compositionally relative to each assignment of values to all variables, in the usual way. For simplicity, I will henceforth leave this relativity to assignments tacit; it only makes a difference to the final truth-value for formulas with free variables. One can define a conclusion to be a *logical consequence* of a set of premises if and only if the conclusion is true in every model in which every premise is true. Similarly, a formula is a *logical truth* if and only if it is true in every model. Famously, there are formal proof-systems for first-order non-modal logic which can be proved *sound* and *complete*, in the sense that if a conclusion is provable in the system from some premises then it is a logical consequence of the premises (soundness), and conversely, if the conclusion is a logical consequence of the premises then it is provable in the system from those premises (completeness).

The non-modal object-language can be expanded to a modal object-language by the addition of modal sentence operators such as ◊ (informally read as 'possibly') and □ (informally read as 'necessarily'). Modal operators do not fit into the standard extensional framework because the extension of a formula in such a model is simply its truth-value, and modal operators are not truth-functional: the truth-value of the output is not a function of the truth-value of the input. For example, if a formula α is false in a model, ◊α may be either true or false in the model, and if α is true, □α may be either true or false. An increasingly urgent question in the 1940s and 1950s was how to adapt models for non-modal logic to modal logic, preferably so as to enable analogous soundness and completeness theorems to be established for appropriate formal proof-systems for first-order modal logic.

A simple, natural, and economical strategy is to treat the modal operators as generalizing over the extensional models themselves. More specifically, for any formula α, ◊α is true in a model if and only if α is true in some model, and □α is true in a model if and only if α is true in every model. Thus, possibility is understood as truth in some model, and necessity as truth in every model. If we regard extensional models as demystified possible worlds, then possibility is equated with truth in some possible world, and necessity with truth in every possible world. Rudolf Carnap (1947) pursued a strategy along these lines, using syntactic 'state-descriptions' rather than extensional models, but to very similar effect. He even compared his state-descriptions to Leibniz's possible worlds (which were ideas in the mind of God). The consequent reduction of modality to syntax was attractive from the perspective of Carnap's logical positivism.

However, for various technical reasons, the Carnapian approach worked poorly (Williamson 2013a: 75–80). In particular, no formal proof-system is sound and complete for the logical consequence relation it generates. Although many logicians in the 1950s contributed to the search for an alternative approach to the model theory of modal logic, it was Kripke who took the decisive step, in effect by sharply separating the role of possible worlds from that of models. He defined a new kind of model. Such 'Kripke models' are *intensional* models. A Kripke model is equipped with a set W, required only to be non-empty, whose members can informally be thought of as possible worlds, although that plays no role in the development of the model theory proper, which involves only mathematical and syntactic reasoning. In a model, the members of W are in effect the available values of the world parameter. The model assigns each 'world' (each member of W) a set of individuals to be its domain of quantification. The model also assigns each atomic predicate an *intension*, a function mapping each 'world' to the predicate's extension at that world, defined over the appropriate domain. Formulas are assigned truth-values compositionally relative to each 'world' (they are also relative as before to an assignment of values to variables, which we can ignore for present purposes). For any formula α, ◊α is true at a 'world' *w* if and only if α is true at some 'world' in W, so possibility is understood as truth in some world, and $\Box\alpha$ is true at *w* if and only if α is true at every 'world' in W, so necessity is understood as truth in every world (in the simplest version of the semantics). The model also singles out one member of W, which is informally understood as the actual world. A formula is evaluated as true in the model, without relativization to a 'world', if and only if it is true at the 'actual world' of the model, but the 'non-actual worlds' are still needed to determine whether modal formulas are true at the 'actual world' of the model, since the modal operators are interpreted as quantifiers over worlds.

The simple structures just described are quite restrictive, because they all validate the strong modal logic S5, on which nothing is contingently possible or contingently necessary. The formulas $\Diamond p \to \Box\Diamond p$, $\Diamond\Diamond p \to \Diamond p$, and $p \to \Diamond p$ are all theorems of S5, but fail on many interpretations of the modal operators. For example, when $\Diamond$ is interpreted in terms of easy possibility (and $\Box$ as $\neg\Diamond\neg$), $\Diamond\Diamond p \to \Diamond p$ is invalid, because even when one can get from A to B by an easy step, and one can get from B to C by an easy step, it does not follow that one can get from A to C by an easy step. When $\Diamond$ is interpreted in terms of permissibility, or compatibility with what one believes, or the past or future, $p \to \Diamond p$ is invalid, for when something happens, it does not follow that its happening is permissible, or compatible with what one believes, or past, or future. Kripke therefore equipped his models with an *accessibility* relation R between 'worlds'. Formally, R can be any binary relation over W. The generality over 'worlds' is then restricted by accessibility, in the sense that $\Diamond\alpha$ is true at *w* if and only if α is true at some world to which *w* has R (possibility is truth in some accessible world) and $\Box\alpha$ is true at *w* if and only if α is true at every world to which *w* has R (necessity is truth in every accessible world). To invalidate $\Diamond\Diamond p \to \Diamond p$, one allows R to be non-transitive; to invalidate $p \to \Diamond p$, one allows R to be non-reflexive. The accessibility relation makes the formal framework much more flexible—and in doing so adds another degree of freedom.

Kripke's work had a profound influence on philosophy. The apparatus of possible worlds soon became a standard part of an analytic philosopher's toolkit, a convenient framework for use in thinking and talking about all sorts of topics. Philosophical theses were increasingly formalized in modal rather than non-modal terms. Quine's arguments had put modal language under a cloud of suspicion, with dark threats of incoherence, especially when the possibility or impossibility at issue concerned individuals themselves, irrespective of how they were designated, and so resisted paraphrase in terms of the consistency or inconsistency of sentences. Although Kripke's formal semantics by itself gives little specific information on *which* such *de re* modal claims are true, it does call the bluff of those threats of incoherence, and demonstrates very clearly that there is no purely logical obstacle to the meaningfulness of *de re* modal claims. Natural versions of his semantics also validate some significant structural principles with a metaphysical edge, such as the non-contingency of identity and distinctness. The result was in effect to give the green light to substantive theorizing about modal metaphysics, in which Kripke himself played a leading role.

On the technical side, the perspicuous formal structure of Kripke models lends itself to mathematical investigation, and the model theory of modal logic became a flourishing branch of mathematical logic. It also found numerous applications in other disciplines, often using models equipped with whole families of accessibility relations, each associated with its own modal operators. For example, in computer science, modal logic is applied to the study of indeterministic computing, where the members of W are interpreted as the possible states of the computer, and each programme is associated with an accessibility relation which one state has to another if and only if running the programme *can* take the computer from the former state to the latter (Pratt 1976 is a seminal paper on *dynamic logic*, Troquard and Balbiani 2022 a recent survey). Kripke models are also standard in epistemic and doxastic logic, where the knowledge and belief operators are indexed to agents, and one state has a given agent's accessibility relation to another if and only if, when the agent is in the former world, for all they know (or believe) they are in the latter world. Such models are used in theoretical economics and computer science as well as in formal epistemology (Fagin, Halpern, Moses, and Vardi 1995).

Here, our interest is in the contribution of Kripke models to the formal semantics of natural languages. Although the object-language for his model theory was a formal language, its operators ◊ and □ were generally understood to be formal representations of modal operators such as 'possibly' and 'necessarily' in natural languages. Discussions of modal metaphysics often moved seamlessly in and out of languages for quantified modal logic and natural languages. From a linguistic perspective, the most common modal terms are auxiliaries such as 'must', 'can', 'could', 'may', 'might', 'would', 'should', 'ought', and so on. They are commonly used to make highly contingent claims, for which Kripke models are far more natural than a Carnapian framework: the accessibility relation can be as local as desired. Linguists soon applied a world parameter to the semantics of modal auxiliaries in natural languages (Kratzer 1977 was especially influential). More generally, the use of an intensional framework with a world parameter for the formal semantics of natural languages became standard.

In short, introducing a world parameter to semantic models proved immensely fruitful in logic, philosophy, linguistics, and beyond. It was clearly a progressive move. Adding a degree of freedom is not *always* bad.

The treatment of context-dependence offers another case of the fruitful addition of new parameters to a formal semantic framework. The occurrence of terms whose reference varies with context is not in doubt: obvious examples include demonstratives like 'this', 'that', 'then', 'there', and 'they', and other indexicals like 'I' and 'now'. Such context-dependence is not ambiguity: that the word 'I' refers to me when uttered by me and to you when uttered by you is explained by the same linguistic rule; we use the word with the same linguistic meaning. Although it is controversial how far such context-dependence extends beyond the obvious cases, the need for a proper semantic treatment of it is clear. Such a treatment will require contextual parameters, in order to formulate general linguistic rules such as the rule of reference for 'I'.

The seminal recent account of the semantics of context-dependence is by David Kaplan (1989). One might hope that the parameters needed to handle intensional operators could also be used to track context-dependence: for example, that Kripke's world parameter for modal operators and an analogous time parameter for temporal operators would in effect track shifts in the world and time of the context. But Kaplan showed that it is not so. Take the word 'tomorrow'. As uttered on a given day D, it refers to the day after D, D + 1. Imagine someone saying on D 'When it's tomorrow, I'll feel better'. To handle the phrase 'when it's tomorrow', which applies 'when' to the sentence 'it's tomorrow', the compositional semantics must evaluate 'it's tomorrow' with respect to different times, to determine which of them it is true at. But that is quite different from determining when one can truly say 'it's tomorrow', for the answer is: never (trick cases aside). To get the right result, the semantics must evaluate 'it's tomorrow' *as uttered on day D* with respect to other days: as uttered on day D, 'it's tomorrow' is true with respect to day D + 1. In Kaplan's terminology, one must distinguish the *context of utterance* (on day D) from the *circumstance of evaluation* (on day D + 1). The reference of 'tomorrow' is fixed in the context of utterance, and then carried over to the circumstance of evaluation. Since the circumstance of evaluation varies independently of the context of utterance, separate time parameters are required for each, and likewise for world parameters. That is how 'tomorrow' manages to be a *rigid designator*, even though its designation varies over time: if the context of utterance is held fixed, its designation remains the same while the circumstance of evaluation is varied. By contrast, context-dependence is variation in reference (or designation) when the circumstance of evaluation is held fixed while the context of utterance is varied; that is why 'tomorrow' is context-dependent. Kaplan uses the distinction between context of utterance and circumstance of evaluation to implement his general theory of content and character, where the content of an expression in a given context is what it contributes to the propositions expressed by sentences containing it as uttered in that context, while its character is the function mapping each context to the expression's content in that context. The content of 'I' in a given context is normally the speaker of that context. The character of 'I' is what remains constant across contexts, a good candidate for its linguistic meaning.

In short, a proper semantic treatment of context-dependence would hardly be possible without something like the distinction between context of utterance and circumstance of evaluation, and the consequent multiplication of parameters.

Both Kripke's work and Kaplan's were, and still are, paradigms of successful innovation in formal semantics. That may well have given semanticists the impression that this is just what progress in semantics looks like: introducing one or more new parameters into the formal semantic framework to explain linguistic data that could not be explained otherwise. That is just what one would expect from a Kuhnian perspective on semantics: scientists recognize solutions to new problems by their similarity to paradigmatic solutions of old problems. The trouble in this case is that if one keeps introducing new parameters into the semantic framework, thereby increasing degrees of freedom, one will sooner or later sink into overfitting.

We cannot reasonably expect a universal formula for when to stop adding parameters, much though some philosophers might demand one. As so often in science, it requires experience and good judgment. But one must at least recognize the problem, and not regard the introduction of a new parameter as cost-free. Each new parameter makes overfitting more likely.

A semanticist might object that if a new parameter is needed to explain the data, it would be a dereliction of duty *not* to introduce one. But that is a generic reply, which can always be offered in defence of overfitting. We must ask whether the data really are all correct, and whether the new parameter really is needed to explain them. If introducing a new parameter is regarded as a paradigmatic form of progress in semantics, or at least as methodologically low-cost, then there is little incentive to probe the data for errors, or to keep seeking an alternative explanation for the data within the current framework.

For example, relativism as a view in contemporary semantics involves adding a parameter to the circumstance of evaluation for something like a *standard of assessment*, in order to explain data about predicates of personal taste and other phenomena (Lasersohn 2005, MacFarlane 2014). That the linguistic phenomena have been correctly described, and can be explained only by adding an assessment parameter to the circumstance of evaluation, is by no means obvious (Cappelen and Hawthorne 2009). For instance, I say to Ana 'Rhubarb is disgusting'; Ana says to me 'Rhubarb is delicious'. In a sense, we disagree; in a sense, we are both right. But if I spoke in a context where the relevant reference class comprised just me, while she spoke in a context where the relevant reference class was just her, then we both spoke truly, and the apparent disagreement was merely verbal, as if I had said 'I like rhubarb' and she had replied 'I don't'. By contrast, if we both spoke in a joint context where the relevant reference class comprised both me and her, then the disagreement was real, but we both spoke tendentiously and falsely. Once such confusions as to the operative context have been cleared up, the invocation of a new parameter in the circumstance of evaluation may have nothing left to explain.

As in the case of philosophical analyses, adding too many parameters is not the only form of over-complication in semantics. One can also overfit by overusing the standard contextual parameters, for example, to gerrymander a complicated contextualist semantics on which content varies with context in ad hoc ways, or by diagnosing context-dependence more widely than necessary.

Not all semanticists accept that simplicity is a theoretical virtue in the semantics of natural languages. Perhaps the concern is that meaning in natural languages may just be very complicated. But that too is just an instance of a generic form of scepticism about simplicity as a theoretical virtue. A scientist in any branch of science, accused of overfitting, can respond that what they are investigating may just be very complicated. Indeed, in semantics, apart from the usual need to avoid overfitting, there is the additional concern that an over-complicated semantic framework may impose infeasible computational burdens on ordinary speakers. In contemporary semantics, one often sees very complex semantic accounts presented with no apparent sense that their complexity might be a theoretical cost.

A current test case is the research programme of *dynamic semantics* (not to be confused with Pratt's dynamic logic). In slogan form, the central idea is that 'meaning is context change potential'. Dynamic semantics is motivated by phenomena such as cross-sentential anaphor. For example, I can say 'Samuel kicked a stone' and later add 'It rolled into a ditch'. Together, my two statements are equivalent to 'Samuel kicked a stone, which rolled into a ditch', but it is broken into two. In a standard formalization of my original statement, the phrase 'a stone' would introduce an existential quantifier, with no implication of uniqueness; he may have kicked several stones. My use of the pronoun 'it' in my second statement is anaphoric on 'a stone', so one wants to formalize it with a variable bound by the existential quantifier, but that does not work because the quantifier's scope is confined to my original statement. Although this is not a straightforward counterexample to a non-dynamic framework, it is unclear how to handle it within such a framework. By contrast, dynamic semantics in effect extends the scope of 'a stone' over the whole subsequent discourse. Dynamic semantics is a generalization of standard truth-conditional semantics, in the sense that the latter can be recovered as a special case of the former, but dynamic semantics is significantly more complex and flexible than standard truth-conditional semantics. As another example, 'A and B' is not in general equivalent to 'B and

A' in dynamic semantics, since the second conjunct is processed with respect to a context updated on the first. A recent introductory survey of dynamic semantic emphasizes its flexibility as a framework (Nouwen, Brasoveanu, van Eijck, and Visser 2022), but, as we have seen, the obverse of flexibility is overfitting. The jury is still out on whether any linguistic phenomena are explicable *only* by dynamic semantics. The risk is that dynamic semantics turns out to be another manifestation of overfitting.

A more specific case is the semantics of conditionals. In their attempts to do justice to the complex ways we use conditionals in natural language, semanticists have offered a wide variety of complex semantic and pragmatic accounts of those conditionals. Elsewhere, I have argued in detail that humans' primary heuristic for assessing such conditionals is the suppositional heuristic described in chapter 1, and that it is implicitly inconsistent (Williamson 2020). *No* semantics will validate all aspects of our use of 'if'. Consequently, the search for a semantics that *does* validate all those aspects is condemned to overfitting. Instead, we do better to accept that our use of 'if' is flawed, the data cannot all be taken at face value, and the semantics of 'if' must be related to our use of it less directly. That opens the way to rehabilitating the simplest of all semantics for 'if', the material, truth-functional interpretation. How far that approach can be generalized to other problem cases for the semantics of natural languages, I leave to the reader as an open question.

2.5 Overfitting in logic

On a popular stereotype of logic, it is not in the business of fitting data and so cannot be guilty of overfitting. Instead, logic is imagined as laying down ground-rules without which our language could not function, let alone express our hypotheses and the data we test them on. But such preconceptions about logic find no support in the actual practice of disputes between proponents of rival logics in the same natural language.

Most famously, Hilary Putnam once argued that data from 'two-slit' experiments in quantum mechanics can best be explained on the hypothesis of a failure in the distributive principle of classical logic, that P and (Q or R) entails that (P and Q) or (P and R) (Putnam 1969). Putnam later withdrew his conjecture, and the programme of 'quantum logic' is generally regarded as a failure, at least in its attempt to explain the puzzling data (Putnam 2012). However, even if Putnam's reasons for making the proposal were confused, there was never a transcendental proof that any such proposal *must* be confused—unless one counts an argument that relies on the classical logical principles in question. Imagine that tomorrow a team of leading experts in logic and quantum mechanics announces that they have found a better way to explain the data from experiments in quantum mechanics on the hypothesis of a failure in some generally accepted principle of classical logic. A philosopher who tells them that they must be confused, because their proposal violates the rules of the language, would not have much credibility. One might be sceptical of their proposal on inductive grounds, because so many similar proposals have turned out badly in the past, but such scepticism is itself data-driven.

Whether a given allegedly logical principle has the status of a rule of some natural language is a question about that language, to be settled on the basis of evidence by the normal standards of linguistics. Such evidence might include data on what speakers of the language are or are not willing to say in various speech situations. The evidence would need to discriminate between linguistic rules and regular theoretical principles to which speakers are deeply committed. Strikingly, philosophers who ascribe the status of a linguistic rule to a logical principle tend to provide little or no linguistic evidence to support their claims (for a deeper and more systematic critique of closely related ideas about 'analyticity', see Williamson 2007, 2021a).

In any case, ascriptions of exceptional linguistic status to logical principles are of scant dialectical use in defending a generalization against alternative logicians who deny that it *is* a logical principle. After all, if the generalization is *not* a logical principle, all kinds of data may be used against it. If someone asserts that Newton's laws of motion are laws of logic, a physicist may appropriately respond by providing experimental evidence against Newton's laws. If an alleged law of logic is false, it is not a law of logic. Thus, when critics of classical logic bring all kinds of data against it, the response that logic is not in the business of fitting data would be question-begging. For instance, linguistic data involving epistemic modals such as 'may', 'might', and 'must' have recently been used as a basis for objections to numerous principles of classical logic (Holliday and Mandelkern 2023). If friends of classical logic decide to take such a critique seriously, they have to get their hands dirty by engaging with the alleged counter-evidence and showing what in particular is wrong with it.

Very schematically, if the criteria for theory comparison are divided into simplicity, strength (informativeness), and fit with data, then proponents of alternative non-classical logics typically have no choice but to make their case on grounds of fit with data. For their alternatives are clearly neither simpler nor stronger than classical logic.

In practice, all kinds of phenomena have been wheeled out against classical logic. For instance, the law of excluded middle has been alleged to fail for the open future, the forgotten past, potential infinity, vagueness, semantic paradoxes, quantum physics, and so on. In each case, the critics willingly give examples where they take the law of excluded middle to have unacceptable consequences. If they often leave it unclear exactly what evidence they are relying on in those cases, it is not for want of trying. But if friends of classical logic manage to show that it can accommodate such challenging phenomena, they have thereby enhanced the case for classical logic. Beyond that, both sides aim at more than mere accommodation: they want to treat the phenomena at issue in their preferred logic smoothly and elegantly, without resort to ad hoc devices.

More positively, proposed laws of logic gain support by identifying a common structural pattern in a mass of examples with diverse subject matters, unifying them by bringing them all under one illuminating generalization. For instance, the gradual identification of modus ponens as a logical principle in ancient Greece was a very significant intellectual achievement; as a general principle, it was not obvious all along (Bobzien 2002). Again, for many readings of modal operators, which principles of modal logic are sound remains unclear—especially for principles where modal operators occur embedded in the scope of further modal operators. Settling such questions is at least in part a matter of data-fitting (see also Ripley 2016). In a non-causal sense of 'explanation', we aim at an inference to the best explanation of the data.

Since logic is involved in data-fitting, it faces the issue of overfitting. Indeed, the issue takes some of the same forms for logic as we saw it take for semantics, for logical consequence is standardly defined by a generalization over semantic models. Standardly, a conclusion is defined to be a logical consequence of some premises if and only if every model of the premises is a model of the conclusion—in other words, the conclusion is true in every model in which every premise is true. Some variations on that theme are played for some non-classical logics, but they all involve generalizations over semantic models. Thus, changing the class of models by adding new parameters can change the logical consequence relation, at least for those connectives whose semantics is sensitive to the change.

For instance, Kripke's semantics for non-modal intuitionistic logic involves adding a new parameter with an associated reflexive, transitive accessibility relation. Informally, the picture is that the parameter's values are states of information, and one state is accessible from another when the latter extends the former. The semantics is designed to make every formula behave monotonically: if a state of information verifies it, so does every extension of that state. Monotonicity requires a tweak to the semantic clause for negation (¬): instead of the classical clause that a state verifies ¬α if and only if it does not verify α, Kripke's semantics requires a state to verify ¬α if and only if *no extension of* that state verifies α, in order to ensure that whenever a state verifies ¬α, so does every extension of that state. As a result, the semantics invalidates the principle of double negation elimination: in some cases, a state verifies ¬¬α without verifying α. For example, in a model with just two states, s and $s+$, where $s+$ extends s, and only $s+$ verifies an atomic sentence p, neither state verifies ¬p, so both states verify ¬¬p, so s verifies ¬¬p but not p.

Without adding new parameters, one can also increase flexibility by extending the range of values available for an old parameter, by adding or subdividing values. Standard semantic models are *bivalent*: at a given point in the model, each sentence is either true or false, and not both. In three-valued logic, the available values are typically truth, falsity, and 'neither'. In four-valued logic, they may be 'just true', 'just false', 'neither true nor false', and 'both true and false' [sic]. Such flexibility is used to deal with semantic paradoxes such as the Liar. In response to paradoxes of vagueness, the values may spread out into a continuum, represented by the real numbers from 0 (perfect falsity) to 1 (perfect truth), allowing the truth-value of the vague sentence 'It's dark' to rise continuously at dusk and fall continuously at dawn. A multi-dimensional space of truth-values may be invoked to track the multi-dimensionally vague sentence 'It's a religion' in truth-value. As truth-values proliferate, so do the different possibilities for defining logical consequence in terms of them. In some three-valued logics, preservation of non-falsity determines a different consequence relation from preservation of truth. In some other many-valued logics, a conclusion is a logical consequence of some premises if and only if no model makes the conclusion worse in truth-value than every premise, and so on.

Conversational virtues may also be built into the definition of logical consequence, by adding new parameters to models. In relevance logic, validity requires the conclusion to be in some sense relevant to the premises, and models are complicated accordingly (see Anderson and Belnap 1975 and Mares 2004; see Burgess 1981 for a critique of the idea of 'fallacies of relevance'). Perhaps someone will propose *politeness logic*, whose models have a politeness parameter taking values in a totally ordered set, informally understood as a scale from the rudest to the politest. A model assigns each atomic sentence a rudeness-value. The rudeness-value of a complex sentence is the maximum (worst) of the rudeness-values of its atomic constituents. An argument is valid only if it is politeness-preserving, in the sense that no model makes the conclusion ruder than every premise (other conditions may also be necessary for validity). In politeness logic, the rule of disjunction introduction is invalid, for if a model makes the atomic sentence r ruder than the atomic sentence p, then it also makes the disjunction $p \vee r$ ruder than p, so $p \vee r$ is not a logical consequence of p.

The semantics for a logic can be complicated in other ways too. Most obviously, the semantic clauses for logical connectives can be gerrymandered to invalidate disliked principles. The possibilities are endless.

Revisions of classical logic are often presented as making for more flexibility. Usually, classical logic can still be recaptured from the proposed alternative as a special case. For example, restricting Kripke models for intuitionistic logic to those with only one state in effect collapses it back to classical logic. Restricting models for many-valued logic to those which assign each atomic sentence one of the two 'classical' truth-values has a similar effect. Thus, the non-classical model theory can be interpreted as recognizing all the possibilities recognized by classical model theory, and more besides. The non-classical logic is strictly *weaker* than classical logic, since some arguments in the object-language validated by all classical models are invalidated by some models in the non-classical semantics, whereas every argument validated by all models in the non-classical semantics is also validated by all classical models.

Another rhetorically ingenious way of marketing weakness in a logic as a virtue is by saying that a weaker logic *makes more distinctions* than a stronger logic. Specifically, given two formulas α and β, α ↔ β may be a theorem of a logic L but not of a weaker logic L⁻, though α ↔ α and β ↔ β are theorems of both. Then friends of L⁻ may say that it distinguishes between α and β, whereas L does not. Of course, the distinctness of the *sentences* α and β is not in dispute. The question is whether α ↔ β is *true* on all relevant interpretations. If it is, what is the virtue in being unable to prove it? Analogously, imagine a theory of arithmetic so weak that it lacks '2 + 2 = 4' as a theorem. It might be advertised as having the advantage of allowing us to distinguish between 2 + 2 and 4. Of course, the distinctness of the *terms* '2 + 2' and '4' is not in dispute. The question is whether 2 + 2 and 4 are the same *number*. If they are, what is the virtue in being unable to prove it?

Proponents of non-classical logic face the challenge of explaining the success of classical logic as the standard implicit background logic for proofs in mathematics for two and a half thousand years, by far the most severe test of any logic in human history. A popular strategy is to claim that the language of pure mathematics satisfies the special conditions for the recapture of classical logic from the preferred non-classical alternative. For example, those who reject excluded middle for languages with vague or meta-semantic vocabulary (such as 'true' and 'false') often accept it for the language of pure mathematics, which they take to lack such vocabulary. However, *applications* of mathematics in the natural and social sciences do involve vague or meta-semantic vocabulary, so the classical-recapture strategy arguably fails to explain the success of classical mathematics in scientific applications (for details see Williamson 2018a). Such alternative logicians cannot escape as easily as they imagine from the daunting challenge of reconstructing mathematics for scientific applications from the starting-point of their weak non-classical logic.

On one view of logic, it is needed to play the role of a neutral arbiter of more substantive disputes in science or metaphysics. That view favours weak logics, because they are neutral on more questions. Strength in a logic tends to compromise its neutrality. But what counts as 'substantive' is never made clear. In any case, the view is hopeless because *any* proposed principle of logic can be attacked on scientific or metaphysical grounds, however mistaken they may be, and so is not neutral on those scientific or metaphysical issues. We have already seen examples of that, and they can be multiplied. Perhaps under the influence of Hegel, some metaphysician claims that all change involves a contradiction (Priest 1985). Even the anodyne structural principle that logical consequence is reflexive, so α is always a logical consequence of α, may be denied by a follower of Heraclitus, on the grounds that one can never grasp the same proposition twice. If a correct logic comprises only principles incapable of being challenged on scientific or metaphysical grounds, then the correct logic is empty.[8]

For present purposes, a key feature of weak logics is how unhelpful they are when we need to identify bad data. For a crude case, take dialetheist logic, which permits true contradictions. When a witness contradicts himself, the dialetheist is not best placed to see the problem. We might also be suspicious of a witness who states 'Not everyone present was invited' but refuses to accept 'Someone present was not invited', a consistent combination of attitudes in intuitionistic logic. Of course, alternative logicians may offer more

---

[8] For a more detailed critique of the idea of logic as a neutral arbiter see Williamson 2014a. For more on strength as an abductive virtue in logic see Williamson 2017b. For how confusion between logic and metalogic has led to scepticism about strength as an abductive virtue in logic see Williamson forthcoming-d. Much of the literature on disagreement in logic is vitiated by similar confusions, for example between disagreement in logic on whether $\forall P (P \vee \neg P)$ (the law of excluded middle) and disagreement in metalogic on whether '$\forall P (P \vee \neg P)$' is a logical truth. For a sympathetic treatment of logical nihilism see Russell 2018.

roundabout reasons for doubting such testimony. More crudely, they may just say that since classical logic is incorrect, we should not be relying on it in our attempts to identify bad data.[9]

Such responses on behalf of alternative logics push the question further back. Were concerns about overfitting given enough weight, or indeed any, when the case for revising classical logic was made? Increases in flexibility make data, including bad data, easier to accommodate, and so incur a significant methodological cost. Sensitivity to this cost is hard to detect in arguments against classical logic. Instead, one finds remarkable levels of implicit trust in unclear data—for example, when the failure of classical logic for vague languages is simply taken for granted. The problem becomes even more acute when the data can be explained as products of imperfectly reliable heuristics, as chapter 1 explained they often can.

One reason the analogy between alternative logics and prototypical cases of overfitting may have been missed is that there are also striking differences. Most notably, in curve-fitting, the old and new curves represent equally specific hypotheses. By contrast, alternative logics are usually less specific—weaker—than classical logic. They withdraw from some consequences of the old hypothesis, without adding new ones to compensate. That is quite different from what happens in the natural sciences. The analogue would be at best a kind of curve-fitting where one specifies upper and lower curves, the hypothesis being that the correct values lie in the band between the two curves. The analogue of weakening the logic would be pushing the two curves further apart, widening the band to include data-points outside the old band, thereby weakening the hypothesis. For some cases, the analogue would

---

[9] Naïve empiricist attitudes to data may lead to errors in logic as they seem to have done elsewhere in philosophical theorizing. According to Ernst Cassirer, in Renaissance Italy 'empiricism leads not to the refutation but to codification of magic' and to 'empirical magic', through its respect for miscellaneous empirical reports of magic (1963: 151-2), whereas rationalists swept such reports aside in their quest for a uniform mathematical theory of nature. In present terms, the empiricists were guilty of overfitting.

be even worse: just crossing out the old curve without proposing a replacement. With such a methodology, the result of erroneous data-points is not a more erroneous hypothesis but just a less informative one. Consequently, one will not get the kind of erratic instability and falsified predictions characteristic of classic overfitting, but just a loss of informativeness.

A logic's predictions can be regarded as its deductive consequences for particular cases. When overfitting produces a weak logic, its predictive failures consist in uninformativeness rather than falsity.

At a more general theoretical level, weakening a logic is analogous to revising a theory in physics by abandoning some of its general principles without replacing them by any alternatives of similar generality. Such a move in physics would look defeatist rather than progressive. Not only would it result in a less informative theory; it would fail to stress-test the crucial data by not trying to explain them on an alternative equally strong theory. That would have in common with overfitting an insufficiently critical attitude towards the data. Proposals for weakening classical logic implicitly treat the relevant data in a similarly uncritical way.

In abductive terms, weakening a logic implies loss of strength rather than loss of simplicity, whereas overfitting in the natural and social sciences typically involves loss of simplicity without loss of strength. In both cases there is a loss of abductive virtue, incurred by an insufficiently critical attitude to the data, but the virtue lost is different. In practice, however, weakening a logic usually involves some loss of simplicity too. In the model theory that almost always happens, since new structure is added to the models to make classical principles fail. It often happens in the proof theory too, since classical rules of inference or axioms are qualified or replaced by more complicated substitutes rather than simply dropped. For example, relevance logics exhibit both loss of strength and loss of simplicity, in both model theory and proof theory. Thus, alternative logics typically enjoy the worst of both worlds, and so do even worse than ordinary overfitting in the natural and social sciences.

2.6 Overfitting in philosophical model-building

When scientists speak of degrees of freedom in a model, the models they have in mind are rarely semantic models such as those in the previous two sections, which assign semantic values to expressions of a language. Although semantic models are a special case of models in the general scientific sense, the scientists are unlikely to have semantic models in mind. Most models of natural or social phenomena imply nothing specific about the semantic values of linguistic expressions—though general methodological morals about models in science are indeed applicable and relevant to semantic models. In the predominant scientific sense, a model of a phenomenon is an intermediary object, which is intended in relevant ways to be easier to study than the target phenomenon itself, but structurally similar enough to it for insights about the model to reveal something about the target phenomenon (for a general treatment of modelling in science see Weisberg 2013). For the model to have well-defined parameters, it must be formally specified, typically in mathematical terms—for example, by differential equations whose coefficients are parameters of the model. Informally, the equations may be conceived as characterizing the development of a closed system over time. By solving the equations analytically, or by approximating their effect for given initial conditions on a computer, scientists can often work out how the model develops, identify patterns, and tentatively transfer them to the target phenomenon. Models of pandemics and of global warming are of this general kind.

Almost always, the model is much simpler than the target phenomenon. For example, it may model a planet as a point mass. Without such massive simplifications, the model would be mathematically and computationally intractable, and so unfit for purpose. Unless the target phenomenon is the whole universe, just modelling it as a closed system—ignoring the possibility of interference from outside the system—is already a massive simplification: in practice, there is always some outside interference (for example, by gravity). Restricting degrees of freedom in models to avoid overfitting is another source of deliberate simplification. In a deterministic model, the implicit assumption that the parameters' values at one time jointly determine their values at any later time is also a simplification. For example, a biological model of predator-prey interaction may treat the sizes of the two populations at any time as jointly determining their sizes at any later time, ignoring obviously relevant factors such as age profile, interactions with a third species, the changing state of the environment, and so on.

Although models in natural and social science tend to be diachronic, that is inessential to the model-building methodology. Probability spaces in the mathematical sense are used to model various kinds of uncertainty, but are synchronic: they specify one probability distribution, not an evolving sequence of distributions. Many models of language in linguistics are synchronic. So is an electoral model of the relation between parties' share of the votes and their share of the seats in an assembly. One can learn about synchronic dependencies between the variables by varying the values of the variables, thereby comparing different models with the same overall structure.

Much progress in the natural and social sciences consists in building better models of natural and social phenomena. The new model may capture all the features of the target phenomenon captured by the old model, and more besides, without becoming mathematically or computationally intractable. That is quite different from the older paradigm of scientific progress as the discovery of new scientific laws. Most macroscopic systems and many microscopic ones are too messy and complicated to satisfy any distinctive universal generalizations, let alone laws, formulated in terms of such systems. Philosophers sometimes try to hold onto a law-based conception of science and absorb such complications by invoking a category of 'ceteris paribus laws', but it cannot do the required work. *Ceteris paribus*—other things being equal—planets are *not* point-masses, and the number of animals in a population does *not* vary continuously over time as a differential equation requires—it is discrete. We can determine by rigorous mathematics or computer simulation what holds in a model; by contrast, the assumption that a law holds *ceteris paribus* is far too vague for us to determine its consequences in any such way. Instead, the appropriate way to study those messy and complicated phenomena is often by building formal models rather than by seeking exceptionless or *ceteris paribus* laws. One may be able to conclude with some rough but robust generalizations drawn from the model, formulated with '*ceteris paribus*' qualifications (Weisberg 2013: 158–9, 167–8), but at the heart of the rigorous scientific action is the model, not a *ceteris paribus* law. The principles that define the model which explains the *ceteris paribus* law do not themselves hold *ceteris paribus*.

Of course, model-building in the natural and social sciences is informed by data. The curves in curve-fitting are more or less simple models. A complication at this point is that the target phenomenon is hardly ever a particular one-off event token, such as the Big Bang or global warming on Earth. Typically, the target phenomenon is a general *type* of event or process, such as the working of some kind of cell or bodily organ, or some kind of interaction between two species. Scientists aim to produce a model of the type, that is, a model generically of a token of the type, without there being any particular token of which it is a model—just as a diagram can be of a human heart without there being any particular human heart of which it is a diagram. Typically, the model will be based on data from many different tokens of the relevant type. Even if there are no *errors* in the data, there may still be *outlying* data, for instance from an abnormal heart. Such outlying data can distort the model, making it a worse model of a normal heart (similar issues would arise in semantics also if it were done in a similarly model-building spirit). Precautions against overfitting can help avoid such distortions too.

Not all model-building concerns quantitative issues. For example, biologists want to understand the predominance of sexual reproduction, since asexual reproduction is also possible and actually occurs in some cases. For such theoretical purposes, biologists use a model-building methodology. In particular, they build models to explore the hypothesis that sexual reproduction makes a population better able to adapt to changes in the environment. Such a model may schematically represent competition between a sexually reproducing population and an asexually reproducing population, with an initial distribution of genotypes, under intense selection from a rapidly changing environment. The hypothesis to be tested is that sexual reproduction is more conducive than asexual reproduction to variance in genotype, and so makes for more adaptability to environmental change (Weisberg 2013: 115-117, Crow 1992). The dynamics of such a model are encoded in simple mathematical rules, whose consequences over time can be computed. The rules are not intended to be a realistic description of actual events, but just to capture general qualitative features of competition between the two forms of reproduction. The rules are best kept as simple as possible, not merely for ease of computation, but because any unnecessary complication or ad hoc feature would risk rigging the model in favour of a desired conclusion. The aim is not data-fitting or quantitative prediction but general theoretical explanation. Still, the model is ultimately constrained by data: for instance, the dynamical rules for how the sexually reproducing population evolves should not diverge too much from known features of the genetics of sexual reproduction.

In brief, simple formal models are used in the natural and social sciences to gain qualitative understanding of very general phenomena, especially phenomena whose instances are too messy and complicated to be governed by informative exceptionless laws at the relevant level. That is evidence that the model-building methodology would be of value to philosophy too. An example was already noted in section 2.3: the use of simple formal models to test the behaviour of the JTB analysis of knowledge. We should expect the model-building methodology to be much more widely applicable in philosophy than that. After all, the human world is fantastically messy and complicated ('Out of the crooked timber of humanity no straight thing was ever made'), and much of human philosophy concerns the human world: human minds and bodies, human knowledge and action, human thought and language, human art and science, human morality and politics, human identity through change and counterfactual variation. Many of those philosophical issues generalize to the wider world of non-human animals and perhaps even of artificial intelligence, but that wider world is fantastically messy and complicated too. Thus, philosophy spends much of its time and energy engaging with phenomena of just the kind better suited to model-building than to the quest for exceptionless laws.

The model-building methodology is already widely used in some areas of philosophy (Williamson 2017a). It predominates in formal epistemology, including Bayesian probabilistic models, models of epistemic and doxastic logic, and more, for both individual and social epistemology. Formal models from decision theory, game theory, deontic logic, voting theory, and evolutionary theory are sometimes used in moral and political philosophy. In metaphysics, the mereology of gunk—the theory of parts and wholes where everything has a proper part—is hard to think about accurately without a mathematical model. When semanticists of natural language state a formal semantic theory, it is usually for a toy model language.

Despite these examples, only a small proportion of contemporary philosophy uses a model-building methodology. One possible explanation is that only a small proportion of contemporary philosophy studies topics for which a model-building methodology would be useful. However, in my experience, there is also widespread ignorance and incomprehension of the model-building methodology amongst philosophers. Many take the falsity of its simplifying assumptions as sufficient reason to reject a model. Most graduate students in philosophy are neither encouraged to build or use models nor trained in how to do so. Consequently, the methodology has not so much been tried and found wanting as not tried. Almost certainly, it could usefully be applied more widely in philosophy than it has been so far, as some examples below suggest.

Unfamiliarity with the model-building methodology helps explain the marginalization of epistemic and doxastic logic in twentieth-century mainstream epistemology, despite the pioneering work of Jaakko Hintikka (1962). For decades, new developments in epistemic and doxastic logic came more from computer scientists and theoretical economists than from philosophers. Notoriously, standard models of epistemic logic validate a strong form of *logical omniscience* for knowledge: automatically, if one knows the premises of a deductively valid argument, then one knows the conclusion too (with no qualifications about knowing the entailment or having competently carried out the deduction). Similarly, standard models of doxastic logic validate the correspondingly strong form of logical omniscience for belief: automatically, if one believes the premises of a deductively valid argument, then one believes the conclusion too (again, with no qualifications). The obvious computational and reflective limitations of actual humans seem to provide innumerable counterexamples to logical omniscience for both knowledge and belief, which were taken to discredit epistemic and doxastic logic: whatever epistemic and doxastic logicians were studying, it was not what interested epistemologists, they thought. Significant opportunities for epistemology were lost. Logical omniscience could have been treated as a legitimate simplification for modelling purposes in order to apply the formal framework of epistemic and doxastic logic to the rigorous exploration of other structural issues in epistemology. But such an outlook on model-building seems not to have been available in epistemology at the time. The required formal skills were also in short supply.

Later work in epistemic and doxastic logic showed how to avoid logical omniscience, and model agents' limited rationality, for example by allowing possible worlds epistemic or doxastic access to 'impossible worlds' where any set of sentences whatsoever can be the set of truths (Rantala 1982). Such models carry a cost, because they drastically increase degrees of freedom. The effect is that the model-builder has to put the agent's knowledge and beliefs into the model 'by hand', so stipulation largely replaces exploration, and many of the potential gains from model-building are lost. Instead of learning from the model, one is just taking out of it what one had explicitly put in.

Some functionalists in the philosophy of mind have argued that, on a proper understanding of knowledge and belief, the failures of logical omniscience are illusory (Stalnaker 1984, 1999). The following chapters will discuss issues about logical omniscience and the individuation of the objects of knowledge and belief more deeply. In any case, technical work on blocking logical omniscience was scarcely noticed in mainstream epistemology, and did not in practice constitute a bridge between mainstream epistemology and epistemic and doxastic logic. Encouragingly, more recent years have seen more interaction between formal epistemology and mainstream epistemology, and consequently more use of the model-building methodology in epistemology by philosophers.

When the model-building methodology is applied in philosophy, issues of overfitting and degrees of freedom arise. We need to be on the alert for complication and ad hoc features as warning-signs of error or distortion. If an example convinces philosophers that a phenomenon can occur, but modelling it requires something reminiscent of gerrymandering, then the example may have been misinterpreted. Even if a phenomenon is genuinely possible, it may be such an outlier that complicating the model to allow for it makes the model less useful for many other purposes.

Often, the dialectic is more intricate. Here is a case from my own experience. I have been interested in using epistemic models to illustrate extreme failures of the 'KK' or 'positive introspection' principle that if one knows that P, one knows that one knows that P, and of watered-down versions of that principle—for instance, that if one knows that P, one is *in a position to* know that one knows that P. In models of epistemic logic, positive introspection provably corresponds to the transitivity of the accessibility relation for knowledge. I have used an example where one is looking from a distance at an unmarked clockface with a single hand, wondering what time it shows. By looking, one learns *something*, but not *everything*, about where the hand is pointing. In the simplest epistemic models of that situation, one can easily show, positive introspection fails drastically (Williamson 2014b). However, friends of positive introspection can approximate those models by slightly more complicated models where positive introspection *holds*, by arbitrarily selecting a coarse-grained partition of epistemic possibilities to determine the accessibility relation in the model. Similar tricks can be played with less grossly simplified models where positive introspection fails.

However, one can show that any model of the situation which validates positive introspection does so at the cost of a sort of *symmetry-breaking* (Williamson 2021d). The basic set-up, including all potential positions of the hand, has a symmetry induced by the underlying rotational symmetry of the clockface about its centre. But one can show that if an epistemic model respects that symmetry, in the sense that the underlying epistemic structure remains invariant under 'rotations' of the model, and the model meets basic epistemic constraints such as avoiding both scepticism and omniscience about where the hand is pointing, then the model violates positive introspection. Symmetry-breaking is not just inelegant; it is a symptom of an ad hoc intrusion. In effect, it means that the model postulates differences in associated epistemological structure between one point on the circumference of the clockface and another, even though the basic set-up does not require any such differences. Of course, in real life, the situation is doubtless not perfectly symmetric: our visual system may well embody a slight bias on one side or another. But for an epistemological theory to insist in advance that there *must* be such a bias or asymmetry in a situation whose basic structure does not impose one looks like gerrymandering. In particular, specifying which way the bias goes would require an extra degree of freedom. Thus, the methodology of model-building tells against symmetry-breaking, and so against positive introspection. In brief, to save positive introspection in this case, you must overfit.

None of this means that *all* epistemic models must invalidate positive introspection. On the contrary: there is often good reason to use epistemic models that validate both positive introspection and the much less plausible principle of *negative introspection*: if one does not know that P, one knows that one does not know that P, which corresponds to the accessibility relation being *Euclidean*, in the sense that all worlds accessible from a given world are accessible from each other. Negative introspection fails in very ordinary cases of confident error, where it is false that P, but one thinks that one knows that P: as a result, one does not know that P, but one also does not know that one does not know that P (in Donald Rumsfeld's phrase, an unknown unknown). Despite such clear counterexamples, it often makes good methodological sense to build negative introspection as well as positive introspection into a model. For many epistemic models are designed for exploring interpersonal effects, such as those which depend on the presence or absence of common knowledge (where everyone knows that P, everyone knows that everyone knows that P, everyone knows that everyone knows that everyone knows that P, and so on). Each agent in the envisaged situation has their own knowledge operator with its own epistemic accessibility relation. The best way to isolate the *inter*personal obstacles to common knowledge is by minimizing the *intra*personal obstacles to knowledge about one's own knowledge states, to avoid interference. That requires assuming that each agent satisfies both positive and negative introspection separately. Unfortunately, epistemic logicians have tended to treat positive and negative introspection not just as convenient simplifying modelling assumptions but as all-purpose epistemological dogmas, brushing aside all the epistemological objections to them. When the focus shifts to intrapersonal epistemology, background assumptions of interpersonal epistemology should be called into question. Which simplifying assumptions are legitimate depends on what questions one is using the model to think about.

2.7 Summing up

As we have seen, the methodological issues around overfitting and degrees of freedom are themselves messy and complicated, both in general and in particular in their application to philosophy. But that is no good reason to ignore them. Overfitting is a trap into which too many philosophers have fallen, or jumped. Although it can be hard to know whether one is overfitting, we need to be alert to the danger. To that end, we should put somewhat more weight on simplicity and strength as theoretical virtues in philosophy, as elsewhere, and be somewhat less trusting than heretofore of data that tempt us to complicate and weaken our theories. Obviously, that does not mean that we should rush to the opposite extreme: having neglected simplicity and strength, we should not switch to neglecting fit with data. We need to be keenly aware that there is a balance to be struck, and that we have not been striking it right. Nothing about the nature of philosophy exempts us from the methodological exigencies that other theorists are used to working under.

Clearly, once we have a plausible explanation of potential errors in those data the theory fails to fit, the lack of fit becomes less serious. As we have seen, in philosophy and elsewhere, our reliance on a fallible heuristic may be central to that explanation.

In abductive methodology, theoretical virtues are often roughly summarized as simplicity, strength, and fit with data. Giving too much weight to any one or two of them at the expense of the remainder distorts our view of comparisons between theories, and is liable to end in error or triviality. By focusing on the more specific theoretical vice of overfitting, we can clarify our sense of what would be involved in properly implementing an abductive methodology in philosophy.[10]

---

[10] See also Williamson 2016c on abductive philosophy.

3
Case Study: Hyperintensionalism

3.1 Two revolutions?

According to a fashionable triumphalist narrative, philosophy is in the midst of a revolution. The cartoon version goes like this. Early analytic philosophy—from Frege to Quine—worked in a coarse-grained *extensional* framework. Around 1960, through the work of Saul Kripke and others, that framework was overthrown in favour of a more flexible, more fine-grained *intensional* framework, implemented in terms of possible worlds. Analytic philosophers started working in the intensional framework instead. That was the *intensional revolution* Much more recently, through the work of Kit Fine and others, the intensional framework has in its turn been overthrown in favour of a still more flexible, still more fine-grained *hyperintensional* framework, implemented in terms of grounding or some such metaphysical relation. Many analytic philosophers have started working in such a framework instead. That is the *hyperintensional revolution*. It began in metaphysics but is spreading to other branches of philosophy. It is where we are now.[1]

Although the most eye-catching features of the three approaches are metaphysical, the underlying structural differences between the frameworks are more abstract. They concern the

---

[1] Nolan 2014 tells such a story, though I am not attributing the cartoon version to him. It is part of current folklore. Of course, plenty of philosophy—including plenty of analytic philosophy—is not usefully classifiable as working within either an extensional, intensional, or hyperintensional framework, because it does not engage with the relevant issues. That may apply to much ordinary language philosophy.

quasi-logical operations available within each framework, hinted at by the contrast between 'coarse-grained' and 'fine-grained'. The differences emerge most clearly when one compares the forms of semantic theory suited to each approach. The intensional revolution corresponded to the transition to possible worlds semantics, discussed in section 2.4 of chapter 2. The hyperintensional revolution is sometimes implemented by *im*possible worlds semantics, sometimes by truthmaker semantics. In brief: extensional semantics operates on extensions; a sentence's extension is its truth-value, an n-place predicate's extension comprises the ordered n-tuples that satisfy it. Intensional semantics operates on intensions; a sentence or predicate's intension assigns it its extension at each world. Hyperintensional semantics operates on . . . something else.

The case for hyperintensionalism is usually made in terms of examples, presented as decisive counterexamples to intensionalism. Perhaps the most famous is due to Kit Fine, in his seminal paper 'Essence and Modality' (Fine 1994). It is directed against attempts by Kripke and others to develop essentialist metaphysics within an intensional framework, by giving a modal account of essence (Kripke 1972, 1980; for Fine's view of Kripke's understanding of essence, see Fine 2022). Such a modal account equates 'It is essential to S that X is F' with 'Necessarily S is F', or with 'Necessarily if S exists then S is F', where 'S' designates S rigidly, the pronoun 'X' is anaphoric on 'S', and the necessity is metaphysical. But consider the contrast between (1A) and (1B):

(1A) It is essential to Socrates that he is Socrates.

(1B) It is essential to Socrates that he is a member of {Socrates}.

If one is willing to think in essentialist terms at all, one is liable to be struck by (1A) as true and by (1B) as false, at least until conscious theoretical commitments intervene: (1A) sounds like a truism, (1B) like the introduction of something extraneous to Socrates himself, his singleton set. Nevertheless, on standard views of the modal metaphysics of sets, being Socrates is necessarily equivalent to being a member of {Socrates}. Thus, 'Necessarily Socrates is Socrates' is equivalent to 'Necessarily Socrates is a member of {Socrates}', and 'Necessarily if Socrates exists then Socrates is Socrates' is equivalent to 'Necessarily if Socrates exists then Socrates is a member of {Socrates}'. Consequently, given that (1A) is true and (1B) false, those modal accounts of essence fail. Other modal accounts will do no better. For the predicates 'is Socrates' and 'is a member of {Socrates}' have the same intension. Since a standard intensional semantic framework operates compositionally on intensions, substituting one predicate for another with the same intension in a sentence makes no difference to its intension, so no difference to its truth-value, since the intension of a sentence determines its truth-value at a given circumstance of evaluation. Thus, whatever semantics is attributed to the sentence operator 'It is essential to S that . . .' in the intensional framework, it will perforce assign the same truth-value to (1A) and (1B). Since any properly developed modal account of essence will correspond to some semantics of the operator in the intensional framework, any such account will assign (1A) and (1B) the same truth-value. Consequently, if (1A) and (1B) differ in truth-value, no modal account of essence is correct, and the standard intensional framework cannot handle the operator 'It is essential to S that . . .'; it is *hyperintensional*.

Another well-known case goes back to Aristotle (*Metaphysics*, book Θ 10: 1051^{b}6–9, cited against intensionalism by Schnieder 2011: 445–6). For any true declarative sentence in place of the schematic letter 'A', consider:

(2A)   The proposition that A is true because A.

(2B)   A because the proposition that A is true.

The natural verdicts are that (2A) is true and (2B) false. The former seems to get the order of explanation right, the latter to get it wrong. Nevertheless, on standard views of truth for propositions, necessarily, the proposition that A is true if and only A. Thus 'the proposition that A is true' and 'A' have the same intension, so, in a standard intensional semantic framework, interchanging them in a sentence makes no difference to its intension, so no difference to its truth-value; the hyperintensionalist argument in terms of (2A) and (2B) goes much like the one in terms of (1A) and (1B). Consequently, if (2A) and (2B) differ in truth-value, the standard intensional framework cannot handle the sentence operator '. . . because ---'; it is hyperintensional.

A third example was used by Elliott Sober to argue that logically equivalent predicates may pick out different properties (Sober 1982). It involves the terms 'triangle', meaning *closed straight-sided figure having three angles*, and 'trilateral', meaning *closed straight-sided figure having three sides*. On the intended readings, being a triangle is necessary and sufficient for being a trilateral, so 'triangle' and 'trilateral' have the same intension (Sober's assumption that the equivalence is *logical* may be too strong, but that does not matter for present purposes). Sober imagines a machine with two components linked in series. The first component is a closed straight-sided figure detector: given a piece of wire as input, the machine outputs it if and only if it is a closed straight-sided figure. The second component is a three-angle detector: given any number of straight pieces of wire, it outputs them if and only if they have three angles. The second component is not a three-side detector because it will output an open four-sided but three-angled figure if given as input. Now one inputs a wire triangle to the machine, which then outputs it. Why? Sober argues that, given how the machine works, the cause was the object's being a triangle, not the object's being a trilateral. The machine outputted the piece of wire because it was a closed straight-sided figure having three angles, not because it was a closed straight-sided figure having three sides. He takes this to show that the property of being a triangle is distinct from the property of being a trilateral. Thus (3A) is true and (3B) false:

(3A) Being a triangle = being a triangle

(3B) Being a triangle = being a trilateral

But 'triangle' and 'trilateral' have the same intension, so, in a standard intensional semantic framework, substituting one of them for the other in a sentence makes no difference to its intension, so no difference to its truth-value. Consequently, if (3A) and (3B) differ in truth-value, and 'being a triangle' and 'being a trilateral' differ in reference, the standard intensional framework cannot handle the construction 'being a . . .', which forms terms for properties; it is hyperintensional.

Examples such as (1A/B), (2A/B), and (3A/B) can be very persuasive. However, they also hint at an asymmetry between the intensional and hyperintensional 'revolutions'. One can of course give similar pairs for the intensional revolution, involving modal operators, for example:

(4A) It is contingent that Scotland is part of the United Kingdom.

(4B) It is contingent that $5 + 7 = 12$.

Since (4A) is true and (4B) false, but 'Scotland is part of the United Kingdom' and '$5 + 7 = 12$' have the same truth-value, so the same extension, the example shows that the standard extensional semantic framework cannot handle the sentence operator 'it is contingent that . . .'; it is intensional.

Such examples can easily be multiplied for any of the usual modal operators. But whereas examples like (1A/B), (2A/B), and (3A/B) are what motivate the hyperintensional revolution, examples like (4A/B) were *not* what motivated the intensional revolution. In 1959,

Kripke did not have to show that modal operators lack truth-tables; that had been obvious for decades. What initiated the intensional revolution was a more theoretical development: the discovery of a technically powerful and philosophically fruitful framework for the semantics of modal languages. By contrast, when examples like (1A/B), (2A/B), and (3A/B) are used to motivate hyperintensionalism, they are typically presented as counterexamples to intensionalism just as they stand, with no hyperintensional semantic framework to back them up. Although some hyperintensional semantic frameworks have subsequently been developed—involving truthmakers, or impossible worlds, or whatever—their putative merits are not what proponents of the hyperintensional revolution present as its driving-force. In that role, they cast the putative counterexamples themselves. Indeed, hyperintensionalists do not agree on any one semantic approach: semantics with impossible worlds differs radically from truthmaker semantics.

As explanatory successes of a hyperintensional framework, its proponents also claim its capacity to make systematic sense of independently attractive metaphysical claims, such as 'the mental is something over and above the physical despite supervening on it' or 'the whole is prior to the parts despite each necessitating the other'. But for those who do *not* find such claims independently attractive, that is a dubious benefit, just as, for classical logicians, allowing one to get away with contradicting oneself is a dubious benefit of paraconsistent logic. Moreover, the intensional revolution bore much more fruit much more quickly than the hyperintensional revolution *outside* metaphysics (see the next section). For serious dialectical traction, the hyperintensional revolution still has to rely mainly on apparent counterexamples to intensionalism.

The terminology of 'extensional', 'intensional', and 'hyperintensional' is already a clue to the difference between the two 'revolutions'. Extensional semantics operates compositionally on extensions. Intensional semantics operates compositionally on intensions. Does hyperintensional semantics operate compositionally on hyperintensions, whatever they are? It does something beyond intensional semantics, but its name does not specify what. Indeed, some versions of hyperintensional semantics fall below the minimum standard of compositionality, an issue discussed later in this chapter.

On the standard use of the terms 'extensional', 'intensional', and 'hyperintensional', there is an asymmetry between the extensional-intensional distinction and the intensional-hyperintensional distinction. If an operator is extensional, it is also intensional, because an operation on extensions induces a corresponding operation on intensions. By contrast, if an operator is intensional, it is *not* also hyperintensional; an operation on intensions may not induce a corresponding operation on 'hyperintensions', whatever they are. I will use the terminology in this standard way.

One might describe hyperintensionalism as a more data-driven approach than either extensionalism or intensionalism. From a methodological perspective, that already raises concerns about overfitting: the data on which subsequent theorizing relies are typically derived from off-the-cuff judgments on examples. Concerns about overfitting intensify when the theoretical frameworks inspired by the data turn out to help themselves to many extra degrees of freedom, as hyperintensional semantic theories do. Still worse, one can give a specific non-hyperintensionalist alternative explanation of the data, in terms of a heuristic of limited reliability. This chapter will treat the hyperintensionalist programme as a case study in overfitting.

Before we get into the methodological details, some more general reflections on the taxonomy of extensional, intensional, and hyperintensional are worth noting.

3.2 Extensional, intensional, hyperintensional

The hyperintensional is defined as what is beyond the intensional, so the boundary of the hyperintensional is no clearer than the boundary of the intensional. The use of impossible worlds in semantics illustrates the unclarity in the boundary. It is usually thought to entail hyperintensionality. But the general structure of intensional semantics does not exclude worlds in which Socrates was a donkey, for example, even if those worlds are metaphysically impossible. Another aspect of vagueness in the term 'intensional' concerns the structure of the semantics. Strictly speaking, if models have a parameter for times as well as the one for worlds, they go beyond the original Kripke models, but the addition is usually understood to be well within the spirit of intensional semantics.

The boundary between the non-extensional but intensional and the extensional is also much less clear than it may first sound. For example, David Lewis is usually regarded as a leader of the intensional revolution, having made possible worlds more central to his theorizing than did any other major philosopher, including Leibniz. Lewis also wrote one of the most systematic early accounts of the semantics of natural languages in the framework of intensional semantics (Lewis 1970). But he designed his modal metaphysics to facilitate his semantic reduction of the intensional language of quantified modal logic to the extensional language of counterpart theory (Lewis 1968). He thereby provided a way of making intensional languages respectable by the extensionalist standards of his old PhD supervisor Quine, though not to Quine's satisfaction. Lewis himself argued that the distinction between extensional and intensional languages is elusive and unimportant (Lewis 1974). Admittedly, Lewis's counterpart theory and modal realism about concrete possible worlds are minority views in metaphysics. But when one applies intensional semantics to a modal object-language, one standardly does so in an *extensional* metalanguage, quantifying over worlds rather than using modal operators. More specifically, work on the model theory of modal logic and formal modal semantics is normally done in the non-modal language of mathematics, with some extra vocabulary to describe the syntax of the object-language. However, when one characterizes the *intended* model(s) for given readings of the modal operators, one may need to use those operators with those readings to pick them out (Williamson 2013a). It's complicated.

Defining 'extensional', 'intensional', and 'hyperintensional' precisely may be more trouble than it is worth. We have clear paradigms of extensional semantics, clear paradigms of intensional semantics, and clear paradigms of hyperintensional semantics. Given a clearly specified formal semantics, we can identify its similarities to, and differences from, those paradigms. We know that any standard intensional semantics assigns the sentences in any one of the pairs (1A/B), (2A/B), and (3A/B) the same truth-value, and that some paradigmatically hyperintensional semantics assigns them different truth-values. That is enough to be getting on with. If someone later claims to have a non-standard intensional semantics that assigns different truth-values to the sentences in such a pair, one should look at the details before passing judgment. Typically, in a perspicuous formal semantic framework, one can define natural formal criteria for an operator to be extensional, intensional, or hyperintensional, but the specific details may vary.

Some philosophers might argue that hyperintensional semantics is nothing new, because Frege's semantics was hyperintensional once he introduced his distinction between sense and reference. For instance, although '2 + 2 = 4' and 'Peano arithmetic is incomplete' are necessarily equivalent, they differ in cognitive significance, and so have distinct Fregean senses. That allows Frege to evaluate 'The children believe that 2 + 2 = 4' as true but 'The children believe that Peano arithmetic is incomplete' as false. The issue is not straightforward, because Frege implemented the compositional aspect of his semantics primarily at the level of reference rather than of sense, so in a way his semantics is extensional. His trick is that when a declarative sentence occurs in the scope of a propositional attitude operator such as 'The children believe that', the embedded sentence refers to its customary sense, not to its customary referent (the true, for '2 + 2 = 4' and 'Peano arithmetic is incomplete'). Thus, rather awkwardly, Frege achieves a hyperintensional effect in a nominally extensional setting. That is yet another hard case for the taxonomy of extensional, intensional, and hyperintensional.

Even at the height of the 'intensional revolution', most philosophers of language and mind in effect treated propositional attitude operators as hyperintensional, in accord with ordinary assessments of propositional attitude ascriptions in natural language. That is exactly why they rejected the standard intensional treatments of operators for knowledge and belief in models of epistemic and doxastic logic, on the grounds that they entailed logical omniscience (see chapter 2.6). In that respect, the 'hyperintensional revolution' was not revolutionary at all.

What was more revolutionary in the 'hyperintensional revolution' was the hyperintensional treatment of constructions characteristic of general metaphysics: for instance, 'It is essential to . . . that ---' in (1A/B), '. . . because ---' in (2A/B), and 'being a . . .' in (3A/B). For hyperintensional distinctions had been widely assumed to make a difference only in cognitive or representational matters: the picture was that there is no hyperintensionality out there in the world as it is independently of how it is conceived. The role of senses in Fregean semantics poses no threat to that picture, because Fregean senses are individuated in terms of cognitive significance.

A further complication is that the talk of 'the world as it is independently of how it is conceived' presupposes a broadly realist approach to metaphysics. A metaphysical idealist who identifies the real with the rational may take cognitive hyperintensionality to *be* fully worldly hyperintensionality. Henceforth, I will follow most advocates of hyperintensionalism in metaphysics by ignoring metaphysical idealism.

Minimally, to draw non-trivial hyperintensionalist morals from examples like (1A/B), (2A/B), and (3A/B), the constructions in them should be free of metalinguistic elements, as should our assessments of their truth-values, beyond the bare minimum required to understand them. For metalinguistic hyperintensionalism comes very cheap indeed, as in (5A/B):

(5A) '2 + 2 = 4' contains '4'.

(5B) 'Peano arithmetic is incomplete' contains '4'.

Obviously, (5A) is true and (5B) false, even though they differ only in the substitution of necessarily equivalent sentences; quotations of meaningful expressions are typically hyperintensional. That shows nothing interesting about hyperintensionality in metaphysics.

Within analytic metaphysics itself, arguments for genuine worldly hyperintensionality went back further than is often recognized, well before the 1990s. For example, the article in which Sober made his case for the hyperintensional individuation of properties was published in 1982. It treats properties as causally potent in mind-independent ways, not as mere projections of predicates or concepts.

Another case concerned the use of a *supervenience* relation to characterize relations between different 'levels'—for instance, mental properties or events and physical properties or events (as in Davidson 1970). Supervenience was standardly defined in modal terms: there is no *possible* difference at the supervening level without a corresponding difference at the base level. That rough statement can be made precise in various non-equivalent ways, yielding various different supervenience relations, but all within an intensional framework. A much-discussed worry was that a modally defined supervenience relation might not capture the full sense in which the base level metaphysically *determines* the supervening level (Kim 1984). For a start, supervenience as modally defined is a reflexive and not anti-symmetric relation: each level supervenes on itself, and two levels can supervene on each other. Although such cases can be excluded by focusing on one-way supervenience, where one level supervenes on another in the original sense but not conversely, not even that gives one what one wants. For instance, the family of two properties {red, not-red} supervenes one-way on the family of four properties {red and round, red and not-round, not-red and round, not-red and not-round}, but the four-property family does not seem metaphysically to determine the two-family property in the right way; it does not seem 'more basic'. I remember a widespread sense in philosophical discussions around 1980 that modal relations were too coarse-grained to capture what was wanted. In current terminology, the complaint was that modal relations are insufficient to *ground* the supervening level in the supervenience base.

Other resources for metaphysical hyperintensionality were also available in that period. In particular, since *propositions* were normally treated as the objects of propositional attitudes, and few were willing to treat propositional attitudes intensionally, hyperintensional theories of propositions were needed. Thus, the sentences '2 + 2 = 4' and 'Peano arithmetic is incomplete' were usually taken to express distinct propositions, despite their necessary equivalence. Philosophers of language tended to accept a theory of direct reference for various expressions, on which sentences do not express Fregean senses, so propositions were not identified with Fregean thoughts. Instead, a sentence was often taken to express a *Russellian proposition*, a complex of the objects, properties, and relations the sentence was about, with a structure somewhat similar to the syntactic structure of the sentence. For example, Nathan Salmón used such an apparatus to give an anti-Fregean treatment of Frege puzzles (Salmón 1986; for more discussion of Frege puzzles see chapter 4). Russellian propositions are worldly entities; they are not individuated by cognitive significance. Nor are they individuated by necessary equivalence. Consider these two sentences:

(6A) Mont Blanc has snowfields and Mont Blanc does not have snowfields.

(6B) Mount Everest has snowfields and Mount Everest does not have snowfields.

Let [6A] and [6B] be the propositions expressed by (6A) and (6B), respectively. On the Russellian picture of propositions, Mont Blanc is a constituent of [6A] but not of [6B], while Mount Everest is a constituent of [6B] but not of [6A], so [6A] and [6B] are distinct propositions, despite being necessarily equivalent, since they are both impossible. That conception should allow one to define a propositional operator O which has nothing to do with cognitive significance but is sensitive to the constituents of the input proposition, so that the proposition O([6A]) is true while the proposition O([6B]) is false. For example, given any proposition P, we could define O(P) as the proposition that Mont Blanc is a constituent of P. Then O is a hyperintensional operator at the purely metaphysical level of Russellian propositions.

As this background suggests, the 'hyperintensional revolution' was not the result of any major new philosophical or technical breakthrough—by contrast with the intensional revolution. Fine's 1994 paper hit intensionalism where it hurt, by casting serious doubt on (many would say 'refuting') one of its supposed successes, Kripke's modal account of essence, but the damage was limited. Still, the paper was eye-catching; perhaps it brought interest in hyperintensional theorizing up to a critical mass.

The hyperintensionalist programme tends to be seen as a comparative newcomer on the philosophical scene, which has to be given time to prove itself. But key hyperintensionalist ideas have been around for forty years or more, so one might be forgiven for starting to feel impatient. By contrast, the intensional revolution had achieved a far broader and deeper transformation of philosophical thinking by the mid-1970s, in the work of Kripke, Lewis, Stalnaker, Kaplan, Barcan Marcus, Plantinga, Fine himself, and many others. Outside philosophy, the breakthrough in modal logic soon had effects in mathematical logic, linguistics, computer science, and theoretical economics. Traces of the 'hyperintensional revolution' are rarer outside philosophy (Fine 2017a: 574–5 lists some examples). Of course, anyone interested in computational phenomena must make syntactic distinction amongst logically equivalent formulas, but such distinctions do not depend on *semantic* hyperintensionality. Still, the main impact of what is called 'the hyperintensional revolution' has been in pure analytic metaphysics itself.

Hyperintensionalist metaphysical theorizing manifests the self-confidence which analytic metaphysics developed through the work of Kripke, Lewis, and others, and so at least in part through the intensional revolution (see Williamson 2014c for discussion). The suspicions of metaphysics associated with the 'Linguistic Turn', in both its logical positivist and its ordinary language manifestations, have been banished. But there is a concomitant danger of over-confidence. The less one doubts that one's judgments are directly responsive to relations out there in the non-linguistic world, with no linguistic bias or projection, the more vulnerable one is to exactly such linguistic biases and projection, because one is not screening for them. That problem will surface in the final section of this chapter. Before that, we will scrutinize some versions of hyperintensional semantics to see how resistant they are to overfitting—for overfitting is a typical effect of over-confidence in one's data.

3.3 Hyperintensional semantics: impossible worlds

The role of 'impossible worlds' in semantics goes back long before the 'hyperintensional revolution'. They were used early on in models of epistemic and doxastic logic to block logical omniscience, in what could be presented as a natural generalization of intensional semantics (Hintikka 1975, Rantala 1982; for more recent developments see Berto and Jago 2019). Even earlier, Kripke had used models with 'nonnormal' worlds at which every formula

CASE STUDY: HYPERINTENSIONALISM 119

of the form $\Diamond \alpha$ is true to handle the non-normal modal systems S2 and S3, though that was a far more restricted use of impossible worlds than was later made of them (Kripke 1965).[2]

If there is a problem with 'impossible worlds' in semantics, it is not that they could not exist. They *do* exist. A model contains a set W, whose members are the values of the 'world' parameter with respect to which formulas of the object-language are evaluated as true; W can be any non-empty set. In models for the semantics, the 'impossible worlds' form a proper subset of W; the semantics imposes no constraints on which formulas of the language are true at an impossible world. Consequently, in some cases, the formulas true at a given impossible world in a given model are not jointly compatible; they may be formally inconsistent or (on their intended interpretations) metaphysically incompossible. The designated actual world of a model is not allowed to be one of the impossible worlds.[3]

To see the attraction of using 'impossible worlds' in the semantics to handle apparent metaphysical hyperintensionality, we will consider *counterpossibles*. A counterpossible is a counterfactual conditional with an impossible antecedent, such as 'If there were true contradictions, Graham Priest would be vindicated'. In semantics, the default reading of counterfactuals is standardly taken to be non-epistemic, though epistemic readings are sometimes available (see Edgington 2008, Vetter 2016, and Williamson 2020: 251–3 for discussion). For example, whether the counterfactual 'If you had pressed the red button, there would have been an explosion', is true

---

[2] A standard Kripke model can have impossible worlds in the less extreme sense that some members of W are inaccessible from the actual world of the model. This can happen even for the intended model structure on a metaphysical reading of the modal operators if metaphysical modality violates the S4 axiom $\Diamond \Diamond p \rightarrow \Diamond p$; some worlds will be possibly possible but not possible (Salmón 1984). Unlike the models with 'impossible worlds' discussed in the main text, such cases involve no relaxation of the standard semantic constraints on the semantic evaluation of formulas at worlds.

[3] The 'impossible worlds' here are impossible only in belonging to a subset of W exempted from the usual semantic evaluation clauses for the connectives. At some such worlds, the sentences evaluated as true are jointly logically consistent and metaphysically compossible on their intended interpretations.

or false depends on the real state of the device, and more generally of the physical world, not on what anyone happens to know about it. Thus, unless one already expects hyperintensionality to be non-worldly, one might expect hyperintensionality in counterpossibles to constitute worldly hyperintensionality.

Standardly, the semantics of counterfactuals is done within an intensional framework, in the tradition of Stalnaker (1968) and Lewis (1973). The general idea—which Stalnaker and Lewis implement in slightly different ways—is that the counterfactual 'If it were that A, it would be that C' is true at a world *w* if and only if 'C' is true at the closest world(s) to *w* at which 'A' is true. In the special case where 'A' is true at *no* world, the counterfactual counts as true, since *a fortiori* there is no world at which 'A' is true and 'C' is not.[4] In brief, if all worlds are possible, then all counterpossibles are vacuously true. My preferred intensional approach to counterfactuals delivers the same verdict on counterpossibles. It treats 'if' itself as the material conditional, but the whole conditional as in the scope of 'would', read as a contextually restricted local necessity operator; composing these yields a contextually restricted strict conditional. In other words, 'If it were that A, it would be that C' is true at *w* if and only if, at every world contextually relevant to *w* at which 'A' is true, 'C' is also true. Thus, if the counterfactual is a counterpossible, it is vacuously true because 'A' is not true at any world (Williamson 2020).

Now take these two counterpossibles:

(7A) If 7 + 5 were 13, 7 + 5 would be 13.

(7B) If 7 + 5 were 13, 7 + 5 would both be 13 and not be 13.

---

[4] Strictly speaking, what Stalnaker (1968) offers is an impossible worlds semantics, since he handles counterpossibles by giving each model one 'absurd' world where every sentence is true, so all counterpossibles still come out true everywhere. This has no hyperintensional effect in the object-language because he could have achieved the same result by eliminating the absurd world and directly stipulating that every counterpossible is true at every world. The variant semantics is strictly intensional.

People are naturally inclined to assess (7A) as true and (7B) as false. Indeed, (7A) sounds utterly truistic, while (7B) is dissonant. On the supposition that 7 + 5 = 13, one accepts that very supposition and rejects a contradiction. But, on the intensional semantics for counterfactuals, both (7A) *and* (7B) are vacuously true. Indeed, *any* treatment of counterfactuals in the standard intensional framework will assign them the same truth-value, because their antecedents are necessarily equivalent (both are impossible) and their consequents are necessarily equivalent (both are impossible). Consequently, some philosophers advocate a hyperintensional treatment, to capture the apparent difference in truth-value between (7A) and (7B). A similar example can be given with a non-obviously logically inconsistent sentence in the language of ordinary truth-functional propositional logic in place of the sentence '7 + 5 is 13', which states a mathematical impossibility.

One can easily validate (7A) and invalidate (7B) in impossible worlds semantics, using Lewis's or Stalnaker's semantic clause for the counterfactual conditional at all *possible* worlds in all models. Trivially, (7A) is true at any possible world (including the actual world) in any model, because its consequent is true at all the closest worlds at which its antecedent is true, since its antecedent and consequent are identical. To invalidate (7B), just take a model where, at one of the closest worlds to the actual world at which '7 + 5 is 13' is true, '7 + 5 is and is not 13' is not true. In that model, (7B) is not true, because at one of the closest worlds to the actual world at which its antecedent is true its consequent is not true. Thus, impossible worlds semantics is well designed to give the desired verdicts on (7A) and (7B).

Impossible worlds semantics pays a high price for such results. The guiding principle of systematic semantics is *compositionality*: it aims to show how the meaning of each complex expression of the object-language is determined by the meanings of its constituent expressions and how they are put together. Compositionality is central to explaining language users' ability to understand unfamiliar sentences composed of familiar words. But impossible worlds 'semantics' sacrifices compositionality. It is like a kind of alternative mathematics where the value of '$x + y$' is not determined by the values of 'x' and 'y'.

Compositionality is not an all-or-nothing matter. Without more constraints on meanings, it can be trivialized in various ways: most blatantly, by assigning all expressions the same meaning, or by assigning all distinct expressions different meanings. With more constraints on meanings, minor violations of compositionality may be explicable and tolerated. The term 'compositional' is not perfectly precise (for a nuanced account, see Szabó 2000). Still, we have both a schematic understanding of the general principle and paradigms of its implementation in standard semantic theories, which together act as strong guidelines for semantic theorizing. In graded terms, the more compositional the semantic theory, the better. But standard impossible worlds semantics violates the spirit of compositionality so grossly that we can legitimately characterize it as non-compositional.

To see how compositionality fails in standard impossible worlds semantics, take the case of negation. In effect, both standard models of possible worlds semantics and standard models of impossible worlds semantics equate the meaning of a sentence with its *intension*, which for present purposes we can simply treat as the set of all worlds in the model at which the sentence is true. In standard possible world semantics, the semantic clause for negation is simply this: in any model, $\neg\alpha$ is true at a world w if and only if α is not true at w. Thus, the intension of $\neg\alpha$ in a model is simply the complement of the intension of α in the set W of all worlds in the model. That is perfectly compositional. The same applies to the evaluation of $\neg\alpha$ at all *possible* worlds in impossible worlds semantics. But the semantic clause for negation does not apply at impossible worlds. Thus, there are impossible worlds models like this: two atomic sentences p and q are true at exactly the same possible and impossible worlds, but at some impossible world, $\neg p$ is true but $\neg q$ is not true. Consequently, in the model, although p has the same intension as q, $\neg p$ has a *different* intension from $\neg q$; the intension of p and q does not determine the intension of $\neg p$ and $\neg q$. This shows that negation does not in general behave compositionally in models for impossible worlds semantics. The same applies to conjunction, disjunction, and conditionals.

A defender of impossible worlds semantics might retreat by consigning the impossible worlds to a purely instrumental role in the semantics, and identifying the meaning of a sentence in a model with its intension restricted to the possible worlds of the model, where the standard semantic clauses still apply. That would restore compositionality to negation, conjunction, disjunction, and the other truth-functors. But it would *not* restore compositionality to the counterfactual conditional. The kind of model used above to invalidate (7B) shows exactly that. In it, the antecedent of (7A) has the same restricted intension as the antecedent of (7B), and the consequent of (7A) has the same restricted intension as the consequent of (7B), the empty set, but (7A) does *not* have the same restricted intension as (7B), since (7A) but not (7B) is true at the actual world, which is a possible world. The very features for which the impossible worlds semantics was designed make it non-compositional with respect to restricted intensions. Whether meanings are equated with restricted intensions or (more plausibly) with unrestricted ones, the semantics is not compositional.

Advocates of impossible worlds semantics rarely mention its violation of the central constraint of systematic semantics. Indeed, they often seem unaware of it. At a conference a few years ago, having heard a talk in favour of impossible worlds semantics, I asked the speaker about its non-compositionality; he replied that it had never occurred to him. Someone could argue that non-compositionality is a cost worth paying, but to do that they would first have to acknowledge that it is a cost.

The way compositionality fails in impossible worlds semantics carries with it a massive increase in degrees of freedom. As already noted, the nature of the subject-matter of semantics implies that each non-logical atomic expression of the object-language adds its own degree of freedom; its meaning has to be written into each model 'by hand'. In a compositional semantics the complex expressions add no further degrees of freedom; their meanings are determined by the meanings of their atomic constituents and how they are put together. By contrast, in impossible worlds semantics, the intension of each complex sentence over the impossible worlds also has to be written into the model 'by hand'. This deprives such models of much of the explanatory power one hopes for in a scientific model, where simple assumptions generate complex effects.

A fan of impossible worlds could restore the letter, though not the spirit, of semantic compositionality by expanding the models with extra worlds to differentiate the input sentences in meaning while fencing the extra worlds off in order not to disturb other hyperintensional features of the model. But that would provide virtually none of the illumination available from standard compositional semantic theories, which *explain* compositionality in terms of simple, natural semantic clauses for the relevant operators. It would achieve compositionality by brute force, and complicate the models still further.

To their credit, Franz Berto and Mark Jago explicitly confront the problem of non-compositionality on behalf of impossible world semantics (2019: 180–4). They restore the letter of compositionality by an elaborate construction that involves a hypothetical 'world-making' language distinct from the object-language under study. Their approach is purely generic, in the sense that it does not depend on any specific features of the object-language operators to which it is applied. This makes it quite uninformative about the object-language. Its hypothetical success consists in *sterilizing* the compositionality constraint, while the constraint's value to semantics has consisted in its fruitfulness.

One could achieve a similar effect more directly with a new semantics on which the meaning of each expression E is the ordered pair <M(E), E>, where M(E) is the meaning of E on the old non-compositional semantics. For any monadic operator O of an appropriate type in the object-language, the new meaning of O(E) is <M(O(E)), O(E)>, which is a function of <M(E), E> through being a function of E, which is in turn a function of the new meaning of E, <M(E), E>; the case of polyadic operators is similar. Tellingly, the new semantics forbids any distinct expressions E_1 and E_2 from having the same new meaning, even if they have the same old meaning, for although $M(E_1) = M(E_2)$, $<M(E_1), E_1> \neq <M(E_2), E_2>$ because $E_1 \neq E_2$. Thus, the new semantics respects the letter of compositionality, but not its spirit. Such trivializations of compositionality offer nothing to our understanding of natural language semantics, or counterfactuality, or propositional attitudes. Compositionality has contributed so much to the development of systematic semantics because it is a demanding yet natural constraint; reducing it to a form of words to which lip-service must and can be paid is a retrograde step.

On the evidence, impossible worlds semantics is a classic case of overfitting of the distinctive kind that sometimes arises in logic and formal semantics, discussed in chapter 2.

The threat of overfitting immediately raises the question: how safe were the originally motivating data? In particular, how safe was the assessment of (7B) as false?[5] The judgment is just what one would predict from the application of the suppositional heuristic. On the counterfactual supposition '7 + 5 is 13', one assesses '7 + 5 both is and is not 13' and denies it; applying the heuristic, one denies (7B) itself. The processing is shallow; it does not take the impossibility of the antecedent into account, but simply reacts in the usual way to 'A and not-A' on the supposition 'A'. Strictly speaking, the heuristic has to be adapted to the presence of the modal operator, by combining it with a heuristic for 'would', but the combined

---

[5] The original judgment that (7A) is true agrees with its evaluation on standard intensional approaches and is not in question.

heuristic turns out to be structurally similar to the original heuristic for 'if' itself; the role of 'would' was acknowledged by qualifying 'supposition' with 'counterfactual' (Williamson 2020: 189–213). But the combined heuristic for 'would if', like the original heuristic for plain 'if', is implicitly inconsistent. Moreover, the heuristic for 'would if' generates contradictions specifically when applied to counterpossibles (Williamson 2020: 205–7). It would be rather rash to rely on the heuristic-generated verdict on (7B) in the very type of case for which the heuristic is known to be unreliable. Other alleged examples of false counterpossibles can be explained in similar ways (Williamson 2020: 256–9).

One could be reassured if the pre-theoretic verdict on (7B) were confirmed by a tight explanatorily powerful semantic theory. But confirmation by a semantic theory as profligate with degrees of freedom as impossible worlds semantics carries little weight. With so many degrees of freedom, one can model almost any behaviour someone might attribute to counterpossibles.

Without even seeing examples, one could have predicted on more general grounds that standard forms of conditional thinking might well run into trouble with impossible suppositions. One need only consider the mathematics of conditional probability; there is a well-documented tendency to associate the probability of a conditional with the corresponding conditional probability, as predicted by the suppositional heuristic (for an introduction to the literature, see Williamson 2020: 31–4). Usually, the conditional probability $Pr(X \mid Y)$ of X on Y is defined as the ratio $Pr(X \cap Y)/Pr(Y)$ of unconditional probabilities, where X and Y are *events*, subsets of the probability space, analogous to sets of possible worlds. Informally, the conditional probability of X on Y is the proportion of the Y-region that is also in the X-region. When $Pr(Y) = 0$, the ratio involves dividing by zero, and so is undefined. Schoolchildren are often fascinated by sophistical arguments for mad conclusions such as $0 = 1$, which non-obviously involve dividing by zero: one shows that $xz = yz$ and divides through by z to conclude that $x = y$.

In thinking with counterpossibles, we must be careful not to do the analogue of dividing by zero. Admittedly, for conditional probability, we have the alternative of treating it as primitive, rather than trying to define it in terms of unconditional probabilities. Of course, we need some constraints on primitive conditional probabilities. Here is a plausible candidate:

[i]   If $Y \subseteq X$ then $\Pr(X \mid Y) = 1$

For if *every* point in the Y-region is in the X-region, the probability of being in the X-region conditional on being in the Y-region should be maximal. Here is another plausible candidate:

[ii]   If $X \cap Y = \{\}$ then $\Pr(X \mid Y) = 0$

For if *no* point in the Y-region is in the X-region, the probability of being in the X-region conditional on being in the Y-region should be minimal.

Now if $Y = \{\}$, $Y \subseteq X$, so by [i] $\Pr(X \mid Y) = 1$, but also $X \cap Y = \{\}$, so by [ii] $\Pr(X \mid Y) = 0$, a contradiction! Despite their plausibility, [i] and [ii] cannot both hold in this special case. Considering probabilities conditional on the null event is the probabilistic analogue of considering counterpossibles. But, for conditional probabilities, we have a clear, agreed mathematical framework to correct our thinking when we stray off the straight and narrow path. By contrast, for conditionals, we have no such clear, agreed framework.

The probabilistic analogy is available before we decide what to make of counterpossibles. It warns us that when we consider them, we are entering a space where normally reliable ways of thinking are liable to break down. With warning signs like that, and the inconsistency of the heuristic for 'would if', to trust our off-the-cuff judgment that (7B) and similar counterpossibles are false, to the point of abandoning a well-tried theoretical framework and taking up instead one with well-known hallmarks of bad science, is an act of alarming methodological naivety. *Sancta simplicitas!*

The perspective *before* we have decided what to make of counterpossibles is also useful for considering another question: *if* impossible worlds semantics involves treating counterpossibles as implicitly metalinguistic, what symptoms of that would we expect to see? The suspicion arises naturally, because the evaluation of sentences at impossible worlds bypasses their semantic structure, as if it were irrelevant.

One salient hypothetical prediction is that if impossible worlds semantics treats counterpossibles as implicitly metalinguistic, substituting synonyms in a counterpossible can change its truth-value, because the sentence is at least partly about the words themselves. Take this pair of counterpossibles:

(8A)   If furze were not gorse, furze would not be gorse.

(8B)   If furze were not gorse, furze would not be furze.

Here 'furze' and 'gorse' are synonymous terms for the same natural kind. Assessing (8A) and (8B) in the same pre-theoretic way as (7A) and (7B), we are naturally inclined to assess (8A) as true and (8B) as false. On the counterfactual supposition 'Furze is not gorse', one trivially assents to that very sentence and dissents from the logically inconsistent sentence 'Furze is not furze': disregarding botany does not force one to disregard logic. Again, the processing is shallow; it does not take the impossibility of the antecedent into account but simply reacts in the usual way to an obviously inconsistent sentence on an apparently consistent supposition. Applying the suppositional heuristic, one therefore assents to (8A) and dissents from (8B). The impossible worlds semantics can then vindicate these verdicts on (8A) and (8B), just as it vindicated the corresponding verdicts on (7A) and (7B). On this view, merely substituting the word 'furze' for its synonym 'gorse' turned the true (8A) into the

false (8B). This reinforces the suspicion that the approach treats counterpossibles as implicitly metalinguistic. More generally, rather than contributing to the development of hyperintensional metaphysics, the impossible worlds framework seems to be used as a device for staying on the linguistic surface.[6]
In short, the impossible worlds framework is bad science.

3.4 Hyperintensional semantics: truthmakers

A less profligate framework for hyperintensional semantics involves *truthmakers*. I will focus on a version developed by Kit Fine (2017a, 2017b, 2017c), since it represents the current state of the art. More specifically, I will assess it primarily as a *semantic* theory, since Fine presents it as such, not as a metaphysical theory. Nevertheless, it is a leading candidate for a systematic framework for hyperintensional metaphysicians to use in explaining how their characteristic statements can be meaningful and true.

In truthmaker semantics, when sentences are true, they are *made* true by *states*, their truthmakers; a *verifier* for a sentence is a state that *would*, if it obtained, make the sentence true. Similarly, when sentences are false, they are made false by states, their falsehoodmakers; a *falsifier* for a sentence is a state that would, if it obtained, make the sentence false. Unlike worlds, states are typically partial, involving only some local aspect of things. Some states are possible: they can obtain. Others are impossible: they cannot obtain. The natural connections with truth and falsity themselves

---

[6] For a long-running debate on counterpossibles and impossible worlds, see Nolan 1997, Dorr 2008: 37, Brogaard and Salerno 2013, Berto, French, Priest, and Ripley 2018, and Williamson 2007: 172–76, 2017c, 2018b, and 2020: 256–9. I hope that setting the debate in a wider methodological context will help to clarify the issues. Of course, since furze = gorse, the claim that (8A) and (8B) differ in truth-value also violates Leibniz's Law, and so is bad logic too, for closely related reasons—a concern to which I have found proponents of impossible worlds semantics strikingly insensitive. Leibniz's Law is not a distinctively intensionalist principle.

are that a sentence α is true if and only if some verifier of α obtains, and α is false if and only if some falsifier for α obtains.[7]

States have mereological structure: some states are parts of other states. Any set of states has a *fusion*, the minimal state of which they are all parts: it is part of any state of which they are all parts. In this semantics, a model assigns each sentence of the object-language a set of verifiers and a set of falsifiers, whose ordered pair is in effect the meaning of the sentence in the model. Unlike impossible worlds semantics, truthmaker semantics is compositional: the meaning of a complex sentence is determined by the meanings of its constituents and how they are put together.

The mereological structure is needed for compositional purposes. In the simplest version of Fine's semantics, for example, since making a conjunction true involves making each conjunct true, a verifier of α ∧ β is a fusion of a verifier of α with a verifier of β. But since making a conjunction *false* just involves making one or other conjunct false, a falsifier of α ∧ β is simply a falsifier of α or a falsifier of β. Similarly, since making a disjunction false involves making each disjunct false, a falsifier of α ∨ β is a fusion of a falsifier of α with a falsifier of β. But since making a disjunction *true* just involves making one or other disjunct true, a verifier of α ∨ β is simply a verifier of α or a verifier of β.

The apparatus of verifiers and falsifiers smoothly handles the semantics of negation: the verifiers of ¬α are the falsifiers of α, and the falsifiers of ¬α are the verifiers of α.

---

[7] Fine's postulation of non-obtaining states undermines one philosophical motivation for truthmaker theory: the idea that a true proposition needs some *thing* to make it true (Armstrong 1997: 115). For if there is a state *s* which, if it obtained, *would* make α true, although in fact α is false and *s* does not obtain, then *s* itself is insufficient for α to be true; what is needed is for *s to obtain*. The distinction between obtaining and not obtaining is just the analogue for states of the distinction between being true and being false; in effect, the property of truth for propositions and sentences gets explained in terms of a truthlike property for states, whereas the original ambition was to explain it in radically different terms: by things *themselves*. For more on these issues, see Williamson 2013a: 391–403. The critique of truthmaker theory there is independent of, and consistent with, the critique in this section.

The semantics is hyperintensional because necessarily equivalent sentences sometimes differ in their verifiers or falsifiers. The most dramatic case is that $α ∧ α$ can differ from $α$ in its verifiers: repetitiousness is logically significant. For the fusion of two verifiers of $α$ is a verifier of $α ∧ α$ even though it may not be a verifier of $α$ itself. However, Fine shows how to avoid that oddity by tweaking the semantics to make every fusion of verifiers of a sentence itself a verifier of it. A more robust hyperintensional feature is that, although the sentence $α ∨ (α ∧ β)$ has the same truth-conditions as plain $α$, they often differ in their verifiers and falsifiers. For some verifiers of $α ∨ (α ∧ β)$ will include verifiers of $β$ as parts, and some falsifiers of $α ∨ (α ∧ β)$ will include falsifiers of $β$ as parts; but if $α$ and $β$ are about quite different topics, no verifier of $α$ will include any verifier of $β$ as a part, and no falsifier of $α$ will include a falsifier of $β$ as a part. For Fine understands verification and falsification as *exact*, so the fusion of a verifier or falsifier of a sentence with some quite irrelevant state is not another verifier or falsifier of that sentence. Capturing such differences in subject matter is an aspect of what Fine intends truthmaker semantics for, so from his perspective the semantic difference between $α ∨ (α ∧ β)$ and $α$ is a feature, not a bug.

One might have the impression that states are in effect partial worlds, and the state parameter is just Fine's analogue of the world parameter in intensional semantics. But that is not Fine's intended understanding of his framework. He treats the apparatus of states as fundamentally *amodal*. Although he permits a distinction between possible and impossible states to be introduced, it is extraneous to the underlying structure of states. Moreover, a one-off distinction between possible and impossible states would not by itself provide for all the more restricted modalities in continual use by speakers of natural languages. The point is not that there is any block in principle to *adding* parameters capable of handling such modalities to the truthmaking framework; it is just that the extra methodological costs associated with states and their mereological structure may not be adequately compensated for by economies elsewhere.

Truthmaker semantics adds another degree of freedom by treating the verifiers and falsifiers of a sentence as independent of each other. Fine uses a complicated example to argue that even when α has the same verifiers as β, ¬α does not always have the same verifiers as ¬β, in which case α does not have the same falsifiers as β (Fine 2017a: 564). With verifiers alone, or with falsifiers alone, the semantics would not be compositional. If a state s is not a verifier of a sentence γ, it does not follow that s is a falsifier of γ, for s may simply be irrelevant to γ. Equally, though less obviously, if s is a verifier of γ, it does not follow that s is not also a falsifier of γ. On Fine's semantics, some states are both verifiers and falsifiers of the same sentence.[8]

The quasi-independence of verifiers and falsifiers clearly adds a degree of freedom to the models, by comparison with classical semantics, which in effect equates falsity with non-truth for sentences. This aspect of the semantics is most striking for atomic sentences. Imagine that you are being taught a foreign language. Your teacher explains to you exactly what would make a given atomic sentence true. Could you then complain to her: "You've only done half your job! You've told me what this sentence's *verifiers* are, but you haven't told me anything about its *falsifiers*"? That sounds quite unreasonable. Your teacher has already done enough to enable you to understand the sentence, by normal linguistic standards. You are not missing half its meaning. Normally, what would make a sentence true does determine what would make it false.

---

[8] Proof: Let s be a verifier of α, t a falsifier of α, and $s \sqcup t$ the fusion of s with t. Then $s \sqcup t$ is a verifier of (α ∨ ¬α) ∧ (α ∨ ¬α) because s is a verifier of α ∨ ¬α and t is a verifier of ¬α and so of α ∨ ¬α. But $s \sqcup t$ is also a falsifier of (α ∨ ¬α) ∧ (α ∨ ¬α) because s is a falsifier of ¬α, and t is a falsifier of α, so $s \sqcup t$ (= $t \sqcup s$) is a falsifier of α ∨ ¬α. The text describes Fine's *bilateral* semantics, with truthmakers and falsehoodmakers treated separately. He also has an alternative *unilateral* semantics, with only truthmakers. To handle negation, it postulates a primitive relation of *exclusion* between states, which is another complication in the models, compensating for the loss of falsehoodmakers. Unlike the bivalent semantics, the univalent semantics fails to treat ¬¬α as expressing the same proposition as α (Fine 2017b: 634–5). That is a loss in both simplicity and strength.

These reflections suggest that, with respect to negation, although the truthmaker semantics complies with the letter of compositionality, it violates the spirit. The slack between α and ¬α on the truthmaking outlook has been dressed up as slack between two components of the meaning of α. Truthmakers are something like old-fashioned *facts*, and the lack of co-ordination between the verifiers and falsifiers of a given sentence is reminiscent of Bertrand Russell's difficulties in finding a metaphysically plausible account of negative facts in *The Philosophy of Logical Atomism* (Russell 1918/1919, lecture III). Stephen Yablo's account of truthmakers faces a similar problem in its treatment of negation (Yablo 2014: 58).

From the truthmaker semantics, Fine extracts a general account of a proposition, a candidate for being expressed by a declarative sentence in a context, as an ordered pair of sets of states, the first conceived as the set of its verifiers, the second as the set of its falsifiers. On this approach, true contradictions come very cheap, without need of independent support from paradoxes such as Russell's, the Liar, or the Heap. Let s be any actually obtaining state. Taking $\{s\}$ as both the set of verifiers and the set of falsifiers yields a perfectly good Finean proposition; as already noted, on Fine's semantics a state may be both a verifier and a falsifier for the same sentence, and so for the proposition it expresses. This proposition <$\{s\}$, $\{s\}$> is both actually true and actually false, since s is both a verifier and a falsifier for it and actually obtains. If a sentence α expresses <$\{s\}$, $\{s\}$>, then the sentence α ∧ ¬α is true (and false) on the truthmaker semantics. Of course, Fine could postulate rules of natural languages forbidding such propositions from being expressed, but that would be ad hoc, and in any case would not prevent us from constructing artificial languages in which such propositions *are* expressed. If truthmaker semantics is on the right lines, such languages could be easily understood.

Fine mentions that one might 'impose' a constraint of Exclusivity on propositions, 'No verifier is compatible with a falsifier' (Fine

2017b: 629). Exclusivity implies that <{s}, {s}> is not a proposition, for if *s* actually obtains then *s* is possible, and so compatible with itself. Two comments are in order.

First, the use of a modal constraint to demarcate propositions violates what Fine himself presents as the spirit of his approach. For he writes (Fine 2017a: 566):

[T]he present point of view is that there is nothing in the general notion of content or meaning or in the most general logical devices that requires us to draw the distinction between possible and impossible states. This freedom from the modal thinking that has been so characteristic of the more usual approaches to semantics is, I believe, one of the most distinctive and liberating aspects of the present approach.

By contrast, an intensional account of propositions requires no such restriction.

Second, by imposing more or less ad hoc constraints on which combinations of verifiers and falsifiers constitute propositions, Fine adds yet more complexity, and more degrees of freedom, to his semantic framework, thereby intensifying the danger of overfitting.

Such speculations are alarmingly under-constrained. They indicate that we have helped ourselves to too many degrees of freedom. At first, Fine's separation of truth and falsity looked like a very mild liberalization of the usual practice. But when we take its implications seriously, we find ourselves glibly talking as though we had forgotten what truth and falsity are. Although truthmaker semantics is much better constrained than impossible worlds semantics, it is still not constrained enough.[9]

---

[9] I have not attempted here to discuss Fine's application of truthmaker semantics to specific linguistic issues: for example, he mentions partial content, subject-matters, counterfactuals, imperatives, and scalar implicature. Elsewhere, I have argued in detail that his case for his alleged counterexamples to intensional accounts of counterfactuals neglects independently confirmed context-sensitivity in counterfactuals (Williamson 2020: 217–21).

3.5 Hyperintensional semantics: Russellian propositions

When hyperintensionality is approached through impossible worlds or truthmakers, the unsatisfactory accounts of propositions are overtly inspired by the semantic framework. An alternative hyperintensional account of propositions is covertly inspired by *syntax*. The picture is that a declarative sentence expresses a proposition with an overall constituent structure—perhaps that of an inverted branching tree—like that of the syntactic constituent structure of the sentence. The qualifier 'overall' is needed because syntactically simple constituents of the sentence may express complex constituents of the proposition: for instance, the single word 'vixen' may express a complex with constituents corresponding to 'female' and 'fox'. In some cases, the syntactic form of the sentence misrepresents its underlying *logical form*, the constituent structure of the proposition it expresses: famously, that was Russell's view of sentences of natural language with definite descriptions.

So far, the account is consistent with treating propositions and their constituents as something like Fregean senses, or concepts. For Russellian propositions, however, the constituents are more worldly: the objects, properties, and relations the sentence is about, and complexes of them. For instance, the atomic sentence 'Brutus stabs Caesar' may express a proposition whose form is something like the ordered pair <stabs, <Brutus, Caesar>>, whose constituents include the stabbing relation and the men Brutus and Caesar themselves, not concepts of them, still less their names. Such propositions and their constituents are individuated in a fine-grained way. More precisely, if the operators O and O* figure in the build-up of propositions, where O is m-place, O* is n-place, $C_1, \ldots, C_m$ in that order are suitable inputs for O, and $C^*_1, \ldots, C^*_n$ in that order are suitable inputs for O*, then this principle holds:

FINEGRAIN   If $O(C_1, \ldots, C_m) = O^*(C^*_1, \ldots, C^*_n)$,
then $O = O^*$, $m = n$, and $C_i = C^*_i$ for $1 \leq i \leq n$

In other words, not only do the inputs of applying an operator uniquely determine the output, the output uniquely determines the input. Forming ordered pairs works like that, for $<w, x> = <y, z>$ if and only if $w = y$ and $x = z$. FINEGRAIN implies a hyperintensional conception of propositions, given minimal assumptions about the proposition-building operations. For example, if they include negation ($\neg$) and conjunction ($\wedge$), then, if p and q are distinct propositions, by FINEGRAIN the logically contradictory propositions $p \wedge \neg p$ and $q \wedge \neg q$ are also distinct from each other, despite being necessarily equivalent.[10]

Unfortunately for such a fine-grained conception of propositions, it is inconsistent on natural background assumptions. The best-known reason for this is the *Russell-Myhill Paradox* (Russell 1903: 527, Myhill 1958, Dorr 2016, Goodman 2017). Here is an informal version of such an argument. Let pp be any plurality of propositions. Then we can define a propositional operator O_{pp} where, for any proposition q, $O_{pp}(q)$ is the proposition that q is one of the pp. For any two extensionally distinct pluralities of propositions pp and pp^*, some proposition q is either one of the pp but not one of the pp^* or one of the pp^* but not one of the pp, so the propositions $O_{pp}(q)$ and $O_{pp^*}(q)$ differ in truth-value, so O_{pp} and O_{pp^*} are distinct operators. Hence, for any given proposition q^*, $O_{pp}(q^*)$ and $O_{pp^*}(q^*)$ are distinct propositions by FINEGRAIN. Thus, the mapping that takes each plurality of propositions pp to the proposition $O_{pp}(q)$ is one-one. This means that there are at least as many propositions as there are pluralities of propositions. But, by Cantor's diagonal argument, there are more pluralities of propositions than there are propositions. Contradiction.

---

[10] In this section, when expressions of the formal language of any type occur in English sentences, unless otherwise specified they are being used as singular terms to refer to what they would ordinarily express on the Russellian semantics. Here, as elsewhere in the book, for ease of reading I also ride roughshod over type distinctions, but the proofs do not exploit that sloppiness. A more exact statement could be laboriously given in higher-order terms.

Many variations can be played on that theme, for example, by using properties of propositions rather than pluralities of them, or by constructing different propositions out of them (Kment 2022; see also Fritz 2022 for a related paradox for fine-grained theories of grounding). Later, Russell evaded the paradox by adopting his 'multiple relation theory of judgment' and denying the reality of propositions. The paradox does not arise in his intricately complicated ramified type theory, though the ramification was not needed to preserve consistency (see Hodes 2015 for discussion of Russell's thinking on these matters).

Since the paradoxical argument is in essence Cantorian, as Russell recognized, one naturally gets the impression that the problem is to be solved by some analogue of measures used in set theory to avoid Russell's paradox of the set of all sets that are not members of themselves, by imposing an iterative hierarchy of propositions, or a limitation of size constraint, or whatever. But the underlying problem is both simpler and deeper than that.

We can begin to appreciate the issues by considering *definitions*. For instance, the material biconditional is often defined in terms of the one-way material conditional and conjunction. We can treat that definition as an equation of propositions:

DEF $\leftrightarrow$ $\qquad (p \leftrightarrow q) = ((p \rightarrow q) \wedge (q \rightarrow p))$

But applying FINEGRAIN to DEF $\leftrightarrow$ gives this absurd result:

DEF $\leftrightarrow$! $\qquad \leftrightarrow\, =\, \wedge,\ p = (p \rightarrow q)$, and $q = (q \rightarrow p)$

For the main connective of the left-hand side of DEF $\leftrightarrow$ is $\leftrightarrow$, while the main connective of the right-hand side is $\wedge$. The result is absurd not merely because the operator it equates $\leftrightarrow$ with is not the one we intended; when p and q are falsehoods, they are falsely equated with the truths $p \rightarrow q$ and $q \rightarrow p$.

The common definition of the necessity operator $\Box$ as the dual of the possibility operator $\Diamond$ creates an analogous problem:

DEF$\Box$ $\Box p = \neg \Diamond \neg p$

Applying FINEGRAIN to DEF$\Box$ gives this absurd result:

DEF$\Box$! $\Box = \neg$ and $p = \Diamond \neg p$

For the main operator of the left-hand side of DEF$\Box$ is $\Box$, while the main operator of the right-hand side is $\neg$. The result is absurd not merely because the operator it equates $\Box$ with is not the one we intended; when p is a necessary truth, it is falsely equated with the falsehood $\Diamond \neg p$.

A fan of structured propositions might respond that definitions of operators yield only identities of operators, not of the propositions to which they are applied. We might express the identities with the abstraction device λ:

DEF$\leftrightarrow\lambda$ $\leftrightarrow = \lambda pq.((p \to q) \land (q \to p))$

DEF$\Box\lambda$ $\Box = \lambda p.(\neg \Diamond \neg p)$

The trouble is that the characteristic effect of applying the λ-operator is given by the standard principle of β-conversion:

βCONV $(\lambda v_1 \ldots v_n.\varphi)a_1 \ldots a_n = \varphi[a_i/v_i]_{1 \leq i \leq n}$

As a rather trivial special case of βCONV, abstracting the operator and then re-applying it to the same variables gives back what one started with:

ABST$\leftrightarrow\lambda$ $\lambda pq.((p \to q) \land (q \to p))pq = ((p \to q) \land (q \to p))$

ABST□λ $\lambda p.(\neg\Diamond\neg p)p = \neg\Diamond\neg p$

Combining DEF↔λ with ABST↔λ yields DEF ↔ (rewriting ↔pq as $p \leftrightarrow q$), and combining DEF□λ with ABST□λ yields DEF□; but DEF ↔ and DEF□ are exactly what we are trying to avoid, given FINEGRAIN. Thus, the fan of structured propositions would have to reject βCONV, and in particular its instances ABST↔λ and ABST□λ. But the general principle of βCONV is the central constraint on the behaviour of the λ-operator. Without it, we are left wondering what λ does, and so what DEF↔λ and DEF□λ mean. Although the symbol λ looks reassuringly familiar, it is cast adrift without its usual logical moorings.

The problem is not confined to definitions. On a structured view of propositions, we can build up more and more complex propositions in stages by applying operators iteratively (to use a more or less dead construction metaphor). This requires that proposition-building operators can be *composed*: given proposition-building operators O_1 and O_2, there is a proposition-building operator $O_{1,2}$ whose result when applied to a proposition p is the result of applying O_2 to the result of applying O_1 to p. Trivially, therefore, we have this equation:

COMP $O_{1,2} p = O_2 O_1 p$

But COMP too yields hopeless results, given FINEGRAIN:

COMP! $O_{1,2} = O_2$ and $p = O_1 p$

For the main operator of the left-hand side of COMP is $O_{1,2}$, while the main operator of the right-hand side is O_2. Thus, COMP implies that we can compose operators only if the first of them makes no difference, so applying them in sequence is the same as just applying the second; in brief, we can compose operators only when doing so is pointless. This trivializes the picture of building up structured propositions iteratively.

One might hope to rescue something from the rubble by postulating that, although proposition-building operators cannot strictly be *composed*, they can somehow be combined in ways that have a roughly equivalent effect. The idea is to replace identity in COMP by something slightly weaker, an equivalence relation ≈ on propositions short of identity:

COMP≈ $\quad O_{1,2}p \approx O_2O_1p$

At the very least, COMP≈ should imply that $O_{1,2}p$ and O_2O_1p have the same truth-value. Similarly, one could weaken the propositional identities DEF↔, DEF□, ABST↔λ, and ABST□λ to the corresponding ≈-equivalences:

DEF↔≈ $\quad (p \leftrightarrow q) \approx ((p \rightarrow q) \wedge (q \rightarrow p))$

DEF□≈ $\quad \Box p \approx \neg \Diamond \neg p$

ABST↔λ≈ $\quad (\lambda pq.(p \rightarrow q) \wedge (q \rightarrow p))pq \approx ((p \rightarrow q) \wedge (q \rightarrow p))$

ABST□λ≈ $\quad (\lambda p.\neg \Diamond \neg p)p \approx \neg \Diamond \neg p$

DEF↔≈ follows from DEF↔λ and ABST↔λ≈, while DEF□≈ follows from DEF□λ and ABST□λ≈. But the lack of a good explanation of ≈ leaves the metaphysical picture cloudy, because we have no prior understanding of ≈. A natural temptation is to interpret ≈ in terms of necessary equivalence, though that risks compromising the hyperintensionalist vision, on which intensions are not where the action is.

Worse, FINEGRAIN undermines even the conversion principles ABST↔λ≈ and ABST□λ≈. For presumably they are to be

CASE STUDY: HYPERINTENSIONALISM 141

explained as special instances of a more general underlying weak β-conversion principle of this form:

BCONV ≈ $(\lambda v_1 \ldots v_n \varphi) a_1 \ldots a_n \approx \varphi[a_i/v_i]_{1 \leq i \leq n}$

For the principles with ≈ to be of any use, ≈ must at least imply material equivalence, so βCONV implies this extensional β conversion principle:

βCONV ↔ $(\lambda v_1 \ldots v_n \varphi) a_1 \ldots a_n \leftrightarrow \varphi[a_i/v_i]_{1 \leq i \leq n}$

But, when combined with FINEGRAIN, even βCONV↔ suffices for a version of the Russell-Myhill paradox (Dorr 2016). Without ABST↔λ≈ and ABST□λ≈ even on a minimal material reading of ≈ as ↔, the 'definitions' DEF↔≈ and DEF□≈ are of little use.

There are other concerns too about COMP≈, even on a minimal reading of ≈. For example, on the fine-grained picture, we might expect a monadic proposition-building operator R which, applied to a proposition of the form Op (where O is a propositional operator), re-applies O to Op and then applies negation to the result:

DEFR   ROp ≈ ¬OOp

FINEGRAIN forbids a proposition Op to also be O*q for some other operator O*, so O can be uniquely extracted from Op: the definition is not ambiguous. Since O and ¬ are well-defined propositional operators, there is such a proposition as ¬OOp. For present purposes, what R does to propositions of other forms is irrelevant. Then, in the special case of DEFR where R = O, we have DEFR!, and so by hypothesis DEFR!↔:

DEFR!   RRp ≈ ¬RRp

DEFR!↔   RRp ↔ ¬RRp

DEFR!↔ is a classical contradiction.

Friends of a fine-grained view of propositions may reply that the argument shows only that there is no such operator as R. But that response is inadequate, since it was the fine-grained view itself that made it seem natural for there to be such an operator as R in the first place. Given FINEGRAIN, proposition-building operators are basic to the individuation of propositions, so what proposition-building operators there are should be a central question for such a theory of propositions. We need a more positive, general account of how proposition-building operators can be defined; *post hoc* denials in particular cases are not enough.

The λ operator seemed to provide for just such a general account of proposition-building operators. However, given FINEGRAIN, λ is unconstrained even by βCONV↔, and in most cases we have very little idea how it behaves. For example, given two monadic predicates F and G, we can define the predicate $\lambda x.(Fx \wedge Gx)$, but we have no guarantee that it will behave conjunctively: $(\lambda x.(Fx \wedge Gx))a$ may not be materially equivalent to $Fa \wedge Ga$. In natural language, 'This is such that it is red and it is round' may differ in truth-value from 'This is red and this is round'. Metaphysically, having the 'conjunction' of some properties would not be equivalent to having each of those properties. Similarly, although we can define the predicate $\lambda x.\neg Fx$, we have no guarantee that it will behave negatively: $(\lambda x.\neg Fx)a$ may not be materially equivalent to $\neg Fa$. In natural language, 'This is such that it is not round' may differ in truth-value from 'It is not the case that this is round'. Metaphysically, having the 'negation' of a property would not be equivalent to not having the property. Such a λ gadget is not well-designed for the purposes of either semantics or metaphysics.

At first sight, the picture of structured propositions seems to present a clear, systematic vision of the structure of propositions. On closer inspection, it turns out to be all, or almost all, smoke and mirrors. The central result is the incompatibility of COMP with FINEGRAIN: if one tries composing the operators needed to build structured propositions in non-trivial cases, FINEGRAIN collapses. Since the composite operators are perfectly well-defined proposition-building operators, FINEGRAIN holds only within some unspecified, privileged subclass of proposition-building operators; it is not the advertised general principle for individuating propositions.

One may wonder how the idea of structured propositions can be incoherent, given that Carnap in *Meaning and Necessity* seems in effect to have provided a good formal model of them as what he calls 'intensional structures' (Carnap 1947: 56–64, applied in Lewis 1970). For present purposes, an intensional structure is the kind of thing one gets by taking an analysis tree for a sentence and replacing the expression at each node by its intension, so the result is not language-specific. As usual in linguistics, trees are inverted, branching outwards from the top node.

Intensional structures satisfy FINEGRAIN. For if the expressions $O(C_1, \ldots, C_m)$ and $O^*(C^*_1, \ldots, C^*_n)$ are associated with the same intensional structure, then the number of nodes immediately below the top node is the same, so $m = n$, and the same intensional sub-structures are associated with corresponding nodes immediately below the top node (counting from the left, say), so the expressions O and O* are associated with the same intensional structure, as are the expressions $C_i = C^*_i$ for $1 \le i \le n$.[11] For example, if the sentences α and β have different intensions, then although the sentences α ∧ ¬α and β ∧ ¬β have the same intension, they are associated with different intensional structures, because the second of the nodes immediately below the top node of the intensional structure associated with α ∧ ¬α is labelled with the intension of α, whereas the second of the nodes immediately below the top node of

---

[11] This paragraph talks about expressions rather than the structured propositions or complexes they express because the existence of the latter is not assumed. This involves some abuse of notation, but the intended meaning should be clear in practice, and the notational measures needed to avoid ambiguity in principle would be quite cumbersome.

the intensional structure associated with β ∧ ¬β is labelled with the intension of β. Why is that not a 'proof of concept' for structured propositions?

The trouble is that although intensional structures encode operators, those are not operators on intensional structures, but operators on *intensions*. If propositions are intensional structures, then the operators encoded in propositions are not operators on propositions. It is analogous to associating the expression '2 + 2' with the ordered triple <+, 2, 2>, which encodes addition, but it is still addition of numbers, not addition of ordered sequences, and <+, 2, 2> is no more the number 4 than is the ordered triple <+, 3, 1>; two ordered triples cannot both be identical with the same thing. Intensional structures cannot square the circle; nothing can. Whatever propositions are, they cannot encode operators on propositions with full generality, because that would involve satisfying both FINEGRAIN and COMP, which is impossible.

Intensional structures are not proof of concept for a full-blooded theory of structured propositions, because intensional structures are parasitic on intensions. That also explains what is wrong with the putative propositional operator R: its definition depends on extracting the operator O from the proposition O*p*, and so does not correspond to any operation on intensions. Similarly, the Russell-Myhill argument fails for intensions, because the intensions corresponding to $O_{pp}(q)$ and $O_{pp^*}(q)$ may be identical even when the pluralities of intensions corresponding to *pp* and *pp** are distinct, so the relevant function is not one-one.[12]

In general, intensionalism faces no analogue of the Russell-Myhill paradox; it is much more robust. Of course, with enough restrictions, some theories of somehow structured propositions may also avoid Russell-Myhill. The danger is that they are inadequately

---

[12] For an attempted solution on behalf of structured propositions to the Russell-Myhill paradox and a critique of it, see Menzel 2024 and Williamson 2024.

motivated.[13] The picture of Russellian propositions looked like a principled, attractively simple fine-grained view. Patching it up in a semi-fine-grained way promises much greater complexity for no commensurate gain—some kind of half-hearted overfitting.

Rather than labour the problems for hyperintensional theories of propositions still further, I will turn to examining the motivation for adopting hyperintensional theories in the first place. As throughout this chapter, the focus will be on alleged *metaphysical* hyperintensionality, in phenomena conceived as non-representational.

3.6 The 'why?' heuristic

In section 3.3, we saw how flimsy are the data of one kind often used to support claims of non-representational hyperintensionality, for counterpossibles. The data are exactly what one would expect on the independently confirmed hypothesis that we use the relevant variant of the suppositional heuristic to assess counterfactuals. That heuristic is implicitly inconsistent, and its inconsistency shows up with counterpossibles, as well as in other cases. Consequently, our pre-theoretic judgments of counterpossibles are an untrustworthy source of evidence for their hyperintensionality.

However, counterpossibles are far from the only cases of alleged metaphysical hyperintensionality. Other, perhaps more central examples come from our pre-theoretic judgments about *explanations*. These are often elicited by the use of the word 'because', or similar words in other languages. For instance, in section

---

[13] Bacon 2023 develops an unorthodox but systematic account of fine-grained structured propositions that avoids the Russell-Myhill paradox by restricting the available operations. For example, conjunctive and negative predicates are indefinable in his canonical language. On whether the theory is well-motivated, Bacon himself expresses doubts. Another watering-down of the theory of structured propositions that avoids the Russell-Myhill paradox is the theory discussed as 'Generalized Qualitative Atomic Structure' in chapter 7 of Dorr, Hawthorne, and Yli-Vakkuri 2021.

3.1, we considered the contrasting schematic pair (2A) and (2B), the opposed 'because' statements about propositional truth. For concreteness, we can instantiate them:

(9A) The proposition that snow is white is true because snow is white.

(9B) Snow is white because the proposition that snow is white is true.

The normal pre-reflective judgments are that (9A) is true and (9B) false. Nevertheless, on standard views of truth for propositions, necessarily, the proposition that snow is white is true if and only if snow is white. Thus, if the normal pre-reflective judgments are correct, 'because' is hyperintensional.

The statement 'A because B' is naturally understood as proposing 'B' as an answer to the question 'Why A?' Indeed, in some languages, such as Italian, the word for 'why' is the same as the word for 'because' ('*perché*'). Thus, an obvious principle for assessing 'because' statements is what we may call the 'Why?' principle:

Accept [reject] 'A because B' if you find 'B' a good [bad] answer to the question 'Why A?'.

The questioner wants to *understand* why A: a good answer helps them understand why A; a bad answer does not. In effect, the questioner asks the addressee to *explain* why A. Philosophers of science have produced a vast literature on the nature of explanation; as its track record attests, the attempt to give informative and precise necessary and sufficient conditions for explaining something is unlikely to succeed; what yields the desired understanding is too sensitive to the vagaries of conversational context, background knowledge, and human psychology. We can usually recognize whether we understand, though of course we often think we understand when in fact we do not. Even when we do understand, we often have difficulty in pinning down just what our understanding consists in. The 'Why?' principle enables us to judge the truth-value of 'A because B' by using our unreflective capacity to recognize *whether* the answer 'B' would help one as questioner to understand why A, without the need for explicit, detailed criteria.

The use of the words 'why' and 'because' depends on conversational context. More specifically, 'why' can be used in causal, constitutive, or evidential ways, and 'because' varies correspondingly. For instance, someone may ask 'Why was NN a murderer?', intending to get at what caused him to become a murderer, so the answer 'His parents violently abused him' would be relevant; the answerer might also say 'NN was a murderer because his parents violently abused him'. Someone else may ask 'Why was NN a murderer?', intending to get at what NN did that counted as murder, so the answer 'He intentionally killed his wife by poisoning her' would be relevant; the answerer might also say 'NN was a murderer because he intentionally killed his wife by poisoning her'. A third person may ask 'Why was NN a murderer?', intending to get at what evidence there is for NN's guilt, so the answer 'He confessed the murder to the police' would be relevant; the answerer might also say 'NN was a murderer because he confessed the murder to the police'. All these cases fit the 'Why?' principle.

The 'Why?' principle also correctly predicts that we will find 'because' doubly factive, in the sense that we accept 'A because B' only if we accept both 'A' and 'B'. For if we do not accept 'A', we will not accept the question 'Why A?', since it presupposes 'A', and if we do not accept 'B', we will not accept it as an answer to 'Why A?'

We can apply the 'Why?' principle to (9A) and (9B). Here, the intended reading of 'because' is neither causal nor evidential but constitutive. The questioner seeks some kind of constitutive *explanation*. In dialogue form, (9A) and (9B) correspond to the question-and-answer pairs (9A^) and (9B^), respectively:

(9A^)   Q: Why is the proposition that snow is white true?
        A: Snow is white.

(9B^)   Q: Why is snow white?
        A: The proposition that snow is white is true.

The explanation is much better in (9A^) than in (9B^), even though both rely on the schematic equivalence of 'P' and 'The proposition that P is true'. But in (9A^) the explanation starts with the simple, easy, familiar, and obvious ('Snow is white') and moves to the more complex, harder, less familiar, and less obvious ('The proposition that snow is white is true'), which is what the most helpful explanations typically do, whereas in (9B^) the explanation moves in the opposite direction (on the psychological preference for simplicity in explanations, see Lombrozo 2007, 2016). More generally, the 'Why?' principle predicts our pre-theoretic preference for schema (2A) over schema (2B).

For similar reasons, we will accept instances of the schemas (10A), (10B) and (10C), given that the sentences flanking 'because' express truths:

(10A)   (A or B) because A.

(10B)   (A or B) because B.

(10C)   Something is F because *a* is F.

In each case, the explanation moves from the simpler and easier to the more complex and harder.

CASE STUDY: HYPERINTENSIONALISM 149

Here is another pair of 'because' statements:

(11A)   Furze is as prickly as gorse because furze is gorse.

(11B)   Furze is as prickly as gorse because furze is furze.

Pre-theoretically, (11A) sounds good, while (11B) sounds bad. In dialogue form, (11A) and (11B) correspond to (11A^) and (11B^), respectively:

(11A^)   Q: Why is furze as prickly as gorse?
         A: Furze is gorse.

(11B^)   Q: Why is furze as prickly as gorse?
         A: Furze is furze.

The explanation is much better in (11A^) than in (11B^). In (11A^), the answer will satisfy a reasonable questioner; it supplies exactly the required information. In (11B^), the answer is likely to baffle a reasonable questioner, since to anyone who needs to ask the question it sounds quite irrelevant.

The trouble is that (11A) differs from (11B), and (11A^) from (11B^), only by the substitution of synonymous terms, 'furze' and 'gorse'. The difference is purely verbal; it corresponds to no difference in a single kind of shrub, which is as prickly as itself. It is not a case of metaphysical, or at least non-representational, hyperintensionality.

One response is to postulate a reading of 'because' on which it creates a metalinguistic context. That is a dubious interpretation of the example, for 'because' is correlative with 'why', and the questioner who asked 'Why is furze as prickly as gorse?' did not intend 'why' in a metalinguistic sense. In any case, going metalinguistic is a dangerous move for hyperintensionalists to make, since it immediately raises the question whether their alleged examples of non-representational hyperintensionality in 'because' should also be understood metalinguistically, and so representationally.

More generally, in using the 'Why?' principle to assess 'A because B', we assess 'B' as an answer to the question 'Why A?', and an answer can be good or bad for almost any mixture of linguistic and non-linguistic reasons. An explanation can be good because it is perspicuous, or bad because it is confusing, which may depend on the order in which information is given, and on whether the explainer follows the stylistic maxim of elegant variation, to refer to the same thing by different terms to avoid plodding repetition, and on whether the explanation is given in common words and short sentences or in uncommon words and long sentences, and so on. The difficulty or ease of following a written explanation depends on the font style and size, the degree of contrast between the colour of the print and the colour of the page, and how well the lines in a graph are differentiated in colour. Likewise, in a spoken explanation, the speaker's accent, diction, speed of speech, and loud or soft voice, and ambient noise all make a difference to comprehension. So do the hearer's familiarity or unfamiliarity with the material, and their levels of alertness and motivation. In evaluating an explanation or argument, it is notoriously difficult to separate in one's own case the influence of form from the influence of content. We don't exactly know what hit us. Psychologists have studied closely related metacognitive illusions (Undorf, Navarro-Báez and Zimdahl 2022).

In consequence, little is to be gained from hiving off special metalinguistic uses of 'why' and 'because', for even when we stipulate that our use of the words is *non*-metalinguistic, in practice we shall still be applying them under the influence of linguistic as well as non-linguistic factors. The linguistic factors may play the role of unconscious biases, and sometimes lead us into error. One cannot stipulate oneself free of bias. Thus, in practice, the 'Why?' principle is less than perfectly reliable. In recognition of that, we may rename it the 'Why?' *heuristic*.

Since the interesting kind of alleged hyperintensionality is not metalinguistic, we may as well specify that for present purposes the intended readings of 'why' and 'because' are non-metalinguistic. Postulating an imperfectly reliable heuristic here is not gratuitous. We have independent reason to classify our assent to (11A) and dissent from (11B) as not both correct, on general semantic grounds. Some mechanism is needed to explain the error, and an imperfectly reliable heuristic is a natural candidate. Compatibly with that, it is a charitable option, since it still allows the mechanism to have a high degree of reliability, short of infallibility.

The problem for hyperintensionalists is that pairs such as (9A) and (9B) become dialectically ineffective as alleged counterexamples to intensionalism, since intensionalists can predict and explain our verdicts on them by our reliance on the 'Why?' heuristic, and observe that an error in those verdicts would be of the same kind as the error in our verdicts on (9A) and (9B): a projection of the pragmatics of explanation onto the semantics of 'because'. That would not make the 'Why?' heuristic too generally unreliable to be useful.

Another indication that 'because' statements may elicit distinctive errors is that, as summaries of explanations, they are structurally awkward, in a subtle way. To see this, we must stake a step back. On a constitutive reading of 'explain', just as any true disjunct explains a true *disjunction*, by the natural deduction rule of disjunction-introduction, so the true conjuncts jointly explain a true *conjunction*, by the natural deduction rule of conjunction-introduction. Both inferential steps go from simpler premises to more complex conclusions. The explanatory steps of disjunction-introduction are naturally summarized in statements where 'because' takes wide scope, in the forms 'A or B because A' and 'A or B because B'. But when one tries to summarize the explanatory step of conjunction-introduction in the same way, one gets only 'A and B because A and B', which is circular. A 'because' statement presents the explanandum and the explanans each in a single sentence, but the point of conjunction-introduction is to unify separate sentences into a single complex one: the syntactic form of a 'because' statement forces the explanans into a form where that step has already been taken, and so misses the point. The form of a 'because' statement represents the explanation in a Procrustean way. In Benjamin Schnieder's logic of 'because', this awkwardness manifests itself in the striking similarity of his rule for conjunction to his rule for disjunction: his system allows for partial explanations of a conjunction by one or other conjunct but not for a full explanation of it jointly by both conjuncts (Schnieder 2011).

Hyperintensionalists themselves sometimes show uncertainty in where to locate the line between linguistic form and non-linguistic content. For example, as noted in section 3.4, Kit Fine presents two versions of truthmaker semantics: in one, the repetitious conjunction $\alpha \wedge \alpha$ can have truthmakers α lacks, so the difference in linguistic form corresponds to a difference in non-linguistic content; in the other, $\alpha \wedge \alpha$ and α always have the same truthmakers and falsemakers, so the difference in linguistic form corresponds to no difference in non-linguistic content. The same principle, under the title of 'idempotence', is also a crux for Cian Dorr (2016). The remark 'It's starting to rain and it's starting to rain' sounds boringly insistent, not like a subtle point about the state of the weather. Compare (12A) and (12B):

(12A)   This ball is round and round because this ball is round.

(12B)   This ball is round because this ball is round and round.

The explanatory direction is clearly better in (12A) (from the simpler to the more complex) than in (12B) (the opposite). The question is whether the difference in linguistic form between 'This ball is round' and 'This ball is round and round' corresponds to a genuine difference in non-linguistic content. If not, on a non-metalinguistic reading of 'because', as a standard intensionalist view implies, (12A) and (12B) have the same truth-value, and appearances to the contrary are an illusion created by the 'Why?' heuristic.

Here is a more extreme example:

(13A) This ball is either round or both round and red because this ball is round.

(13B) This ball is round because this ball is either round or both round and red.

The interchanged sentences are necessarily equivalent to each other because $α ∨ (α ∧ β)$ is truth-functionally equivalent to $α$. The explanatory direction is clearly much better in (13A) than in (13B). Not only is the explanatory direction from the simpler to the more complex in (13A) and the opposite in (13B), the explanation introduces irrelevant subject matter in (13B) but not in (13A). The question is whether that linguistic intrusion corresponds to a genuine difference in non-linguistic content. If not, on a non-metalinguistic reading of 'because', (13A) and (13B) have the same truth-value, and appearances to the contrary are an illusion created by the 'Why' heuristic. Compare the property of being round to the property of being either round or both round and red. They *sound* different on first hearing, but do properties *have* subject matters?[14]

Should we rely on the 'Why?' heuristic as applied to (9A) and (9B)? Does the difference in linguistic form between 'Snow is white' and 'The proposition that snow is white is true' correspond to a genuine difference in non-linguistic content? If not, on a non-linguistic reading of 'because', (9A) and (9B) have the same truth-value, and appearances to the contrary are another illusion created by the 'Why?' heuristic. The difference between (9A) and (9B) in direction of explanation may *feel* metaphysical, but that does not mean that it is. If we had a well-working hyperintensional framework in which to explain the difference in metaphysical terms, that would

---

[14] For hyperintensional theories of subject matter and aboutness see Yablo 2014, Fine 2017c, and Brast-McKie 2021.

support the heuristic-driven verdicts. However, the considerations in sections 3.3–5 indicate that hyperintensionalists are not in that happy position. Instead, their case is still largely driven by examples, and the examples are turning out to be quite shaky.

To widen the inquiry, we can recall another example of alleged hyperintensionality: Sober's alleged difference between the properties of being a triangle and being a trilateral. In brief, his argument was that, in the causal-explanatory context of his example, (14A) is true while (14B) is false:

(14A)   The figure was outputted because it was a triangle.

(14B)   The figure was outputted because it was a trilateral.

When we apply the 'Why?' heuristic, we have two rival answers to the same causal-explanatory question, as in these question-and-answers pairs:

(14A^)   Q: Why was the figure outputted?
A: It was a triangle.

(14B^)   Q: Why was the figure outputted?
A: It was a trilateral.

Uncontroversially, the figure's angles played a more significant role than its sides in the causal process which led to the outputting of the figure; being an angle of a given figure and being a side of that figure are extensionally different properties. Consequently, a good answer to the causal-explanatory question will be cast in terms of angles, not sides. Moreover, speakers of English are more likely to connect the word 'triangle' with the description 'figure with three angles' and the word 'trilateral' with the description 'figure with three sides' than the other way around (the difference may be more marked for those who know some Latin and pick up the etymology). Thus, the causal explanation will be more perspicuous if it uses the word 'triangle' than if it uses the word 'trilateral'; speakers will tend to make the required inferential connections more easily. But none of that requires being a triangle and being a trilateral to be distinct properties.

Here is an analogy. Imagine a student canteen where it is common knowledge that an alarm sounds if anyone takes twelve or more pieces of fruit. The alarm sounds. Compare two dialogues:

(15A^) Q: Why did the alarm sound?
A: A student took 7 apples and 5 oranges, so they took 7 + 5 pieces of fruit, and 7 + 5 = 12.

(15B^) Q: Why did the alarm sound?
A: A student took 7 apples and 5 oranges, so they took 6 + 6 pieces of fruit, and 6 + 6 = 12.

Surely the answer in (15A^) is more perspicuous than the answer in (15B^); it is a better explanation. But none of that requires 7 + 5 and 6 + 6 to be distinct numbers.

What about Fine's signature example for a hyperintensionalist account of essence?

(1A)   It is essential to Socrates that he is Socrates.

(1B)   It is essential to Socrates that he is a member of {Socrates}.

The words 'because' and 'why' do not occur in (1A) and (1B), nor do those sentences purport to explain anything. However, the kind of essentialism that Fine uses such examples to motivate is broadly Aristotelian in spirit. In that tradition, essences are regarded as starting-points for explanation (see *Posterior Analytics* 75a42–b2,

Metaphysics 1041a25–32, and Charles 2000: 197–309 on Aristotle's explanatory conception of essence). After all, what is special about essential natures if they play no explanatory role? Thus, explanatory considerations should be relevant to (1A) and (1B). The introduction of the singleton set in (1B) will indeed tend to detract from the quality of explanations, by interpolating an irrelevant complication. In response to the question 'Why does that man keep accosting people in the street?', 'He is Socrates' makes a better starting-point than 'He is a member of {Socrates}'. A more natural case involves a less trivial essentialist claim than (1A):

(16A)   It is essential to Socrates that he is a human.

(16B)   It is essential to Socrates that he is a member of the set of humans.

Necessarily, all and only humans are members of the set of humans (in the world in question). Still, 'He is a human' is a better explanatory starting-point than 'He is a member of the set of humans'. The introduction of sets in (16B) will also tend to detract from the quality of explanations, by interpolating an irrelevant complication. But the question remains: do such differences in the linguistic form of explanations correspond to differences in non-linguistic content? As the earlier examples suggest, we may be quite susceptible to illusions of difference in non-linguistic content created by differences in the linguistic form of explanations. Thus, Fine's examples are far from decisive.

Other kinds of example are also used to argue for hyperintensionalism about causal contexts. Here is one of a kind I have heard used:

(17A)   The plane crash made Mary an orphan.

(17B)   The plane crash made Mary a self-identical orphan.

CASE STUDY: HYPERINTENSIONALISM 157

The plane's crash killed Mary's parents, so (17A) is true. But one is tempted to assess (17B) as false, on the grounds that the plane crash did not make Mary self-identical; she was self-identical already. Nevertheless, 'orphan' is necessarily equivalent to 'self-identical orphan'. If (17A) and (17B) differ in truth-value, the causal verb 'made' has created some sort of hyperintensional context.

Here is a similar example. It concerns events in 1461, during the English War of the Roses. Richard is Richard Neville, Duke of Warwick, known as Warwick the Kingmaker; Edward is Edward Plantagenet, who became King Edward IV.

(18A)   Richard's actions made Edward a king.

(18B)   Richard's actions made Edward a male monarch.

Richard's actions, given other contributory factors, brought it about that Edward became king, so on the relevant causal reading (18A) is true as a matter of historical fact. But one is tempted to assess (18B) as false, on the grounds that Richard's actions did not make Edward male; he was male already. Nevertheless, 'king' is necessarily equivalent to 'male monarch'. If (18A) and (18B) differ in truth-value, the causal verb 'made' has again created some sort of hyperintensional context.

The trouble is that 'male monarch' is an easily available reading of 'king' in standard English, and that reading is applicable to (18A).[15] Thus, by compositional semantics, (18A) is synonymous with (18B), so they cannot differ in truth-value. Since (18A) is a well-known historical truth, (18B) is true too. Thus, although Richard's actions did not make Edward male, it does not follow that they did not make Edward a male monarch. But that has implications for

---

[15] Are emperors male monarchs without being kings? An emperor is sometimes defined as a king of kings; on that definition, emperors *are* kings. In any case, the differential reactions to (18A) and (18B) are not sensitive to such issues. Quibbling about the particular case is pointless because there are so many similar ones—for example, the old-fashioned words 'actress' and 'poetess'.

our assessment of (17B) too: although the plane crash did not make Mary self-identical, it does not follow that it did not make her a self-identical orphan. Making a conjunction hold does not entail making a given conjunct hold. Consequently, the example of (17A) and (17B) constitutes a poor case for the hyperintensionality of making.

What has gone wrong this time? Most likely, it is a very ordinary case of Gricean conversational implicature. As a hearer (or reader), one expects the speaker (or writer) to have bothered including the apparently redundant words 'self-identical' and 'male' for some purpose, and the best one's brain can come up with on the spot is that they (foolishly) meant to suggest that the self-identity or maleness was also made the case by the plane crash or Richard's actions. That is another case where there is evidence of comparatively superficial linguistic phenomena having been misunderstood as manifestations of hyperintensionality. More specifically, one can connect it to the 'Why?' heuristic: we assess 'The plane crash' as a better answer to the causal-explanatory question 'Why did Mary become an orphan?' than to the causal-explanatory question 'Why did Mary become a self-identical orphan?'

Reading all this metaphysics into the pragmatics of explanation looks like a classic case of overfitting.[16] Pre-theoretic verdicts on examples have been uncritically accepted as refuting intensionalism and motivating hyperintensionalist theories with many more degrees of freedom. Since philosophers did not recognize the proliferation of degrees of freedom as a serious cost, they were comfortable accepting the data at face value and accommodating them within such a theory. They felt no incentive to scrutinize the data more carefully, and to check for potential sources of error. As a result, those most concerned to separate metaphysical reality from the linguistic appearances have become the most susceptible to mistaking the appearances for the reality.

---

[16] Philip Kitcher (2023: 69) briefly makes the related suggestion that 'logics of ground' look like projections of the pragmatics of explanation.

4
Frege Puzzles

4.1 Representational hyperintensionality

On the evidence of chapter 3, hyperintensionality in metaphysics is an illusion, an artefact of overfitting heuristic-generated data. On a conservative interpretation of this outcome, extending hyperintensionality to metaphysics was always implausible: its natural home is in matters of *representation*, not in the world as it is prior to being represented. Once things start being represented, the same thing can be represented in different ways, for instance, as Hesperus or as Phosphorus, which naturally yields familiar, harmless forms of hyperintensionality, in knowledge, belief, hope, fear, and other intentional attitudes.

We have already seen evidence that the conservative interpretation is too complacent. Both impossible worlds and structured propositions have been used in attempts to capture the supposedly hyperintensional semantics of propositional attitude ascriptions, but the representational nature of the states ascribed does not magic away the methodological problems those frameworks face (chapter 3), though it might somehow make those problems a price worth paying. We also glimpsed how heuristics for belief ascription can generate errors in describing Frege puzzles (chapter 1.5), which substantiates the concern that apparent hyperintensionality may be an artefact of overfitting even in representational matters. The case for representational hyperintensionality is weaker than it looks.

In formal epistemology, especially epistemic and doxastic logic and Bayesian probabilistic approaches, the most useful and most used models are coarse-grained and purely intensional: they obliterate cognitively significant differences for the sake of mathematical simplicity, tractability, and power. Although one can add complications to such models to induce hyperintensional behaviour, the results tend to be unilluminating, since one has to insert by hand the very features one is trying to explain. In sharp contrast, when model-building is done well, one *learns* from the model: its behaviour can take one by surprise.

In natural language, ascriptions of knowledge and belief look more fine-grained: they seem sensitive to the cognitive differences the formal models flatten. Yet developments in the formal semantics of natural language threaten to undermine that contrast by analysing the truth-conditions of propositional attitude ascriptions as less sensitive to cognitive differences than they seem.

These issues matter for epistemology, because it is mostly done in natural language, which even formal epistemologists use to explain the intended applications of their mathematical models. If discourse in natural language about knowledge, belief, and other epistemologically interesting relations does not work in the way it seems to do, then arguments in epistemology may be led astray by misleading appearances. For instance, when in testing an epistemological generalization we have to assess sentences of the form 'S knows that P' as true or false in actual or hypothetical cases, our assessments may go wrong because we confuse semantic and pragmatic aspects of knowledge ascriptions in English, perhaps through relying on a fallible heuristic. Although indiscriminate scepticism about our assessments would be unwarranted, they may well need some fine-tuning.

Traditionally, Frege puzzles have been central to discussion of the semantics of propositional attitude ascriptions. But we can also use them as a clue to the heuristics on which we rely in making such ascriptions. Once we appreciate the role of those heuristics, we should be much less inclined to treat propositional attitude ascriptions as hyperintensional. This chapter explores such issues around Frege puzzles in detail, though far from comprehensively.[1]

4.2 The Fregean consensus

In the old days, philosophers took it as a datum that someone can believe that Hesperus is Hesperus without believing that Hesperus is Phosphorus. Thus, substituting co-referential proper names in the 'that'-clause of a belief ascription does not always preserve truth. Presumably, one who believes the truism that Hesperus is Hesperus also *knows* that Hesperus is Hesperus, while one who fails to believe that Hesperus is Phosphorus also fails to *know* that Hesperus is Phosphorus, because knowing requires believing. Hence someone can also know that Hesperus is Hesperus without knowing that Hesperus is Phosphorus. Thus, substituting co-referential names in the 'that'-clause of a knowledge ascription also fails to preserve truth. Ascriptions of other propositional attitudes such as wondering, doubting, hoping, and fearing behave likewise.

Some version of Frege's distinction between sense and reference was widely (though not universally) taken to explain this phenomenon. The names 'Hesperus' and 'Phosphorus' have different senses, different modes of presenting the same planet, which their occurrences contribute as components of the senses of simple sentences in which the names occur; the senses of the sentences are

---

[1] Much of this chapter draws from 'Epistemological consequences of Frege puzzles', *Philosophical Topics*, (2021) 49: 287–319 (Williamson 2021b), which benefitted from written comments by Daniel Kodsi, Anna Mahtani, Jennifer Nagel, Luis Rosa, Mona Simion, and Juhani Yli-Vakkuri, and conversation with Jeremy Goodman. Section 4.8 is based on part of 'Where did it come from? Where will it go?', in Arturs Logins and Jacques-Henri Vollet (eds.), *Putting Knowledge to Work: New Directions for Knowledge-First Epistemology*. Oxford: Oxford University Press, forthcoming (Williamson forthcoming-b). The second half of section 4.10 and all of sections 4.11–12 are new. This chapter does not address the critique of the reliability of attitude ascriptions in natural language implicit in the 'negative programme' of experimental philosophy; it was briefly discussed in chapter 1.7.

Fregean thoughts or propositions. Thus, the sentences 'Hesperus is Hesperus' and 'Hesperus is Phosphorus' express different propositions. There is no obstacle in principle to having an attitude to one proposition without having it to the other. On Frege's own version of the view, words in the 'that'-clause of an attitude ascription refer to their usual *senses*, not their usual *referents*, so the names were not even co-referential in the context in which the substitution was made, though the general consensus did not extend to that reference-shifting mechanism. The consensus was just that some account or other of the semantics of attitude ascriptions would explain how the propositional content of the ascribed attitude depends on the ordinary senses, not just the ordinary referents, of expressions in the 'that'-clause.[2]

On that consensus, Frege puzzles presented no special danger to epistemology. One had to be careful not to make illicit substitutions when characterizing what was putatively known or believed, but that was a matter of fairly straightforward professionalism.

4.3 The failure of the Fregean consensus

Famously, the work of Saul Kripke (1972, 1979, 1980) and others overturned the consensus. Proper names in natural language have no Fregean senses, at least of anything like the kind traditionally assumed by Fregeans. A more promising approach to the semantics of both names and indexicals treated them as *directly referential*: such an expression contributes *only* its ordinary referent and not also a sense to the proposition expressed by a sentence in which it occurs (Kaplan 1989). But the direct reference view gives new menace to Frege puzzles, since it seems to make the relevant

---

[2] Throughout this chapter, occurrences of terms in the complement clause of an attitude-ascribing verb are treated as semantically in its scope; if the distinction makes sense, they are *de dicto*, not *de re*.

substitutions truth-preserving for names and other directly referential terms, though not for definite descriptions. A long and complicated debate ensued, and still rumbles on, about the semantics and pragmatics of attitude ascriptions. I will not attempt to summarize all the moves and counter-moves, though I will sketch some reasons why Fregeanism failed to fulfil its initial promise. This chapter considers some implications of anti-Fregeanism for both general methodology and specific epistemological theses.

Frege puzzles gave Fregeanism a large head start over direct reference theories, of which Fregeans proved unable to take much advantage. What gradually became clear was that even where it seems most promising to associate an expression with a mode of presentation of its referent, that mode does not play the semantic role in natural language that Fregeanism would lead one to expect.

An example is the first-person pronoun. For Fregeans, the indexical 'I' is naturally associated with the distinctive mode of presentation of oneself to oneself *as oneself*, as 'I', which we can call the *first-personal mode of presentation*. Now consider my ascription of a belief to you:

(1)   You believe that I was born on 6 August 1955.

Background: I was indeed born on that date; for the sake of the example, I will assume that you were not. Let p be the proposition which, in uttering (1), I report you as believing. Since 'I' occurs in (1) firmly within the 'that'-clause, on the most straightforward Fregean approach it contributes a mode of presentation to p. Since 'I' is associated with the first-personal mode of presentation, it presumably contributes that mode of presentation to p. Thus, in uttering (1), I say that you believe p, where p is the proposition made up of the first-personal mode of presentation and a mode of presentation of something like the property of having been born on 6 August 1955. But, in your beliefs, the first-personal mode of presentation picks out *you*, not me, as the referent. Thus, in uttering (1),

I end up attributing to you a false belief about your own birthday, not a true belief about mine. That is absurd. Such a reading is just not available for the indirect speech ascription (1), by contrast with a direct speech ascription such as (2):

(2)   You accept 'I was born on 6 August 1955'.

Of course, Fregeans can and do postulate various more convoluted readings of my utterance of (1), on which I am saying in effect that you have a belief in some non-first-personal proposition q suitably related to the first-personal proposition which *I* express by the sentence 'I was born on 6 August 1955', while not myself expressing q. But the supposed availability of such readings is not to the point, which is rather the *unavailability* of the absurd reading generated by the flat-footed application of the Fregean approach, on which I am attributing to you a false belief about your own birthday. As a normal speaker of English, I cannot hear such a reading, no matter how hard I try. I do not hear it only to exclude it immediately on pragmatic grounds; I just do not hear it in the first place. Something is wrong with an approach that gets anywhere near such a reading.

How might some version of Fregean semantics avoid generating the absurd reading of (1)? Suppose that the customary referent of an expression E (for example, 'I') in the given context of utterance is x (for example, me). Then a Fregean might propose that in that context, an occurrence of E in the content clause of an ascription of an attitude to a subject S (for example, you) refers only to a sense under which S can think about x. But one can meaningfully utter (1) without grasping any such sense, indeed, even when there is no such sense—for example, when I address (1) to someone I see on television, under the narcissistic illusion that they must have heard of me. That utterance of (1) is simply false. Even if S *can* think about x, the speaker may not grasp the sense under which S does so. In response, the Fregean might be tempted to interpret the speaker as quantifying over senses under which S can think about x. But that would miss the intended point of the Fregean semantics, for to think about Hesperus just is to think about Phosphorus, so the senses under which S can think about Hesperus just are the senses under which S can think about Phosphorus; thus, substituting 'Hesperus' for 'Phosphorus' in the content clause of an attitude ascription will not affect the ascription's truth-value, on the revised semantics.

The sheer complexity of the Fregean apparatus, how many moving parts or degrees of freedom it offers a theorist to play with, tends to obscure the lack of progress—especially when the focus is on making ad hoc moves for particular examples, instead of proposing a more general, systematic compositional semantics for the constructions at issue. That lack of progress after more than a century is good evidence that, despite its initial promise, the distinction between sense and reference is not the key to the semantics of Frege puzzles. The Fregean approach is in deep trouble even with very simple cases that seem at first sight well-suited to such a distinction.

Although philosophers from Descartes on are used to giving the first-person very special treatment, there is no evidence that the semantics of natural language affords it any such privilege. Linguistically, it would be quite implausible to dismiss examples like (1) as a special case.[3] As seen in chapter 1.5, the required transformations of personal pronouns and similar devices are automatically applied in semi-disquotational reports of others' propositional attitudes, with a focus on preserving reference, not on preserving sense.

Of course, such examples will not silence Fregeans; nothing will. But they do suggest that the appeal to modes of presentation in semantics is much less natural, much less in tune with the workings

---

[3] For relevant discussion of the supposed '*de se*', see Cappelen and Dever 2013 and Magidor 2015.

of natural language and the needs of communication, than it first seemed.

We may well have to live with the conclusion that, despite appearances, the substitutions in Frege puzzles are truth-preserving. I will use some ideas in Kripke's classic paper 'A Puzzle about Belief' (1979, 1988) as a starting-point from which to explore and extend a non-Fregean approach to Frege puzzles, though I will intersperse further comments about Fregean approaches. In the closing sections, I will discuss some implications for issues about evidence and subjective or epistemic probability.

'A Puzzle about Belief' is most famous for its examples, especially Pierre, who asserts 'Londres est jolie' but denies 'London is pretty', and Peter, who does not realize that the pianist Paderewski is the statesman Paderewski. Here, we will be more concerned with some of the more general themes in Kripke's discussion.

4.4 Frege puzzles and synonymy

Kripke emphasizes that Frege puzzles can arise for expressions of many kinds, even when the two expressions are normally regarded as *synonymous*, not just as co-referential. Thus, one cannot simply diagnose Frege puzzles as arising when two terms have the same reference but different meanings, for by normal standards they can arise even for two terms with the *same* meaning. Of course, whether meaning is anything more than reference is itself contested in the semantic debate, but that is not our present concern. Many direct referentialists hold that co-reference varies with context while synonymy requires co-reference across all contexts; thus 'Timothy Williamson' and 'I' are co-referential in my context, but not synonymous, for they are not co-referential in your context.

One of Kripke's examples concerns the synonyms 'furze' and 'gorse', which are simply two terms for the very same kind of shrub (1988: 134). The two words may have originated in different dialects of English. The shrub itself changes in appearance from one season to another, sometimes having dull brown needles and no flowers, sometimes bright green needles and yellow flowers. There is no *general* correlation between how the shrub appears and which word is applied, though for accidental reasons there may be such a correlation in how a particular speaker applies the words.

Suppose that Penny learns the term 'furze' somewhere by being shown various samples with bright green needles and yellow flowers, and learns the term 'gorse' separately somewhere else by being shown various samples with dull brown needles and no flowers. By normal linguistic standards, she understands both terms. Nevertheless, she may be in no position to know that the two terms co-refer. In that case, if one uses both terms with their normal meanings and happens to know that they co-refer, one may still feel tempted to describe Penny's situation by asserting (3) and denying (4):

(3) Penny believes that furze is furze.

(4) Penny believes that furze is gorse.

But, as discussed in chapter 3.3, the guiding principle of formal semantics is *semantic compositionality*, according to which the meaning of a complex expression is determined by the meanings of its simpler constituents and the way in which they are put together. Since (3) and (4) are put together in the same way out of corresponding words with the same meanings, in the absence of semantic 'funny business' compositionality requires (3) and (4) to have the same meaning too. But since meaning and context determine truth-value, it follows that they also have the same truth-value in any given context, such as a context in which one both asserts (3) and denies (4). Thus, such a combination can hardly be the right way to describe Penny's situation.

One might worry that the repetition in (3) and lack of repetition in (4) make a structural difference between (3) and (4). That would be insufficient to block the argument from a standard version of semantic compositionality, but we can anyway finesse the issue by using a pair without repetition, such as (5) and (6):

(5)   Penny believes that furze has yellow flowers.

(6)   Penny believes that gorse has yellow flowers.

There is the same temptation to assert (5) and deny (6), but there is also the same semantic reason as before to resist that temptation.

What kind of 'funny business' could make trouble for the arguments from semantic compositionality? In principle, verbs like 'believe' could introduce some sort of covert sensitivity to context, where uttering 'S believes that P' creates a context in which that sentence is true only if S assents to the proposition expressed by 'P' as presented in some way contextually relevant to the sentence 'P'. Without violating semantic compositionality, such an account permits a situation where uttering (3) would create a context in which (3) and (4) were both true, whereas uttering (4) would create a context in which (3) and (4) were both false, or uttering (5) would create a context in which (5) and (6) were both true, whereas uttering (6) would create a context in which (5) and (6) were both false. For example, when the speaker is using the choice between 'furze' and 'gorse' to mark a contrast, uttering (5) might create a context in which the truth of (5) and (6) requires Penny to assent to the proposition that furze has yellow flowers under the guise of the sentence 'Furze has yellow flowers', whereas uttering (6) would create a context in which the truth of (5) and (6) requires her to assent to the same proposition under the guise of the sentence 'Gorse has yellow flowers'. Since Penny assents to the proposition only under the guise of the sentence 'Furze has yellow flowers', an utterance of

(5) would be true while an utterance of (6) would be false.[4] Strictly speaking, none of that yields a single context in which (3) and (4) or (5) and (6) differ in truth-value, but the effect is similar.

However, such contextualist hypotheses look ad hoc. Normally, just one of 'furze' and 'gorse' is used in a given conversation, and, although the example made Penny a native English speaker, the truth of (5) or (6) does not *require* her to know a word of English; she could use a natural kind term in her own language for the shrub. More radically, nothing in the semantics of English requires Penny to have a language of any kind for (3)–(6) to be true. Imagine a species of languageless animals whose diet consists solely of gorse (like giant pandas with bamboo shoots); they need and have a recognitional capacity for gorse, to which the belief that gorse has yellow flowers is crucial. Various forms of functionalism about the metaphysics of belief allow such a case; to exclude those theories in the philosophy of mind seems to be no business of the semantics of English. But then, if the truth-conditions of belief ascriptions are normally indifferent to the guise (if any) under which a believer believes a proposition, it seems unlikely that natural languages would have a special semantic mechanism waiting to spring into action just to resolve Frege puzzles and a few related difficulties. Theoretically, a more explanatory account of Frege cases would be derived from more general principles needed far beyond Frege cases, rather than relying on semantic structure postulated ad hoc just to handle those very cases.

Grice's category of *conversational implicature* has the requisite generality, since he combines quite general principles of conversation with simple semantic assumptions to predict context-sensitive conversational implicatures (Grice 1989). Indeed, in some contexts, a speaker might well refrain from uttering (4) because uttering

---

[4] See Crimmins and Perry 1989 for a similar account, and Goodman and Lederman 2021 for a more recent version, with extensive references to the literature. Salmón 1986 uses the apparatus of guises but his account is not of the envisaged kind. For the differences between Salmón's guises and Fregean senses, see Branquinho 1990.

(4) would have the false conversational implicature that Penny would assent to 'Furze is gorse'. In the same context, the speaker might also utter (5) rather than (6) because uttering (6) would have the false conversational implicature that Penny would assent to 'Gorse has yellow flowers'. That is compatible with (4) and (6) semantically expressing true non-metalinguistic propositions in that context, which do not entail those metalinguistic conversational implicatures. In Nathan Salmón's terminology (1986), the metalinguistic information is pragmatically imparted, not semantically encoded.

Unfortunately, even granted that there are such conversational implicatures, they do not explain all the phenomena in Frege cases. For speakers do not merely refrain from asserting (4) and (6); they may actively *deny* (4) and (6), regard them as false, and assert their negations. Normally, if uttering a sentence would have a false conversational implicature, that does not justify one in uttering the negation of that sentence. If saying 'The Professor is sober this morning' would have the false conversational implicature that the Professor is often drunk, that does not justify one in saying 'The Professor is not sober this morning'. On an anti-contextualist anti-Fregean semantics, (4) and (6) are true in the example, their negations are false, and whoever asserts them speaks falsely. Similar behaviour is observable with other attitude verbs, such as 'realize', for which parallel issues arise. For example, a botanically well-informed native speaker of English may well assert both (3r) and (3rn), or both (5r) and (6rn):

(3r)   Penny realizes that furze is furze.

(4rn)   Penny does not realize that furze is gorse.

(5r)   Penny realizes that furze has yellow flowers.

(6rn)   Penny does not realize that gorse has yellow flowers.

If one asks the speaker 'Do you mean that literally?', the answer is likely to be an impatient 'Of course'. Thus, some sort of error theory is needed.[5] Even if the error involves some confusion between conversational implicatures and truth-conditional consequences, that confusion would need to be explained, since it is untypical of conversational implicatures.

If anti-contextualist anti-Fregeans can resort to error theories, so can contextualist anti-Fregeans.[6] However, positing *both* contextualist *and* error-theoretic mechanisms to explain the data is unattractively uneconomical. If one has to posit an error-theoretic mechanism anyway, why not let it do all the work, and avoid the need to posit a contextualist mechanism as well? Contextualist anti-Fregeans might respond that a principle of charity in interpretation demands that we posit as little error as possible, and so explain as much of the data as we can with the contextualist mechanism. But if the errors are systematic, not just random performance errors, a well-developed error theory will posit a *specific* mechanism to explain them, which should indicate how widespread we can expect the errors to be. Thus, we will need to know more about the putative error mechanisms before adjudicating the issue. Section 4.6 will discuss such mechanisms in detail.

Faced with these difficulties, some philosophers deny that such differences in cognitive significance between synonyms can arise for competent speakers. One form of denial is to insist that Penny is not fully competent with the terms 'furze' and 'gorse', perhaps on the grounds that her understanding of them involves deference to expert botanists. That is not a promising strategy, for several reasons. First, the original description of the case did not mention semantic deference or a recognized scientific community, and does not require such elements. It simply involves some people being

---

[5] There is no sign that the negation used in denying (4) and (6) has to be *metalinguistic*, as in 'The food wasn't *good*, it was *great*'. For evidence of error even in assessments of simple sentences in Frege cases, see Saul 1997 and 2010.

[6] See, for example, the section on 'Error' in Goodman and Lederman 2021.

better than others at recognizing particular natural kinds, which happens in any community and does not entail semantic deference. Second, the strategy does not vindicate the observed combinations at issue, asserting (3) and (5) while denying (4) and (6). For if Penny's alleged lack of full competence with the terms is relevant at all, it undermines reading off what she believes from her use of those terms; but we are happy to assert (3) and (5) *on the basis of* such reading off. Third, more generally, if having attitudes about a natural kind requires a perfect recognitional capacity for that kind, virtually no one has attitudes about any natural kind. Given that imperfect recognitional capacities suffice, Frege puzzles like this cannot be excluded.

Another form of denial is to insist that Penny has her own personal senses for 'furze' and 'gorse', which are different from each other and from ours. That too is an unpromising strategy. It rests on a misunderstanding of how attitude ascriptions work in natural language. When we make such ascriptions, the words in the 'that'-clause mean what *we* mean by them, not what the subject to whom we are ascribing the attitude does. That already emerged in the discussion of the role of 'I' in sentence (1). Similarly, if Penny happened not to know the word 'yellow', which is quite consistent with the original scenario, that would not make 'yellow' in (5) and (6) *meaningless*; at worst, (5) and (6) might turn out to be false. Nor do we somehow try to make 'furze' and 'gorse' in (3)–(6) mean what Penny personally means by them. After all, we do not know exactly what she means by them, in the intended personal sense. If we simply defer to her for their meanings in these sentences, we undermine the individualistic conception of meaning on which the objection initially relied, with its talk of Penny's personal senses. Anyway, vicariously using the agent's meaning is not an option once we generalize over the agent parameter: for example, when one asks 'How many people know that gorse has yellow flowers?', the embedded sentence 'Gorse has yellow flowers' does not have someone else's meaning.

What matters for what (3)–(6) mean in our mouths is what 'furze' and 'gorse' mean in our mouths; they are synonymous in our mouths, and remain so when we utter (3)–(6). Thus, denying that Penny uses the words 'furze' and 'gorse' in their normal English senses is not just implausible; like the previous strategy for denial, it fails to vindicate the combinations at issue, asserting (3) and (5) while denying (4) and (6).

Of course, there are metalinguistic variants of the sentences at issue. For example, instead of (5) and (6), we can consider:

(5m)   Penny believes that the sentence 'Furze has yellow flowers' expresses a truth.

(6m)   Penny believes that the sentence 'Gorse has yellow flowers' expresses a truth.

There is no Frege puzzle here, because the metalinguistic beliefs are about distinct sentences. Even if (5m) is true, it obviously does not follow that (6m) is true. But that does not explain the Frege puzzle with (5) and (6). After all, (5m) and (6m) are not in general good paraphrases of (5) and (6), respectively. In a quite different scenario, where 'Penny' refers to someone who knows no English, (5m) and (6m) are typically false, while (5) and (6) may easily be true—for example, she may be an expert botanist, who would express the knowledge ascribed in each of (5) and (6) using the same word for the shrub in her own language.

In short, we must learn to live with the conclusion that, read strictly and literally, (3) has the same truth-value as (4), and (5) the same as (6), even when are talking about someone like Penny. Analogous considerations apply when 'believes' is replaced by 'knows' or 'realizes' in (3)–(6). More generally, epistemologists should not assume that Frege puzzles can be handled in some vaguely Fregean or contextualist way. We must be ready to be much more revisionary in treating the initial judgments.

4.5 Frege puzzles from the inside

A Fregean might concede that the sense-reference distinction is ill-adapted to the semantics of natural language, which is tailored to the needs of inter-personal communication, but still insist that it is just right for the needs of individual thought, including reflection on the epistemic status of one's own beliefs. On this view, the problems we have in saying what Pierre, Peter, or Penny believes are fundamentally problems in using a public natural language to describe a private cognitive perspective. This concession would have been unwelcome to Frege himself, for he emphasized that thoughts (the senses of declarative sentences) can be part of the common heritage of humankind—for example, in the case of mathematical theorems. But we can still consider individualistic Fregeanism in its own right.

By itself, the restriction to first-person ascriptions is insufficient. When Pierre later learns that 'Londres' and 'London' refer to the same city, and when Penny later learns that 'furze' and 'gorse' refer to the same shrub, they can wonder what beliefs they had before the discovery, and find the case just as puzzling to describe as we outsiders do. To avoid such problems, what is needed is at least a restriction to first-person *present-tense* ascriptions. But that is still not enough. For Pierre and Penny can entertain the possibility of co-reference even before they know or believe that it obtains. Suppose that Penny is agnostic as to whether 'furze' and 'gorse' co-refer. She can think to herself: 'Perhaps furze *is* gorse; in that case, since I believe that furze has yellow flowers, do I also believe that gorse has yellow flowers?' Pierre can ask himself analogous questions. Even in the first-person present-tense, such questions remain puzzling.

The Fregean must go further, by postulating new attitudes to Fregean thoughts, rather than using the natural language apparatus for attitude ascription. Let the underlined expression 'e' refer to the postulated Fregean sense which the sentence 'e' has for Penny right now, in her agnostic state. The idea is that furze and gorse are distinct, since 'furze' and 'gorse' currently differ in sense for Penny. Thus, furze has yellow flowers and gorse has yellow flowers are distinct Fregean thoughts, for the sense of a complex expression is supposed to be a structured entity built of the senses of its simpler constituents, a strong form of semantic compositionality for senses. Let belief$_s$ be the attitude analogous to belief which one has to some Fregean thoughts.[7] The idea is that Penny believes$_s$ furze has yellow flowers but does not believe$_s$ gorse has yellow flowers; there is no paradox in her believing one Fregean thought and not another. She can use this apparatus to reflect on her own beliefs and their epistemic status. Presumably, she knows both that she believes$_s$ furze has yellow flowers and that she does not believe$_s$ gorse has yellow flowers, from which she can infer that furze and gorse are distinct, by compositionality. At this level, Frege puzzles are easily resolved.

When Penny later learns that 'furze' and 'gorse' are synonyms, she can conveniently fuse the information she associates with each, thereby giving the two words the same sense for her. Since they have distinct senses right now, at least one of the words will change its sense for her; by the symmetry of the situation, both will. Any sentence in which either word occurs will change its sense for her correspondingly. Hence, she cannot now rely on underlining (or her mental equivalent of it) to characterize her future thoughts, since underlining is tied to the senses expressions have for her right now. This already indicates a serious limitation of the envisaged Fregean apparatus for purposes of her epistemic deliberation. In considering what to believe, she must think about what her belief state will be after a potential change. For example, when she considers whether to accept 'Furze is gorse' or 'Gorse has yellow flowers', she must think about what senses they will have for her after she has

---

[7] Belief$_s$ need not be some sort of secondary meaning of 'belief' in English; it is just a theoretically postulated attitude to Fregean thoughts loosely modelled on belief. Presumably, there would be analogous attitudes loosely modelled on knowledge, hope, fear, and so on, though the subscript 's' does not refer to an operation defined for all expressions of English.

accepted them, which depends on the new sense 'furze' and 'gorse' will have for her; but it is not the sense of any of her current words, and it is unclear how she can even entertain it until she has made the very belief change whose merit she is currently trying to asses. By contrast, if Penny works in a natural language, these difficulties do not arise: if she makes the envisaged change, she will believe that furze is gorse, but presumably will not believe$_s$ <u>furze is gorse</u>, since she will no longer have words with the senses <u>furze</u> and <u>gorse</u>.

A further concern for the Fregean apparatus can be explained with a variant of Penny's case. Pat acquired 'furze' and 'gorse' separately as natural kind terms, in a completely normal ostensive way, though in circumstances she no longer remembers. She applies 'furze' by using a reliable recognitional capacity, and she applies 'gorse' by using an exactly similar and so equally reliable recognitional capacity. For her, the *only* differences between 'furze' and 'gorse' in associated descriptions and recognitional capacities are metalinguistic: 'furze' and 'gorse' are different words. However, she does not treat them completely interchangeably, for she has a slight concern that they may not co-refer: she worries that she may have been introduced to 'furze' as a word for one kind of shrub and to 'gorse' as a word for a different kind of shrub, though they are so similar in appearance that she cannot recognize the difference. In fact, that is not what happened; she was shown the same kind both times. Still, her doubt need not be neurotic: she may have had ample experience of lookalike species. Thus, she is slightly more confident of 'Furze is furze' than of 'Furze is gorse'. In Fregean terms, she is slightly more confident$_s$ of <u>furze is furze</u> than of <u>furze is gorse</u> (here the underlinings are for Pat's senses, not Penny's). Consequently, <u>furze</u> and <u>gorse</u> are different senses. But, for Pat, 'furze' and 'gorse' do not differ qualitatively or in individualistic meaning in any non-metalinguistic way at all; the difference is purely verbal.

Although Pat was described as thinking about the words themselves, that is not crucial to the example. Her slightly greater confidence$_s$ in <u>furze is furze</u> than in <u>furze is gorse</u> suffices for the argument and does not require her to think metalinguistically.

What is wrong with building the words themselves into their Fregean senses for a given thinker? Such metalinguistic senses do not fit the usual conception of Fregean senses, but that is not the main problem. Instead, it is an issue of motivation. The required theoretical apparatus of individualistic Fregean senses is elaborate, unclear, and ill-developed. It is not useful for natural language semantics. Nor does it look useful for epistemology, given the problem of incommensurability of senses between different cognitive states. After all, a significant part of epistemology concerns the communication of knowledge across such differences—by memory, from earlier to later states of the same individual, and by testimony, from states of one individual to states of another. Learning itself—the acquisition of knowledge—constitutes a change in cognitive state. What gets preserved through such transactions is likely to be at least somewhat coarse-grained.

Once the senses of words are individuated in terms of the words themselves, the senses risk being redundant. We already have the words themselves, and their meanings in natural language. The senses add another level of theoretical entities with no clear explanatory value. We can make the distinctions we need without them.

4.6 The necessary a posteriori and the contingent a priori

As Kripke recognizes, his revisionary treatment of Frege puzzles affects even some of his own signature doctrines in *Naming and Necessity*, especially concerning the necessary a posteriori and the contingent a priori (1988: 135, 147n44). For example, on Kripke's view of the necessary a posteriori as often expounded, we know the necessary truth that Hesperus is Phosphorus only a posteriori, so while (7) is of course true, (8) is false—otherwise the case would not illustrate the key claim that some necessary truths are knowable only a posteriori:[8]

(7)   We know a priori that Hesperus is Hesperus.

(8)   We know a priori that Hesperus is Phosphorus.

This is just another Frege puzzle. Kripke is open to the possibility that, on the correct semantics, (7) and (8) have the same truth-value (with 'Hesperus' and 'Phosphorus' treated as directly referential proper names).

Kripke suggests a metalinguistic fallback for the problematic claim 'It was once unknown that Hesperus is Phosphorus': 'we can still say that there was a time when men were in no epistemic position to assent to "Hesperus is Phosphorus" for want of empirical information, but it nevertheless expressed a necessary truth' (1988: 135). He explains: 'I was aware of this question by the time "Naming and Necessity" [Kripke 1972] was written, but I did not wish to muddy the waters further than necessary at that time'.

For the contingent a priori, imagine a variant of Kripke's scenario in which we fix the reference of the rigid, directly referential term 'metre' by the non-rigid description 'the length of stick S', and we fix the reference of the rigid, directly referential term 'metre*' by the non-rigid description 'the length of stick S*'. As it happens, and unknown to us, the two sticks S and S* are exactly the same length. Consider these four statements:

(9)   We know a priori that stick S is one metre long.

(10) We know a priori that stick S* is one metre* long.

---

[8] Here and elsewhere, some readers may prefer to insert 'if Hesperus exists' after 'that'; doing so makes no difference for present purposes.

(11) We know a priori that stick S is one metre* long.

(12) We know a priori that stick S* is one metre long.

On Kripke's view of the contingent a priori as often expounded, in all four cases, the embedded proposition about the length of the stick is contingent; (9) and (10) are true, but (11) and (12) are false. For (9) and (10) follow the definitional connections, while (11) and (12) cut across them. But 'metre' and 'metre*' are directly referential terms for the very same length; on the revisionary view of Frege puzzles, substituting one for the other in such contexts preserves truth-value. Thus (11) has the same truth-value as (9) and (12) the same truth-value as (10). Moreover, since (9) and (10) uncontentiously have the same truth-value as each other because the two cases are exactly parallel, (9)–(12) all have the same truth-value. That is quite contrary to the standard account.[9]

As with the necessary a posteriori, metalinguistic fallbacks may still be available, for example about people in no epistemic position to assert 'Stick S is one metre* long' or 'Stick S* is one metre long' for want of empirical information. More generally, Kripke comments that when he wrote his (1972), 'I regarded the distinction between epistemic and metaphysical necessity as valid in any case and adequate for the distinctions I wished to make' (1988: 147n44).[10]

A problem for Kripke's fallbacks is that both epistemic necessity and empirical informativeness are also subject to problems of substitutivity:

(13) It is epistemically necessary that Hesperus is Hesperus.

(14) It is epistemically necessary that Hesperus is Phosphorus.

---

[9] Salmón 1987/88 raises some epistemologically relevant issues about Kripke's example.
[10] In semantics, epistemic necessity and epistemic possibility can be relativized to any given stock of knowledge. For Kripke, they concern specifically *a priori* knowledge.

(15) The information that Hesperus is Hesperus is empirical.

(16) The information that Hesperus is Phosphorus is empirical.

We might expect (13) and (16) to be true and (14) and (15) to be false. But if substituting 'Phosphorus' for 'Hesperus' preserves truth from (7) to (8), as Kripke holds it may do, it should also preserve truth from (13) to (14) and from (16) to (15). Thus 'epistemic necessity' and 'empirical information' will have to be reconstructed in some other form if they are to play the required role in proofing the categories of the necessary a posteriori and the contingent a priori against substitutivity problems. A more thoroughly metalinguistic approach may be needed.

To some, Kripke's appeal to the distinction between epistemic and metaphysical necessity will suggest two-dimensional semantics, for example, as developed by David Chalmers (2006), with one dimension epistemic and the other metaphysical. Chalmers conceives his semantics as Fregean in spirit, by contrast with two-dimensional semantics in the tradition of David Kaplan (1989), which is motivated by more purely linguistic considerations, treats proper names as directly referential, and has no epistemic dimension. For instance, Kaplan assigns exactly the same semantic properties to the names 'Hesperus' and 'Phosphorus', whereas Chalmers distinguishes them on the epistemic dimension of his semantics. In 'A Puzzle about Belief', Kripke holds open the possibility of a semantic theory such as Kaplan's with directly referential terms, and so cannot simply appeal to Chalmers' quite different approach.

In effect, for Chalmers a word has a Fregean sense (or 'narrow content') only relative to a given individual at a given time. The individualistic Fregean senses in section 4.5 might be fitted into the framework of Chalmers's semantics, but that gives a hint of the difficulties it faces. It also contrasts methodologically with Kripke's strong emphasis on the sharing of linguistic meaning, for instance, as names are passed down reference-preserving historical chains.

A further concern for the use of Chalmers's framework to stabilize the distinction between epistemic and metaphysical modality is his appeal to a priori knowability in characterizing epistemic modality, given that the distinction between a priori and a posteriori knowledge is itself destabilized by substitution arguments, as in (7)–(12). Clearly, this is not the place for a detailed assessment of Chalmers's grand programme, with its speculative reductionist ambitions, though the problems raised in section 4.5 are very relevant.[11] Were his Fregean programme on the right lines, that would have many ramifications for epistemology. In what follows, I will assume that his programme is *not* on the right lines, so we face the task of working out the epistemological consequences of an anti-Fregean approach.

Clearly, the anti-Fregean treatment of Frege puzzles has non-trivial consequences for the epistemological distinction between a priori and a posteriori knowledge. In particular, it raises concerns about the reliability of our pre-theoretic assessments of attributions of those types of knowledge. That leaves us with a picture significantly less clear than the one to be found in *Naming and Necessity*.[12]

4.7 Heuristics for belief ascription

In 'A Puzzle about Belief', Kripke suggests an explanation for our difficulties in knowing what beliefs to ascribe in Frege puzzles. He formulates three principles which he takes to guide our ascription of beliefs but which jointly generate problematic consequences when applied to cases like that of puzzling Pierre. The first he calls

---

[11] For a recent book-length critique of Chalmers's approach, see Yli-Vakkuri and Hawthorne 2018.
[12] For a debate on the significance or otherwise of the a priori/a posteriori distinction, see Boghossian and Williamson 2020.

the '*disquotational principle*' (1988: 112–13; I have made the schematic letter 'p' upper-case to conform with the rest of this book):

DP   *If a normal English speaker, on reflection, sincerely assents to 'P', then he believes that P.*

The second is a strengthened biconditional form of the disquotational principle (1988: 113):

SDP *A normal English speaker who is not reticent will be disposed to sincere reflective assent to 'P' if and only if he believes that P.*

The third he calls the '*principle of translation*' (1988: 114); unlike DP and SDP, it is not specifically about belief, or even propositional attitudes in general:

PT   *If a sentence of one language expresses a truth in that language, then any translation of it into any other language also expresses a truth (in that other language).*

Kripke stipulates that the schematic letter '*P*' in DP and SDP 'is to be replaced, inside and outside all quotation marks, by any appropriate standard English sentence', which 'is to lack indexical or pronominal devices or ambiguities that would ruin the intuitive sense of the principle' (1988: 112–13). Kripke seems to understand both DP and SDP as implicitly generalized to other natural languages too—in particular, to French. While admitting that DP may need further qualifications, he says of DP: 'Taken in its obvious intent, after all, the principle appears to be a self-evident truth' (1988: 113).

To appreciate the interplay between these principles, we start with DP. Working in English, we apply DP to Pierre's linguistic behaviour in English, and conclude 'Pierre believes that London is not pretty', because he is a normal English speaker who on reflection sincerely assents to 'London is not pretty'. Working in French, we then apply DP for French to Pierre's linguistic behaviour in French and reach the French translation of 'Pierre believes that London is pretty', because he is a normal French speaker who on reflection sincerely assents to 'Londres est jolie'. Finally, by applying PT, we conclude 'Pierre believes that London is pretty'. Thus, we are led to ascribe contradictory beliefs to Pierre: he both believes that London is pretty and believes that London is not pretty. That is paradoxical because (we may assume) by normal standards Pierre is eminently rational; he may even be the world's greatest classical logician.

When we apply SDP and PT to Pierre's linguistic behaviour in French and English, we ourselves are led to make contradictory statements about Pierre's beliefs—unlike the previous case, where we just attribute contradictory beliefs to Pierre. Working in English, we apply the right-to-left direction of SDP to Pierre's linguistic behaviour in English, and conclude 'Pierre does not believe that London is pretty', because he is not reticent yet is not disposed to sincere, reflective assent to 'London is pretty'. Working in French, we then apply the left-to-right direction of the analogue of SDP for French to Pierre's linguistic behaviour in French. Since he is a normal French speaker who is not reticent and *is* disposed to sincere reflective assent to 'Londres est jolie', we again reach the French translation of 'Pierre believes that London is pretty'. Finally, applying PT as before, we again conclude 'Pierre believes that London is pretty'. Thus, we have contradicted ourselves.

Kripke argues that since our normal practice of belief attribution suffices to generate the problem, given a mild principle of translation, with no appeal to substitutivity, it would be wrong-headed to blame the problem on the latter. Indeed, as he notes, not even the principle of translation PT is really essential to the underlying problem, since similarly paradoxical cases arise for synonymous pairs in the same language. The principle that synonymous sentences have the same truth-value (in a given context) will do instead. We have already been using one of his examples: the synonymous natural kind terms 'furze' and 'gorse'. The example also shows that the underlying problem is not specific to proper names.

Kripke concludes his paper by saying that the puzzle cases lie 'in an area where our normal apparatus for the ascription of belief is placed under the greatest strain and may even break down' (1988: 136). But what would it be for 'our normal apparatus for the ascription of belief' to 'break down'? Kripke writes of it as an extreme outcome which 'may even' occur. Thus, it must be something worse than just our finding ourselves unsure what to say about the puzzle cases, since, as he emphasizes, that obviously does occur.

Is Kripke hinting that the very distinction between believing and not believing may not apply to such cases? That is what some people would expect if, for example, SDP had some sort of analytic status, making it quasi-definitional of 'believe'. But SDP is nothing like analytic. For instance, a congenital liar may believe that P without being at all disposed to sincere reflective assent to 'P'; he may non-reticently deny 'P' (he is still a normal English speaker in his linguistic capacities). Even DP may have counterexamples, unless 'sincerely' is tied too closely to the expression of belief for DP to be a helpful guide to belief ascription; if 'P' is a complicated sentence with several negations, a normal English speaker might make a performance error in processing it and, even on reflection, sincerely assent to 'P' although it in fact expresses the opposite of what he believes. Kripke himself expresses doubts on the matter: he writes of DP 'I fear that even with all this [qualification] it is possible that some astute reader—such, after all, is the way of philosophy—may discover a qualification I have overlooked, without which the asserted principle is subject to counterexample', and of SDP 'Maybe again the formulation needs further tightening, but the intent is clear' (1988: 113–14).

Disappointingly, the subsequent literature has treated 'A Puzzle about Belief' mainly as a source of especially recalcitrant Frege puzzles, with not much focus on the suggested breakdown of our practice of ascribing belief. Perhaps Kripke's conclusion has had so little take-up because it was felt to be too radical. After all, our practice of belief ascription is crucial to the mature human capacity for *mindreading*, without which we could hardly survive as language-using social animals. How could that capacity be comparable to a broken-down machine? But just rejecting Kripke's conclusion does not explain how DP and SDP relate to our practice of belief ascription.

A more promising view of DP and SDP is that they are versions of a standard *heuristic* for belief ascription, in both speech and verbalized thought, of the kind discussed in chapter 1 (especially 1.5 on disquotation). Kripke's puzzle cases then illustrate just the sorts of limitation we might expect of such heuristics. That hypothesis explains our pre-theoretic reactions when faced with cases like that of Pierre. Our sheer puzzlement, confusion, ambivalence, rightly emphasized by Kripke, are not well explained as outcomes of a smoothly functioning semantics alone (such as a contextualist semantics). In Kripke's cases, we don't know what to say. Our reactions make much more sense on the hypothesis that, at some level, we are relying on an imperfectly reliable heuristic, whose outputs are not always mutually consistent.

A much simpler basic heuristic may indeed underlie both DP and SDP:

BDP   *English speakers assent to 'P' if and only if they believe that P.*

The idea is that the putative assent is in circumstances where the question whether P arises.

All the qualifications in DP and SDP about normality, reflection, sincerity, reticence, and dispositionality look like exception-barring clauses inserted to guard against defeaters. BDP is easier to use than DP or SDP: not only is it simpler, but it provides an overt criterion—assent to a sentence—for belief in a proposition, while all the qualifications concern less easily observed matters (normality, reflection, sincerity, reticence, dispositionality) from the perspective of another person. Of course, our capacity to recognize such exceptions shows that BDP does not *exhaust* our understanding of belief, but such defeasibility is typical of heuristics. As Kripke's uncertainty over the formulation of DP and SDP suggests, being a native speaker does not put one in a position to survey all possible ways for the heuristic to be defeated; as one tries to think of as many as one can, pre-theoretical reflection gradually becomes more theoretical. When we use a heuristic, we may easily be unaware of its merely heuristic status, or indeed of what principle we are using, if any.[13]

Heuristics are very different from conversational implicatures. Unlike the latter, heuristics play a direct role in assessing statements as true or false. Also, conversational implicatures are more or less predictable on general social grounds, whereas heuristics are cognitive devices applicable to specific kinds of statement. Of course, heuristics may help to generate conversational implicatures. For instance, if John asks 'Does Penny believe that gorse has yellow flowers?', and Mary replies 'She believes that furze has yellow flowers', John may take Mary to imply that the literally correct answer to his question is negative, or at least that she does not know it to be positive, since otherwise the switch from 'furze' to 'gorse' would be pointless. But such conversational phenomena are derivative.

One limitation of DP, SDP, and BDP is that they are applicable only to the ascription of beliefs to speakers of a language. But we

---

[13] Our reliance on a disquotational heuristic such as BDP in belief ascription may explain the data used by various authors to argue that belief is weak in the sense that one's 'best guess' amounts to belief (Hathorne, Rothschild, and Spectre 2016, Rothschild 2020, Holguín 2022). In restricted circumstances like those envisaged in the literature, one assents to (or says) one's best guess; although that is a marginal case of assent, it may easily be enough to trigger the disquotational heuristic and so to generate the corresponding belief ascriptions. That is shaky evidence for the truth of 'belief is weak'. For other reasons to doubt that belief is weak, see Williamson forthcoming-e.

often ascribe beliefs to non-speakers, such as non-human animals and very young children, by observing their non-verbal behaviour. For example, to explain why the cat jumped into the bathtub, we assume that she believed (falsely) that it was empty. Frege cases arise for such creatures too. To explain why a cock robin in his own territory who sees himself in a mirror flies aggressively at the mirror, we assume that he believes (falsely) that he is a rival. To keep track of the robin's mental states, we may distinguish guises: he believes that he [under a visual demonstrative guise] is a rival, but does not believe that he [under a self-relating guise] is a rival. In effect, we treat the robin as having a belief state aptly manifested by saying 'He is my rival' but no belief state aptly manifested by saying 'I am my rival', although of course we know that the robin himself cannot manifest his belief in words. Obviously, such verbalized belief states will not be fully faithful to how the robin thinks, but they may still be a decent first approximation. Similar examples could be given for very young children. Like non-human animals, they can be tricked by Frege cases into false belief without being able to grasp what false belief is.[14] To grasp such cases firmly, we may need to conceive them in terms of such as-if saying, and make implicit notional use of BDP. Unsurprisingly, given the limitations of BDP, we may have difficulty in trying to describe the situation consistently: does the robin believe that he is his rival?

Of course, we can ascribe beliefs to older children and adult humans on the basis of either linguistic or non-linguistic behaviour. Which sort of heuristic is more reliable, and which is more convenient, depends on the case. If we lack the time or opportunity to observe someone's non-linguistic behaviour but want to know whether they believe that P, just asking them 'P?' is often a good way to find out.

---

[14] Rackoczy, Bergfeld, Schwarz, and Fizke 2015 provides evidence that children acquire a basic understanding of aspectuality (guise-sensitivity in attitude ascription) at the same age, 4–5, at which they acquire a basic understanding of false belief.

A more general limitation of Kripke's account in the paper is that it is specific to belief, although Frege puzzles arise just as much for other attitudes, such as knowledge, hope, and fear. It is not obvious how to generalize DP, SDP, or BDP to those other attitudes. Still, DP, SDP, and BDP are a start. Given that knowledge entails belief, whenever SDP indicates the absence of belief, it also indicates the absence of knowledge. On the positive side, someone's assent to 'P' might be taken as a highly defeasible sign that they know that P; our knowledge that it was not the case that P would be a salient defeater. At a more general level, the same mindreading capacity used for knowledge ascription is also used for belief ascription (Nagel 2013). The case of knowledge ascription will be discussed in more detail in section 4.8.

For any propositional attitude φ, if one wants to know whether a normal speaker φs that P, in many circumstances a quick and moderately reliable way to find out is by asking them 'Do you φ that P?' We can call this the 'Just Ask' heuristic. It is not quite a generalization of DP, SDP, or BDP, for in the case of belief it tells one to ask 'Do you believe that P?', whereas for DP, SDP, and BDP one would ask simply 'P?' The questions are not equivalent. If you ask honest agnostics 'Do you believe that there is a god?' they will answer 'No' (agnostics are not theists); by contrast, if you ask them 'Is there a god?' they will not answer 'No' (agnostics are not atheists), but instead 'I don't know', or the like. Nevertheless, the 'Just Ask' heuristic has a key feature in common with DP, SDP, and BDP: all these tests are sensitive to differences between the *sentences* 'P' and 'Q', even if the *propositions* that P and that Q are identical. Consequently, they may help explain our troubles in Frege cases for any attitude. If the propositions that P and that Q are identical, a rational person may still give conflicting answers to the questions 'Do you φ that P?' and 'Do you φ that Q?' Heuristics for attitude ascription with this feature are *language-sensitive*.

By contrast, the factivity principle 'If not-P, the agent does not know that P' is language-insensitive. For if the propositions that P and that Q are identical, then not-P if and only if not-Q, so the principle never yields conflicting answers to the questions 'Does the agent know that P?' and 'Does the agent know that Q?', though we may of course misapply the principle if we are confused about the relation between 'P' and 'Q'.

When φing is a factive attitude, the question 'Do you φ that P?' normally presupposes that P. For example, the question 'Do you regret that you never told him what you thought of him?' presupposes that the addressee never told the relevant male what they thought of him. The fact itself is taken for granted; the question concerns the addressee's affective attitude to the fact. That in itself poses no problem for the 'Just Ask' heuristic.

However, when φing is a more purely cognitive factive attitude, such as knowing, seeing, or remembering, often one asks whether someone φs because one wants to *learn* the fact at issue; one is in no position to ask 'Do you φ that P?' because one does not yet know whether P. In such cases, a slightly more complex variant of the 'Just Ask' heuristic is needed. Unless one already knows that the train stops at Ardlui, one does not ask 'Do you know that the train stops at Ardlui?' (which could elicit the answer 'I do now'); one asks 'Do you know whether the train stops at Ardlui?' If one gets the rather uncooperative answer 'I do', leaving one still not knowing whether it stops there, one can follow up with 'So *does* it stop there?' More generally, the variant of the 'Just Ask' heuristic has one ask 'Do you φ whether P?', with 'P?' as the potential follow-up to an uncooperatively minimal positive answer. Similarly, one might ask 'Do you remember whether I locked the door?' or 'Can you see whether the light is on?' Rather than directly asking the question one is really interested in, one checks whether one's interlocutor is in a position to answer it. This variant of 'Just Ask' is, of course, equally language-sensitive.

'Just Ask' and its variants are more general than DP, SDP, and BDP because one can apply the former but not the latter to any attitude one can articulate. Obviously, they are not fully reliable, because even a speaker who is trying to be honest may lack self-knowledge or be self-deceived. Nevertheless, they may be better than the available alternatives. One can also use 'Just Ask' in the past tense to probe the speaker's past mental states, by asking questions of the form 'Did you believe/hope/fear that . . . ?', 'Did you already know that . . . ?', 'Did you remember that . . . ?', 'Could you see whether . . . ?' By contrast, DP and SDP target only the speaker's *present* beliefs; if 'P' is in the past tense, they target the speaker's present beliefs about the past.

The primary use of these language-sensitive heuristics is 'on-line', to find out the attitudes of a living person with whom one can communicate. But of course that is not what readers of Kripke's article are doing when they wonder what Pierre in the story believes. If they are applying DP or SDP, they are doing it 'offline', in their imaginations. Such offline uses of heuristics for attitude ascription are quite common; we make them all the time when reading novels. In the case of Pierre, we need not imagine him talking to us or anyone else; we can simply imagine him saying 'Londres est jolie' or 'London is not pretty' to himself; DP and SDP are still applicable.

When we read works of analytic epistemology, we are often expected to do something similar, although the attitude at issue may be knowledge or justified belief rather than plain belief. The reader is asked to imagine fictional cases and, within the fiction, to make positive or negative attitude ascriptions. The content of the putative attitude is normally presented to the reader as expressed by a sentence. Naturally, we will use offline whatever heuristics we have for ascribing the attitude at issue, which will often involve a language-sensitive heuristic. This is a potential source of error in our use of the case method in epistemology. Of course, if the fictional scenario involves an obvious Frege case, experienced philosophers are likely to be on the alert for associated problems, but in some cases even the unmentioned possibility of a Frege case may make problems. For instance, when one considers the assertive use of Moore-paradoxical sentences of the form 'I falsely believe that P', it may not be immediately obvious that, given anti-Fregeanism, such uses can be legitimate in Frege cases (Crimmins 1992).

Our reliance on imperfectly reliable heuristics in assessing attitude ascriptions also threatens the standard methodology for studying the semantics of such ascriptions. The assessments of attitude ascriptions with respect to hypothetical cases are standardly treated as the central data for that study. Normally, a semantic theory of the truth-conditions of attitude ascriptions is expected to explain the data by vindicating the assessments, predicting their correctness. But if the assessments are the outputs of imperfectly reliable heuristics, then they may be *incorrect*, in which case a semantic theory should not predict their correctness. Thus, the literature on the semantics of propositional attitudes may have fallen into the trap of overfitting, producing increasingly complicated theories to fit unreliable data (see chapter 2). If the errors result systematically from reliance on comparatively simple heuristics, semanticists need to know what those heuristics are, so that they can be taken into account in a correspondingly systematic way. We can still expect a semantic theory to treat the heuristics as charitably as possible, by not imputing errors needlessly, but to do that we must first understand how the heuristics work. A more sophisticated methodology is called for, with a more critical attitude to the data.

One consoling thought is that when the heuristics for ascribing attitudes are shared by the participants in a conversation, the errors they induce may often 'cancel out'. For example, if—in that limited context—they all erroneously treat 'Penny believes that furze has yellow flowers' as if it expressed the proposition that Penny believes that furze has yellow flowers under the guise of the sentence 'Furze has yellow flowers', they may still succeed in communicating the latter information among themselves. For reasons already explained, one should not conclude that in that context the sentence really did express that proposition about the guise. After all, if the participants in a conversation all misconstrue the grammar of a sentence in the same way, among themselves they may succeed in using it to communicate a thought quite different from the one it really expresses. Such error-based communicative successes tend to be local, but they still help explain why the heuristics' limitations do much less harm than one might have expected.

4.8 Heuristics for knowledge ascription

Knowledge ascription is arguably more fundamental than belief ascription and works in rather different ways. It therefore deserves a section to itself. In this section, Frege puzzles will be marginal, even though they do of course arise for knowledge ascription too; instead, the focus will be on differences between knowledge ascription and belief ascription. But heuristics for knowledge ascription will later cast light on our difficulties with Frege puzzles.

In *Knowledge and Its Limits*, I made a case for knowing as a core mental state, based mainly on general philosophical considerations about externalism, causal explanation, self-knowledge, the logical form of attitude ascriptions, and so on (Williamson 2000). One footnote cites a discussion by the psychologist Josef Perner (1993) of evidence that children understand knowledge and ignorance *before* they understand belief and error, and so do not understand knowledge in terms of belief. I found that encouraging, but did not build on it. However, as Jennifer Nagel later noted (2013), psychologists routinely classify knowing as a mental state. That is not just a terminological point; it draws substance from how they treat the attribution of knowledge as just as central and basic an application of the human mindreading capacity as the attribution of beliefs or desires (see also Nagel 2017). In effect, the human cognitive system thrives on treating knowledge as a mental state.

There is increasingly strong evidence that the capacity to distinguish knowledge from ignorance is cognitively more basic than the capacity to distinguish true belief from error (for an introduction to the recent literature, see Phillips, Buckwalter, Cushman,

Friedman, Martin, Turri, Santos, and Knobe 2020 and associated discussion). Humans attribute knowledge and ignorance before they can attribute true belief and error, and they tend to do it faster and more automatically. Non-human primates attribute knowledge and ignorance to each other, but not true belief or error. Indeed, that combination may extend much more widely across species. The best available explanations of much animal behaviour interpret them as making such distinctions. Reductive attempts to re-explain the behaviour in terms of mere reflexes become ever more ad hoc when faced with the complexity and flexibility of the behaviour. Claims to have found belief attribution at much earlier stages have not proven robust (see Nagel forthcoming for discussion).

What very young children and nonhuman primates attribute is clearly knowledge-like, not some doxastic *ersatz* such as true belief. It is even sensitive to Gettier cases. For example, here is the experimenters' summary of two experiments with rhesus macaques (Horschler, Santos, and MacLean 2019):

In Experiment 1, monkeys watched an agent observe a piece of fruit (the target object) being hidden in one of two boxes. While the agent's view was occluded, either the fruit moved out of its box and directly back into it, or the box containing the fruit opened and immediately closed. We found that monkeys looked significantly longer when the agent reached incorrectly rather than correctly after the box's movement, but not after the fruit's movement. This result suggests that monkeys did not expect the agent to know the fruit's location when it briefly and arbitrarily moved while the agent could not see it, but did expect the agent to know the fruit's location when only the box moved while the agent could not see it. In Experiment 2, we replicated and extended both findings with a larger sample, a different target object, and opposite directions of motion in the test trials.

In the background is a generic presumption of persistence, in other words the persistence heuristic discussed in chapter 1.3: the default is that if the fruit is somewhere, it continues to be there, and that if the agent knows that it is there, the agent continues to know that it is there. In effect, when the monkeys see the agent see the fruit put in the box, they treat the agent as coming to know that it is in there. They continue to treat the agent as knowing that it is in there when the agent's view is temporarily occluded but the fruit remains in there. Thus, they are surprised if the agent reaches for the wrong box, presumably in order to get the fruit. But when the fruit moves out of the box, the monkeys cease to treat the agent as knowing that the fruit is in there, since they can see that it isn't. When the fruit moves back into the box, they do not treat the agent as again coming to know that the fruit is in it, since they can see that the agent did not see it moving back. Thus, they are not surprised if the agent reaches for the wrong box. Had the monkeys been thinking in doxastic terms, they would have treated the agent in both conditions as believing throughout that the fruit is in the box (this is simply a point about belief; it does not depend on the assumption that knowledge entails belief). Thus, there would be no difference in surprise between the two conditions when the agent reaches for the wrong box. Indeed, the belief that the fruit is in there is true in the final stage of both conditions, and even justified, given the presumption of persistence. Since the monkeys reasonably treat the agent as not knowing that the fruit is in there after it has moved and returned, that is in effect a Gettier case—although, of course, the monkeys do not think of it as a case of justified true belief.

The experimenters themselves interpret the monkeys as attributing only an 'awareness relation' rather than knowledge to the agent. However, their distinction between knowledge and awareness is unclear, and seems to depend on an unnecessarily doxastic conception of knowledge. The results of the experiments make just as good sense on the assumption that the monkeys are distinguishing between knowledge and ignorance (see Nagel forthcoming for more discussion, including of similar results for young children).

Many philosophers have found the idea that attributing knowledge is easier than attributing belief 'counterintuitive'. They assume that attributing knowledge *must* be harder, and require more sophistication, than attributing belief. Sometimes, the assumption comes from a vision of attributing knowledge as attributing some post-Gettier multi-clause analysans of knowledge in terms of belief, truth, and other factors, which would of course be much harder, and require much more sophistication, than attributing belief alone. But even philosophers who do not envisage knowledge as having such an analysis often seem to assume that attributing knowledge must require *more* than attributing belief, simply because knowledge itself requires *more* than belief. Even on the knowledge-first view in *Knowledge and Its Limits*, knowledge entails belief, while belief does not entail knowledge. At a more general level, a similar thought may influence many internalists in epistemology: broad mental states must be harder to identify than narrow mental states because identifying broad states requires monitoring *both* the internal *and* the external, whereas monitoring narrow states only requires monitoring the internal.

Such preconceptions are not surprising for *self*-attributions of mental states. But if, as is likely, mindreading capacities evolved through *social* life, their primary role is in attributing mental states to *others*. For that task, states purely internal to the other may be harder to determine than states involving the mutually observable environment. A simple initial case is the *absence* of factive states. Just from knowing that you didn't eat the banana, you can conclude that I don't know that you ate the banana—but you may still wonder whether I *believe* that you ate the banana.

Of course, attributions of positive mental states are central too. A good place to start is with *seeing an object*. When you see an apple and I see it too, typically, each of us can also see that the other sees it. We can check open eyes, direction of gaze, potential occlusions. That will not satisfy sceptics about other minds, but their sceptical scenarios were scarce in our evolutionary history. Similarly, when two people walking together both hear a loud noise, typically, each of them also knows that the other heard it. On the negative side, one may know that the alpha male can't see the apple, because a bush is in the way, or one may know that he is too far away to hear one's breathing. Such knowledge about what others do or don't perceive plays a large role in communication—for example, in the use of perceptual demonstratives. When young children interact with other children or adults, mutual gaze at an object is often crucial to communication.

The internal analogue of object-seeing is as-if object-seeing, being in a mental state internally the same as (really) seeing an object. Attributing as-if object-seeing is much more laborious. When I see that you see the apple, I can reason that since every mental state is internally the same as itself, you also as-if see an apple, but that is an artificial intellectual exercise. To consider cases where really seeing and as-if seeing come apart, we can suppose that dreaming that one sees an object involves as-if seeing an object without really seeing it. If you see me when I'm asleep, gently snoring with my eyes shut, you know that I am not really seeing an apple, but you cannot tell whether I am as-if seeing an apple.

Although object-seeing is not itself a propositional attitude, it is closely related to propositional attitudes. One can see an apple without seeing *that* it is an apple, because it has an unusual shape, or one thinks it might be a wax replica, or one has been brought up in ignorance of apples. Still, normally, when one sees an apple, one also sees that it is an apple. Conversely, when one doesn't see an apple, one also doesn't see that it is an apple. Thus, it is unsurprisingly typical that when we see an apple together, each of us is in a position to know that the other sees that it is an apple. Seeing-that, 'fact-seeing', *is* a propositional attitude.

Psychologically, perhaps we model seeing that P on seeing an object, treating the state of affairs that P like an object. Just as you can't (really) see what isn't there, you can't (really) see what isn't the case. On this analogy, we treat the non-obtaining of the state of affairs that P like the absence of an object. Just as an object *o* must be there for you to see *o*, it must be that P for you to see that P. Moreover, both object-seeing and seeing-that normally require a suitable causal connection to what is seen: a merely accidental match of your visual image to something external, *e*, does not constitute seeing *e*.

In *Knowledge and Its Limits*, I argue that seeing that P is a specific form of knowing that P. Thus, when we see the apple together, typically, each of us is in a position to know that the other knows that it is an apple. There would be little point in my judging merely that you *believe* that it is an apple, for why should I make that judgment if I doubt that you see that it is an apple?

Psychologically, seeing-that seems to be treated as a paradigm of knowing-that. 'See' is often used in an extended sense for a wide range of cases of knowing or recognizing (coming to know): 'I see your point'; 'I don't see how that follows'. What drives the generalization from literal seeing and other forms of sense perception to knowing? A key factor is *memory*. When you turn away, you no longer *see* that there are apples on the tree, but you still *remember* that there are (or at least were), and many of the effects on action are similar—you may still go to the tree when hungry. Remembering that P is another form of knowing that P. Having seen the agent see the fruit put somewhere, the rhesus macaques continue attributing knowledge that it is there to the agent even when they can see that the agent can no longer see the fruit. A large part of the excess of knowledge over sense perception is simply what remains when sense perception ceases.

In light of these considerations, knowledge attribution looks rather easier and more natural than philosophers' preoccupations make it seem. We should not be surprised that the level of cognitive sophistication required for attributing knowledge turns out to be *lower* than the level of cognitive sophistication required for attributing belief—just as it can take less to recognize whether someone knows that P than to recognize whether they have an attitude internally similar to knowing that P.

Knowing also takes primacy when we learn from others about the world (Phillips et al. 2020). If you want to know whether P, but are not in a position to perceive whether P, it matters to you whether *I* know whether P. If I do, you can learn from me (whether I happen to have a *belief* as to whether P is not the issue). Imagine us facing each other. You can see things behind my back that I can't see; I can see things behind your back that you can't see. We may wish to share our knowledge: one of us sees signs of a predator and sounds the alarm. Or we may wish *not* to share our knowledge: one of us sees some delicious food and tries not to react, hoping to eat it once the other has gone. The other can benefit by spotting tell-tale signs that the first has spotted something. In such cases, to focus on the other's internal states is to miss the point.

A converging line of argument comes from considerations of cognitive efficiency, as Robert Gordon has observed (Gordon 2000, 2021, forthcoming). Minded creatures put huge effort into learning about their environment and what is happening in it, and into keeping their information up to date—it can literally be a matter of life and death, as it is for predators and prey. Creatures capable of mindreading use it to keep informed of similar cognitive states and processes in others. Imagine that whenever they represent something they must also separately represent how each of the others represent it (for instance, whether they believe, disbelieve, suspend judgment, or have some degree of a credence). That is a massive multiplication of effort. Indeed, it threatens to be infinite: I represent X, you represent how I represent X, I represent how you represent how I represent X, you represent how I represent how you represent how I represent X, ... For example, each creature maintains something like a map of its environment. But it also needs to track how each of the others maps the environment, so for each of the others it maintains another map of the environment, representing the other's map. That already threatens to be computationally infeasible, even before we start worrying about the infinite regress of maps of maps.

A much more efficient method would be to maintain just one map, but to try to mark the location of other knowers on it. That already captures something of their different perspectives on the world. For example, it encodes information about what you can see but others can't, because their view is obstructed by an intervening obstacle. Similarly, it also encodes information about places they can see but you can't. Of course, that is only a start. The rhesus macaques already go further by tracking which present states of affairs another can still access through memory though no longer through sight. The older child, in attributing false beliefs, is doing something much more complex. Still, the underlying principle may be the same: in mindreading, the default is to treat the other as knowing; the work goes into tracking deviations from that. In Gordon's terms, the default is 'the shared world' (Gordon 2021 connects his arguments about the shared world and cognitive efficiency to the predictive coding model of perception). Harvey Lederman, crediting Taylor Carman for the observation, pointed me to a passage in Merleau-Ponty 1945: 407–8 about the cognitive attitude of young children where he seems to endorse a similar conception of the shared world. By contrast, on the mistaken but widespread alternative, the default is to treat the other as a *tabula rasa*, so that attributing any positive mental state requires work.

Watering down the default from knowledge to true belief would make no sense. By default, everything lies open to everyone's view; in those circumstances, there is knowledge, not just true belief.

To make knowledge the default is not to assume that most agents know most truths. Even when that assumption is restricted to simple truths about the environment, it is surely false: think of all the truths about what insects are under what stones, and the like. In practice, mindreading is typically used for matters of actual or potential interest to the agents concerned. The point is that, on such matters, it is typically easier to work down from an initial hypothesis of total knowledge than to work up from an initial hypothesis of total ignorance.

Of course, so far as the world is open to everyone's view, there are no Frege cases, since they involve something hidden. But the shared world default still leaves room for such cases to arise, because the default's inhibitors may be guise-sensitive. Imagine this. You and I both know Snežana. I can see both you and her, and that you are in a position to hear her but not to see her. She sneezes. Pre-theoretically, I do not assume that you know 'Snežana is the sneezer'.

The shared world default may well have been ecologically valid in the conditions under which mindreading evolved: small groups of conspecifics in a local environment, interactions between a predator and prey, and so on. One can worry, though, how much sense it makes in the modern world of highly complex, diverse societies. But that worry may underestimate the epistemic diversity already present under those evolutionary conditions. Even in a small group of hunter-gatherers, there are obvious epistemic asymmetries between adults and children. Children know that they know less than adults, and adults know that they know more than children. Mindreading in both directions guides how children learn from adults. Within a group, differences in life history, recent experience, skills, and abilities, can all make for significant differences in knowledge and belief. When one group of hunter-gatherers encountered a new group, perhaps with alien customs, how each group mindread the strangers in those sensitive circumstances could make the difference between things going very well and things going very badly—crudely, between sex and death. Human history is not a simple narrative of increasing diversity; notoriously, imperialism and globalization work in the opposite direction. Even in the modern world, people of very different cultures and mindsets do manage to communicate, using a robust capacity for mindreading that evolved under radically different conditions. For that to happen, the shared world is a more effective default than the *tabula rasa*.

The shared world default may also help solve a long-standing problem in game theory and theoretical economics. Many results depend on the hypothesis that various background conditions such as rationality are *common knowledge* amongst the relevant agents: everyone knows that everyone is rational, everyone knows that everyone knows that everyone is rational, everyone knows that everyone knows that everyone knows that everyone is rational, and so on ad infinitum. Demanding such common knowledge of normal humans seems unrealistic. One might expect that, in practice, a finite approximation to common knowledge would do instead, but that is not always so. Some apparently realistic forms of coordinated action can be achieved under common knowledge but not under 'almost common knowledge' (Rubinstein 1989). Moreover, even a few iterations of 'everyone knows' can be unachievable for epistemological reasons explained in *Knowledge and Its Limits*, since each iteration requires a further margin for error (see also Hawthorne and Magidor 2009, 2010; for a different approach to the problem see Lederman 2018a, 2018b). Yet an announcement over a loudspeaker can surely *seem* to create common knowledge amongst the people in a room. What is going on?

The knowledge default is implicitly a *common* knowledge default. For substituting 'everyone knows that P' for 'P' in the default schema 'If P, everyone knows that P' gives 'If everyone knows that P, everyone knows that everyone knows that P', and so by transitivity 'If P, everyone knows that everyone knows that P'. Repeating the argument yields arbitrarily many iterations of 'everyone knows that'. Obviously, an articulated inferential process like that is psychologically unrealistic. The point is rather that if everyone treats the world as open to view by default, and nothing inhibits the default, then the effect is in many ways similar to common knowledge. Of course, the default does not mean that there really is common knowledge, in the sense of infinitely many levels of iterated knowledge. It just means that, when nothing inhibits the default, everyone acts as they would if everything were common knowledge. But that may suffice for coordination to be achieved. It may even be achieved, just as it often seems to be, with no iteration of epistemic operators, indeed with no epistemic operators at all: the phenomenology is just that of a world open to view. Since the coordination is the predictable result of deeply rooted forms of human thinking, it may even be safe enough for those involved to know in advance that they will coordinate. Naturally, all this needs to be worked out in much more detail. But it promises to be a far more psychologically realistic picture of the cognitive processes underlying apparent common knowledge than any elaborate reconstruction in epistemic logic.

Whatever our heuristics for ascribing knowledge, belief, or other epistemic states, we will be relying on them in epistemology too, when we ascribe such states with respect to hypothetical cases. That does not warrant the panicky response that in epistemology we should stop using our ordinary means of ascribing attitudes, any more than visual illusions warrant the response that in science we should stop using vision. But it does indicate that we need some checks and balances. In particular, we should beware of letting epistemology be a largely data-driven inquiry, where so much of the data is supplied by our ordinary means of ascribing epistemic states. We need to put more weight on theoretical virtues, such as simplicity and strength.

4.9 Evidence

We can now return to exploring consequences of an anti-Fregean treatment of Frege cases. For simplicity, I will assume that the anti-Fregean can explain all the systematically recalcitrant data in Frege cases as effects of reliance on imperfectly reliable heuristics for attitude ascription without resort to contextualist semantics. In that respect, our anti-Fregean will henceforth be an anti-contextualist anti-Fregean.

Normally, whether it is rational for one to believe a proposition *p* is sensitive to how *p* relates to one's total evidence. Thus, if one's evidence can be *non-transparent*, in the sense that what it seems to one to comprise is not what it does comprise, one may be in no position to know how *p does* relate to one's total evidence, and so in no position to know whether it is rational for one to believe *p*. Similarly, whether it is rational for one to do an action *A* is normally sensitive to how *A* relates to one's total evidence. Thus, if one's evidence can be non-transparent, one may be in no position to know how *A does* relate to one's total evidence, and so in no position to know whether it is rational for one to do *A*. Even the cleverest agents can be in such circumstances, whether they know it or not. Such possibilities matter for how we understand the normative claims of rationality.

But can evidence be non-transparent? Anti-Fregeanism about Frege puzzles suggests that it can. For the time being, we may assume that evidence consists of propositions, since it can be *incompatible* with hypotheses and stand in other such propositional relations (Williamson 2000: 194–200). In particular, we may assume that it can include such propositions as that furze has yellow flowers. Recall Penny from section 4.3. Under the guise of the sentence 'Furze has yellow flowers', but not under the guise of the sentence 'Gorse has yellow flowers', she knows that furze has yellow flowers. We may assume that her evidence includes that furze has yellow flowers; after all, she observed that furze has yellow flowers when she was introduced to the word 'furze'. If you ask her 'Does your evidence include that furze has yellow flowers?', on reflection she will sincerely answer 'Yes'. If you ask her 'Does your evidence include that gorse has yellow flowers?', on reflection she will sincerely answer either 'No' or 'I don't know' or 'Perhaps', in part depending on whether *she* is a Fregean or an anti-Fregean. But, if anti-Fregeanism is indeed correct, for her evidence to include that furze has yellow flowers just is for her evidence to include that gorse has yellow flowers. Thus, her evidence includes that gorse has yellow flowers. Consequently, her failure on reflection to answer 'Yes' to the question 'Does your evidence include that gorse has yellow flowers?' looks like a case of non-transparency. After all, by normal linguistic standards, she understands the question.

We must go carefully here. Consider (17) and (18):

(17)   Penny knows that her evidence includes that furze has yellow flowers.

(18)   Penny knows that her evidence includes that gorse has yellow flowers.

In the scenario, (17) may well be true. One can know something by knowing it under one linguistic guise without knowing it under all its linguistic guises. Penny has the knowledge attributed in (17) under the guise of sentence (19), even though she does not have it under the guise of sentence (20), and that seems enough for the truth of (17):

(19)   My evidence includes that furze has yellow flowers.

(20)   My evidence includes that gorse has yellow flowers.

But, given anti-Fregeanism, (17) and (18) have the same truth-value. Thus (18) is true too. Since Penny *knows* that her evidence includes that gorse has yellow flowers, where is the alleged non-transparency?

Unfortunately, (18) does not resolve the problem of non-transparency. For Penny *also* has a psychologically real attitude of *doubt* towards the same proposition, where doubt is understood as an active attitude, not simply as absence of knowledge. Consider (21) and (22):

(21) Penny doubts that her evidence includes that furze has yellow flowers.

(22) Penny doubts that her evidence includes that gorse has yellow flowers.

In the scenario, (22) seems true, because she doubts the proposition under the guise of sentence (20), even though she does not doubt it under the guise of sentence (21). If the knowledge attributed in (17) under the guise of (19) is enough for the truth of (17), why should the doubt attributed in (22) under the guise of (20) not be enough for the truth of (22)? After all, the doubt in (22) is just as psychologically present as the knowledge in (17). But, given anti-Fregeanism, (21) and (22) have the same truth-value, so (21) is also true. Yet Penny knows the very truth she doubts, because she knows it under the guise of (19), even though she does not know it under the guise of (20).[15] In such a case, once we eliminate the relativization to guises, the non-transparency takes the form of the presence of doubt, rather than the absence of knowledge.

In some variants of the scenario, Penny believes that furze and gorse are distinct kinds. In that case, presumably, she will on reflection sincerely answer 'No' to the question 'Does your evidence include that gorse has yellow flowers?'. Consider (23) and (24):

(23) Penny believes that her evidence does not include that furze has yellow flowers.

(24) Penny believes that her evidence does not include that gorse has yellow flowers.

---

[15] Salmón 1986: 111 gives a similar treatment of *withholding* belief.

In this scenario, (24) seems true because Penny believes the proposition under the guise of the negation of sentence (20), even though she does not believe it under the guise of the negation of sentence (19). Given anti-Fregeanism, (23) and (24) have the same truth-value, so (23) is also true. Thus, Penny believes contradictory propositions about her evidence. She believes that it includes that furze has yellow flowers (under the guise of (19), because she knows it under that guise and knowledge entails belief), but she also believes that it does *not* include that furze has yellow flowers (under the guise of the negation of (20)). The non-transparency takes the form of mutually contradictory beliefs as to what her evidence includes.

Even where there is no Frege case, the *epistemic threat* of a Frege case may result in non-transparency which may take the form of ignorance. For example, suppose that Dominic suspects that K2 (under that name) and Kangchenjunga (under that name) are the very same mountain. For all he knows, 'K2' and 'Kangchenjunga' co-refer. He knows that K2 is 8,611 metres high. He is not sure how high Kangchenjunga is, though of course he suspects that it is 8,611 metres high. In fact, they are different mountains, and Kangchenjunga is slightly lower than K2. Thus, we may assume, his total evidence includes that K2 is 8,611 metres high but does *not* include that Kangchenjunga is 8,611 metres high. Consider (25):

(25) Dominic knows that his evidence does not include that Kangchenjunga is 8,611 metres high.

In this scenario, given anti-Fregeanism, (25) is false. Everything Dominic knows is compatible with a scenario in which 'K2' and 'Kangchenjunga' co-refer and his evidence includes that Kangchenjunga is 8,611 metres high, because it includes that K2 is 8,611 metres high. Although he entertains the proposition that Kangchenjunga is 8,611 metres high, and his evidence does not include it, he is in no position to know that his evidence does not include it. Dominic is ignorant of the limits of his evidence.

Incidentally, not even the supposition that Fregeanism is true rules out this example of non-transparency, for it does not entail that Dominic *knows* that Fregeanism is true; thus, everything he knows may be compatible with a scenario in which anti-Fregeanism is true, 'K2' and 'Kangchenjunga' are intersubstitutable in propositional attitude ascriptions, and his evidence includes that Kangchenjunga is 8,611 metres high, because it includes that K2 is 8,611 metres high. By itself, the truth of Fregeanism would not put Dominic in a position to know the limits of his evidence.

Despite all these problems, some anti-Fregeans may suspect that there is something right about the transparency of evidence. The preceding discussion makes one fallback salient: to postulate transparency of evidence at the level of guises, instead of at the level of propositions. On this view, although it is not transparent to Penny whether her evidence includes the proposition that gorse has yellow flowers, and not even transparent to her whether it includes that proposition under the guise of the sentence 'Furze has yellow flowers' (since she doubts that 'Furze has yellow flowers' is a guise of the proposition that gorse has yellow flowers), it *is* transparent to her that her evidence includes whatever proposition is expressed by the sentence 'Furze has yellow flowers'. More generally, the strategy would be to finesse the problem of non-transparency by doing as much of the epistemological work as possible with the guises themselves.

Kripke's example of Paderewski the pianist and Paderewski the statesman raises immediate questions for the metalinguistic strategy. Non-transparency can arise even at the level of names and sentences. Similarly, as David Kaplan (1989) points out, it may be unclear whether two occurrences of 'that' as a perceptual demonstrative refer to the same object. Thus, individuating guises by expression types in a natural language is insufficient.

Proponents of the strategy are likely to respond by going ever more psychological, perhaps treating the word types as mere proxies for underlying 'mental files'.[16] For example, Peter has one mental file associated with the phrase 'Paderewski the pianist' and another associated with the phrase 'Paderewski the statesman'; each time we use 'that' non-anaphorically as a perceptual demonstrative, we open a new associated temporary mental file, and so on. Such mental files are reminiscent of the individualistic Fregean senses discussed in section 4.4, and raise related questions.

There may indeed be the postulated mental files, but they are not well-suited to rehabilitating the transparency of evidence, because they face their own Frege puzzles.[17] After all, a paper file can have one label on the front and another on the back. I do not know whether I associate the English word 'dog' and the French word 'chien' with the same mental file or with two different but cross-referenced mental files, possibly with different contents. Nor is it clear to me how much my postulated mental file(s) contain. Similarly, Pat in section 4.4 may not know whether her words 'furze' and 'gorse' are associated with the same mental file or two different ones. The mere difference of words enables her to ask herself the non-trivial question 'Is furze really gorse?', irrespective of how the words are hooked up to mental files. Issues about the underlying organization of our mental filing system call for investigation by cognitive psycholinguistics; they are not settled by introspection. The problem is not with the specific metaphor of mental files, but with the more general strategy of postulating unconscious cognitive architecture in order to solve the problem of the non-transparency of evidence. Such architecture cannot do the job it was called in to do.

A further problem for the attempt to do epistemology with propositional guises rather than propositional contents is that many epistemological relations are best understood at the level of content. For example, suppose that you are trying to determine whether a

---

[16] See, for example, Recanati 2012; the application of the idea to Frege puzzles goes back to Strawson 1971, 1974, and is made in the Fregean theory of Forbes 1990.

[17] For more detailed discussion, see Goodsell 2013 and Yli-Vakkuri and Hawthorne 2018: 149-66.

tree is dead by looking at it. The hypothesis to be assessed has a primarily linguistic guise: 'This tree is dead'. The evidence by which it is to be assessed has a quite different, primarily visual format. Yet the latter may bear strongly on the former. At a first pass, we can put it in terms of a space of possible worlds: let S be the region where what you can see to be the case holds, and D be the region where the tree is dead; then most of S may be inside D (the hypothesis is very probable on your evidence), or most of S may be outside D (the hypothesis is very improbable on your evidence), or neither (the hypothesis is neither very probable nor very improbable on your evidence). That is a relation between the content (truth-conditions) of the evidence and the content (truth-conditions) of the conclusion. By contrast, if we compare the visual guise of the evidence with the linguistic guise of the hypothesis, they are quite disparate; the evidential relations cannot be properly understood at that level. We need the common currency of content.

All this suggests that there is no level at which evidence or some proxy for it is transparent. Elsewhere, I have argued for the same conclusion on more purely epistemological grounds (Williamson 2000); here, my interest is in showing that it can also be reached by consideration of Frege puzzles.

Still, for modelling purposes, we can mitigate the problem in ad hoc ways (see Williamson 2017a for a general discussion of model-building in philosophy). For instance, to see how things look from the perspective of Penny or Pat, we can treat 'furze' and 'gorse' *as if* they were semantically independent, by allowing metaphysically impossible pseudo-worlds at which they are not coextensive, but which otherwise behave normally. Such worlds may later be epistemically ruled out for the agent by subsequently acquired evidence. That is not a semantic insight, for the words are in fact synonymous, but it does help us understand how Penny and Pat are thinking. Similarly, to see how things look from the perspective of Kripke's Peter, we can work *as if* there were referentially distinct names 'Paderewski$_1$' and 'Paderewski$_2$', by allowing metaphysically impossible pseudo-worlds at which they do not co-refer, but which otherwise behave normally. Such worlds may later be epistemically ruled out for Peter by evidence he subsequently acquires. That is not a semantic insight, for the names would in fact be synonymous (on a direct reference account, since they are actually co-referential), but it does help us understand how Peter is thinking and predict how he will act. The models enable us to apply the formal apparatus of content-based evidential relations to such cases, in a way which takes account of agents' distorted perspectives on their own contents. These artificial modelling devices require nothing as elaborate as a fully developed framework of propositional guises, nor do they rehabilitate a genuine distinction between metaphysical and epistemic modality.

Sometimes, of course, as theorists we want to step back from such models and talk about their limitations. In that case, we need to drop the semantic fictions and separate the real contents from their various guises. We need to be able to track how the agent may have conflicting attitudes to the same content under different guises. But our ability to do so does *not* mean that guises are transparent after all. Quite generally, in describing specific ways in which a given model over-simplifies messy reality, we have to be opportunistic, using ad hoc means to capture specific differences. For example, in Penny's case, the ordinary English words 'furze' and 'gorse' suffice as guises, whereas in Peter's we need to manufacture new names, 'Paderewski$_1$,' and 'Paderewski$_2$.'. For agents uncertain or confused about the individuation of their own mental files, still further layers of differentiation may be needed, and so on.

If we had a one-size-fits-all framework for perspicuously characterizing all the complexities the model ignores, there would be much less need of the model in the first place. In reality, a one-size-fits-all framework would not enable us to characterize anything perspicuously, because it would be cluttered with far too many parameters. Building perspicuous models requires ruthlessly paring away any such clutter.

Once we recognize that transparency is an unattainable ideal, we cannot even use it as a constraint to narrow down what guises must be for that constraint to be satisfied, although under given conditions some things may do better than others in the role of guises, by permitting a closer approximation in relevant cases to the ideal of transparency. Unsurprisingly, on this view, real-life cognition is non-transparent all the way down.

4.10 Probability

Frege puzzles arise for subjective and epistemic probability too. Subjective probabilities (credences) are meant to be degrees of (rational) belief. For Fregeans, just as one can believe that Hesperus is Hesperus without believing that Hesperus is Phosphorus, that Hesperus is Hesperus can be subjectively more probable for one than that Hesperus is Phosphorus; that furze has yellow flowers is subjectively more probable for Penny than that gorse has yellow flowers. The same applies to epistemic probabilities, such as probabilities on one's evidence; they are in effect graded forms of epistemic modality. For Fregeans, one's evidence can entail that Hesperus is Hesperus without entailing that Hesperus is Phosphorus; that Hesperus is Hesperus can be more probable on one's evidence than that Hesperus is Phosphorus; that furze has yellow flowers is more probable on Penny's evidence than that gorse has yellow flowers.

For reasons analogous to those Kripke explains in 'A Puzzle about Belief', such Fregean claims are deeply problematic. Indeed, the traditional use of someone's betting behaviour to measure their credences is a paradigm of a language-sensitive heuristic for attitude ascription. Whether one accepts a bet depends on how it is specified to one. Penny may be willing to bet on 'Furze has yellow flowers' but unwilling to bet on 'Gorse has yellow flowers' at the same odds. In this respect, the betting criterion is like the heuristics

BDP, DP, and SDP for belief ascription. As is now widely agreed, betting behaviour is not definitional of credences, it is at best a fallible heuristic guide to them. For instance, someone may belong to a religious sect which considers all betting sinful; she would start accepting bets only if she left the sect, in which case her credences would be different, so her (absence of) betting behaviour does not measure her current credences. She is actually certain that betting is sinful, but if she were willing to accept bets, she would bet that betting is not sinful.

Anna Mahtani has recently highlighted ways in which Frege puzzles make trouble for current practice in welfare economics (2017, 2023). Standardly, a person's *prospect* under a policy is defined as their expected welfare under that policy. In welfare economics, such expectations are normally calculated in terms of notional subjective or epistemic probabilities. One policy is *ex ante* Pareto inferior to another if and only if no one has a better prospect under the first policy than under the second and someone has a better prospect under the second policy than under the first. A reasonable principle seems to be that one should not adopt a policy if it is *ex ante* Pareto inferior to an alternative policy, which is to say that one should adopt only Pareto optimal policies. But, on a Fregean view, the prospect for a particular person under a policy can depend on how that person is presented, as Mahtani shows in realistic cases, because the subjective or epistemic probabilities used to define the prospect so depend. That seems to make the standard definition of the 'prospect' for the person under the policy break down, since it specifies nothing about modes of presentation. That in turn undermines the definitions of standard welfare-economic ideas such as *ex ante* Pareto optimality. If prospects are ill-defined, so is *ex ante* Pareto optimality. Mahtani proposes complex ways of defining something reminiscent of *ex ante* Pareto optimality within the Fregean framework, by generalizing across a range of admissible assignment functions from people to modes of presentation.

The problem raised by Mahtani is *not* solved by the modelling devices sketched at the end of the previous section. They merely enable one to simulate Fregean effects artificially, from an anti-Fregean starting point: but Fregean effects are the source of Mahtani's problem. On a resolutely anti-Fregean approach, subjective or epistemic probabilities are assigned to coarse-grained propositions, such as the proposition that x has π, where x is a person and π a property, with no mediating modes of presentation, so the original definition of expected welfare would stand, and Mahtani's objection would not arise.

The trouble for the resolutely anti-Fregean approach is that it is unclear how to determine the subjective or epistemic probability of a coarse-grained proposition, given the cognitive impact of modes of presentation. Indeed, the problem is even sharper for probability than for ordinary propositional attitudes. In the case of belief, we may consistently suppose that one believes a proposition p if and only if one believes p under at least one guise; such a guideline was tacitly followed in the discussion of Frege cases above. But if we try ruling that one's subjective probability for p is v if and only if it is v under at least one guise, the result is inconsistency, since in Frege cases the rule will assign conflicting values to the agent's subjective probability for p.[18] The mathematical structure of probability as a function from propositions to numbers forbids such a rule. The same problem arises for epistemic probability too. This does not mean that resolute anti-Fregeans cannot postulate subjective or epistemic probabilities at all, just that their relation to linguistic behaviour and verbalized thought will be even more indirect than for ungraded attitudes.

However, even for Fregeans, the relation of numerical credences to linguistic behaviour and verbalized thought is already quite indirect. Without (rational) betting behaviour, it is very unclear

---

[18] For a proposed non-Fregean treatment of this problem, see Braun 2016; for a Fregean approach, see Chalmers 2011.

how to determine specific numbers. The task is no easier for epistemic probabilities. They cannot simply be *read off* the linguistic behaviour and verbalized thought. Similar difficulties face anti-Fregeans if they try to assign specific numerical credences to coarse-grained propositions relative to guises.

Further challenges arise for diachronic or inter-personal applications of subjective or epistemic probabilities. Imagine a shipwrecked sailor trying to keep track of time on a desert island. When he updates his probabilities overnight, his new probability for 'Today is my birthday' should be his old probability for 'Tomorrow will be my birthday', not his old probability for 'Today my birthday'. Similarly, imagine a young boy deferring to his mother's opinions. His probability for 'Today is my birthday' should be her probability for 'Today is your birthday', not her probability for 'Today is my birthday'. In such cases, letting the probabilities follow sentential guises, or Fregean senses that behave in a similar way, gives exactly the wrong results. The probabilities need to follow something more like objective states of affairs or events. To model properly what is going on, we need both yesterday's probabilities and today's, or both the mother's probabilities and her son's, to be defined over the same space of events. Individuating those events in terms of sentential guises or their Fregean analogues would send us in quite the wrong direction.

Invoking numerical subjective or epistemic probabilities *at all* is a matter of model-building, not of observation, though it still might be justified by an appropriate level of explanatory success. That is not to say that subjective or epistemic probabilities have no basis in reality, just to acknowledge that for theoretical purposes they vastly simplify and tidy up a complicated, messy reality in order to give us some understanding of it. On that view, the simplification built into assigning subjective or epistemic probabilities to objective events may often be the best modelling choice, because it is so unclear how to do better in diachronic and inter-personal cases. The objective approach promises to be a better match with the semantics of natural language, and its capacity to make sense of theoretically powerful welfare-economic ideas such as *ex ante* Pareto optimality as they stand can be used as another argument in its favour. Greatly complicating a good model for a small gain in descriptive detail is often a poor bargain.

Probability theory itself is a case in point. The insights it provides depend crucially on its perspicuous and tractable mathematical structure. When one tries to model extremely bounded rationality in terms of subjective or epistemic probability, it becomes very tempting to weaken the standard Kolmogorov axioms. The result tends to be only slightly closer to psychological reality, but *much* less mathematically tractable. The point is worth exploring in more detail.

A standard probability space is in effect a space of possible worlds, though the terminology is different. The probability space has an underlying set Ω, whose members are *outcomes*, conceived as mutually exclusive and jointly exhaustive; subsets of Ω, sets of outcomes, are *events*. Thus, outcomes correspond to worlds, events to intensional propositions, and Ω to W, the set of all possible worlds. Probabilities are real numbers assigned to some or all events, in conformity with the usual Kolmogorov axioms. For example, if an event X is a subset of an event Y, then the probability of Y is at least as high as the probability of X. This looks like a strong form of logical omniscience for probability (including subjective probability). At the level of propositions as sets of worlds, no proposition is more probable than a proposition it entails, and mutually entailing propositions are equiprobable (indeed, identical). The probability assignment can be extended to *sentences* by mapping them to events (propositions), and assigning to each sentence the probability of the event to which it is mapped. A natural mapping of sentences to events treats logically complex sentences in the obvious ways: a conjunction is mapped to the intersection of the events to which its conjuncts are mapped; a disjunction is mapped to the union of the events to which its disjuncts are mapped; the negation of a sentence is mapped to the complement in Ω of the event to which the unnegated sentence is mapped. Thus, a form of logical omniscience for probability also holds at the level of sentences: the conclusion of any valid argument in classical truth-functional logic is at least as probable as the conjunction of the premises.

The credences of a boundedly rational agent may violate those constraints: most obviously for computational reasons, but also because the agent may be ideologically committed to a non-classical logic. One can model such failures of logical omniscience at the level of sentences by not constraining the mapping from sentences to events in the natural ways. For example, a conjunction may be mapped to an event other than the intersection of the events to which its conjuncts are mapped; a disjunction may be mapped to an event other than the union of the events to which its disjuncts are mapped; the negation of a sentence may be mapped to an event other than the complement in Ω of the event to which the unnegated sentence is mapped. Thus, at the level of sentences, the conclusion of a valid argument in classical truth-functional logic may be less probable than the conjunction of the premises.

From the perspective of this book, ditching the structural constraints on mappings from sentences to events looks like an obvious case of overfitting. Just as in impossible worlds semantics, each complex sentence introduces another degree of freedom. The explanatory power of the probabilistic framework is thrown away, because no general non-trivial probabilistic calculations can be done at the sentential level. Of course, one may be able to do such calculations for a particular model, but that is just articulating what one has put into the model by hand. In the by now familiar way, removing or weakening the structural constraints removes or weakens one's ability to *learn* from probabilistic models.

Although these general reflections on weakening standard probability theory do not by themselves solve problems such as Mahtani's, they do suggest a relevant methodological moral, consonant with the broader themes of this book: beware of tailoring your theoretical framework to fit the limitations of individual agents.

In the case of welfare economics, that moral may have already been flouted by the definition of the key theoretical term 'prospect' in terms of credences, used to calculate the agent's 'expected welfare' under the given policy. This in turn led to the difficulty that prospects must be attached to individuals, irrespective of guise, to play their role in a well-motivated criterion of *ex ante* Pareto optimality, whereas subjectively expected welfare varies over different guises for the same individual.

An alternative is to understand 'expected welfare' and 'prospect' in terms of more *objective* probabilities. Such probabilities may simulate a better-informed perspective—possibly unoccupied—for which no relevant Frege puzzles occur, though not so well informed as to exclude the possibility that any given policy under consideration will be implemented, otherwise expectations conditional on its implementation would be ill-defined.

One might worry that objectifying prospects only postpones the problem, without solving it, for when someone comes to *apply* the objective Pareto criterion, Frege puzzles can still affect their *beliefs* about the quasi-objective prospects of individuals under policies. Fortunately, that worry is mistaken. In effect, the subjective Pareto criterion risks unintelligibility because it involved quantification into a relevantly guise-sensitive epistemic context: a quantifier over individuals (unrelativized to guises) binds the variable 'i' in the context 'the expected welfare of i under the policy', which is sensitive to the guise of i. By contrast, the quasi-objective Pareto criterion runs no such risk of unintelligibility, since it does not involve quantification into a relevantly guise-sensitive context: on the quasi-objective reading, 'the expected welfare of i under the policy' is not sensitive to the guise of i. Of course, the policymaker may still be uncertain or mistaken about whether one policy is *ex ante* Pareto inferior to another, given their ignorance about the individuals in the relevant population, but that is just ordinary uncertainty or error, to be treated in the ordinary way (whatever that is): it is not a problem specific to the Pareto criterion.

Extreme subjectivists may still complain that the quasi-objective Pareto criterion is not 'operational' because it can be unclear which policy, if any, meets it. But that complaint rests on a fanciful standard of epistemic transparency which no reasonable criterion for decision-making could meet (Williamson 2000). Even our own subjective dispositions are often unclear to us, as well as to others. In making a difficult decision, the advice 'Maximize subjective expected utility' is in practice no more useful than 'Do the best thing': it is just as unclear to the agent which choices would maximize their subjective expected utility as it is which would be doing the best thing. In particular, it is often unclear which policy, if any, meets the original subjective Pareto criterion or any given variation on it. Which option an agent chooses can depend on context, mood, or whim. Full operationality is a will-o'-the-wisp.

At first sight, the trouble Frege cases make for welfare economics is surprising. If general decision theory can take Frege puzzles in its stride, why should they be so disruptive for more specific applied inquiries in economics and politics? On second thoughts, however, it is less strange. In economic and political inquiry, theorists must engage with the structure of the world external to any one agent's perspective on it—in particular, with the presence of all the actual individuals in a given society, irrespective of the guises under which they may appear to themselves or to any other agent. A case in point is the quantification over all those individuals in the Pareto principle. As a natural by-product, structural mismatches can occur between the real world and the agent's representation of it—for instance, when the same individual appears to the agent under many different guises (representations). By contrast, when general decision theory is done in the usual subjectivist fashion, it ignores the actual structure of the world, dealing only with the structure of the given agent's representations of it (to which subjective credences and utilities are attached), so no mismatch can arise. On such a subjectivist approach, rationality is understood as a purely formal matter of internal coherence. Troubles with Frege cases manifest one limitation of such an approach.

More generally, if decision theory is to cast light on behaviour, not just on internal representations of behaviour, the actions between which the agent is supposed to be deciding must involve behaviour, at the very least bodily movements, not just internal representations of such movements. Typically, the agent's options involve the environment beyond their body, such as buying one or other item on sale. Since decision theory studies the interplay of a rational agent's probabilities, preferences, and actions, the events for which those probabilities are defined must also involve the external world: for example, probabilities conditional on a given action. In practice, and with good reason, even subjective Bayesians usually describe the contents of agents' credences in external terms: 'a credence of 75% that *it will rain this afternoon*'.

Agents who mindread each other have even more need to ascribe intentional attitudes to contents in a shared space of possibilities, as we have repeatedly seen in various ways. If I want to ascribe credences to you in trying to predict your actions, I will not make much progress by constructing a new possibility space for you incommensurable with my own possibility space and then ascribing to you credences and preferences defined on events in the new space, since I have to map those events to events in my own space to understand *what* you believe and want.[19] At most, to interpret you, I may have to expand and refine my own space in order to separate possibilities between which you distinguish (a 'fusion of horizons'). In game theory, such a shared space of possibilities is normally taken for granted, as when the structure of the game is assumed to be common knowledge amongst the players (it is

---

[19] The space also includes one impossible event, the empty set of outcomes. Of course, an agent may assign probability 0 to some possible (that is, non-empty) events.

common knowledge that player 2 can make move M). This is all just as one would expect given the shared world heuristic for knowledge ascription (section 4.8).

When a game theorist comes to study the game, the shared world heuristic still operates. The theorist works with a possibility space that incorporates the players' own possibility spaces. If the game is just hypothetical, as often in game theory, the theorist incorporates the players' possibility spaces hypothetically.

None of this means that agents cannot in practice differ from each other, and from reality, in their possibility spaces. Of course they can, and do. But the best case for understanding involves a shared possibility space, deviations from which must be handled in more or less opportunistic ways.

For a rough analogy, imagine a formal dance. Mostly, what the dancers do can be explained in terms of the rules of the dance. But when the line the dancers form is not straight, or a clumsy dancer trips and falls, or the dance is interrupted by a fire alarm, the rules do not explain what has happened. A different sort of explanation is needed, even though a general intention to deviate as little as possible from the rules may still guide the dancers' reactions. Should we conclude that the rules the dancers are *really* following are more general, and specify what to do in such eventualities? That sounds like a case of being vicariously wise after the event. The rules are just the original ones, and make no pretence of covering such mishaps and interruptions. The latter should be understood as deviations from the simple rules, not as exemplifications of more complicated rules.

Similarly, with Mahtani's puzzle case in welfare economics, we do best to understand expected welfare and Pareto optimality in terms of probability assignments to coarse-grained propositions, and leave Frege puzzles to be dealt with ad hoc when they arise, as epistemic problems for applying the criterion. In particular, we should not think of guise-insensitive credences as somehow derivative from guise-sensitive credences. Instead, we should regard guise-sensitive credences as ad hoc variations on guise-insensitive credences. After all, as already seen (sections 4.4–5), Frege puzzles can arise even when the underlying content is the same, so guise-sensitivity introduces an extra dimension.

Confusingly, we can often be more precise about guise-sensitive credences than about guise-insensitive ones. For example, we may determine on the basis of betting behaviour that someone has an 80% credence in a proposition *p* under the guise of the sentence 'George Eliot wrote *Middlemarch*' and only a 5% credence in *p* under the guise of the sentence 'Mary Ann Evans wrote *Middlemarch*', while being merely confused as to their guise-independent credence in *p*. But such cognitive asymmetries make a poor guide to explanatory priority. Another analogy: it may be very clear that an action was unfair according to Janet and fair according to John, yet very unclear whether the action *was* fair; nevertheless, such examples do not show that what is fair or unfair is somehow derivative from what people think is fair or unfair. Instead, the distinction between being *thought* fair and being *thought* unfair is derivative from the distinction between *being* fair and *being* unfair. Similarly, guise-relative distinctions may be derivative from guise-independent distinctions.

Even for credences, the asymmetry can run in the opposite direction to that with 'George Eliot' and 'Mary Ann Evans': it may be very clear that a bird knows and has high credence roughly that its nest is in that tree, yet very unclear under what guise it has the knowledge.

Such cognitive asymmetries are natural by-products of our reliance on heuristics in ascribing intentional states. For example, the use of betting behaviour to measure credence is a language-dependent heuristic, mediated by the bettor's understanding of the sentences the bookie uses to state the terms of the bet, so its results are naturally sensitive to those sentential guises. By contrast, when we judge that the bird knows and has high credence that its nest is in that tree, we do so to explain the bird's non-linguistic behaviour.

Our heuristic or method is not mediated by the bird's understanding of a sentence, and no alternative guise is salient. We may guess that the bird has the knowledge and credence under some visual guise or other, but our guess is vague and unspecific. What *is* a guise for the content of a non-linguistic creature's background intentional state? Whatever the guise, an ascriber's awareness or unawareness of the state will be sensitive to the heuristic used (if any) in ascribing the state, not just to the nature of the specific knowledge or credence itself.

4.11 Epistemic and doxastic logic

The challenges raised by guise-sensitivity for epistemic and subjective probability have simpler analogues for epistemic and doxastic logic, as applications of possible worlds semantics, in a tradition going back to Hintikka (1962). Both traditions use models based on the mathematical framework of state spaces (section 4.10). Both do so in ways that naturally validate strong forms of logical omniscience. That is the main source of their computational and explanatory power, but also of their apparent lack of psychological reality. Yet both traditions have played a significant role as frameworks for formal inquiry in social sciences. For example, subjective Bayesian probabilistic approaches to welfare economics and decision theory are widespread, while epistemic logic provides the natural framework for articulating standard game-theoretic assumptions of agents' common knowledge of their rationality and the structure of the game.

For both epistemic logic and epistemic probability, quantification into epistemic contexts is a crucial test case. We have already seen its key role for epistemic probability in welfare economics. For epistemic logic, it is needed to formalize statements such as 'I don't know what anyone else prefers', when the speaker quantifies over the members of a large anonymous crowd.

More generally, in the standard framework of epistemic logic, common knowledge is implicitly treated as guise-independent. When a state of affairs is assumed to be common knowledge for a group of agents, typically no account is taken of differences between them in their guises for that state. Taking account of such diversity would undermine the usual game-theoretic arguments that rely on those assumptions; likewise for applications of doxastic logic to common belief. If one is serious about guises, one will not treat them as uniform across agents.

To see the problem from another angle, recall that if a proposition p entails a proposition q in a model of epistemic or doxastic logic, in the sense that every world in p is also in q, then any agent who knows p also knows q, and any agent who believes p also believes q.[20] Call two worlds w_1 and w_2 *indiscriminable* for an agent S just

---

[20] In the paragraph, knowledge, belief, and indiscriminability are all ascribed with respect to a fixed world in a fixed model. In standard models for epistemic logic, an agent knows a proposition p at a world w if and only if every world epistemically accessible for the agent from w is in p. Consequently, if a set of propositions X entails a proposition p (every world in the intersection of the members of X is in p), an agent who knows each member of X at w automatically also knows p at w: a strong form of logical omniscience, *multi-premise closure* (the argument in the text uses only the special case where X is a singleton set, *single-premise closure*). Neither multi-premise closure nor single-premise closure follows from the treatment of propositions as sets of worlds alone; they depend on the specific way in which knowledge is characterized in terms of accessibility. The model's constituents include a binary relation between worlds for each agent, informally understood as epistemic accessibility, in the sense that a world x is epistemically accessible from the world w just in case whatever the agent knows at w is true at x (for all the agent knows at w, they are at x). Although epistemic accessibility is informally understood in terms of knowledge, formally it is the other way round, with knowledge defined in terms of epistemic accessibility: think of the epistemic accessibility relations as encoding epistemology in the model, and the formal definition of knowledge as decoding it. Standard models for doxastic logic work analogously, with doxastic accessibility relations informally understood in terms of the agent's belief instead of knowledge. The main formal difference is that epistemic accessibility is required to be reflexive (every world has epistemic access to itself), corresponding to the factiveness of knowledge: an agent knows p at w only if w is in p (p is true at w). By contrast, doxastic accessibility is not required to be reflexive, since some beliefs are false, though it may be required to be serial (every world has doxastic access to some world), corresponding to the postulated consistency of (rational) belief: an agent who believes p at w does not also believe ¬p at w. Of course, guises make trouble for the consistency condition for rational belief: a logically impeccable agent may accept both 'Hesperus is inhabited' and 'Phosphorus is uninhabited'. By contrast, guises make no trouble for the factiveness condition for knowledge, which also entails the consistency condition for knowledge.

in case for every proposition p for which S has a guise, w_1 is in p if and only if w_2 is in p (S has no way of distinguishing between w_1 and w_2). Suppose that two worlds w_1 and w_2 are indeed indiscriminable for a given agent S, and that under some guise S knows some q that excludes w_1 (w_1 is not in q). Since w_1 and w_2 are indiscriminable for S, and S has a guise for q, w_2 is also not in q. But S has no guise for the proposition $q \cup \{w_1\}$, since it contains w_1 but not w_2. However, since q entails $q \cup \{w_1\}$, and S knows q, S also knows $q \cup \{w_1\}$, by standard epistemic logic. Thus, S knows something for which S has no guise. Similarly, using standard doxastic logic, one can set up cases where S believes something for which S has no guise. In both the epistemic and the doxastic case, the required assumptions are realistic. But cases of guiseless knowledge or belief undermine the theoretical role guises were introduced to play.

Could we ban such cases by stipulating that the worlds in the model must be individuated only as finely as the relevant agent S can discriminate? The trouble is that, for purposes of game theory and other applications of epistemic and doxastic logic to the social sciences, we need *multi-agent* models. Often, in such models, some agent other than S *will* discriminate between w_1 and w_2, so the model must separate them. To model common knowledge or common belief, we need a common space of possibilities.

In principle, we can expand the model by building in guises for each agent, and specifically excluding guiseless knowledge and belief. In practice, however, doing so may be a bad bargain, buying a little more faithfulness to the phenomena at the price of enormous complication, perhaps to the point of mathematical intractability, or more likely forcing theorists to put into the model by hand whatever they hope to get out of it: yet another case of overfitting.

For many purposes, assuming logical omniscience and ignoring guises is a legitimate modelling choice. It can be compared to the use of differential equations to model population-sized processes over time, such as the recurrent rise and fall of interacting predator and prey populations, or the spread of a pandemic. Differential equations presuppose differentiable functions, which are continuous, 'smooth'. But the biological processes under study involve populations of many discrete animals and so are not really continuous in the way presupposed: answers to the question 'how many?' are natural numbers, not arbitrary real numbers. Of course, one can try to model the process at the level of individual animals, but that involves throwing away the mathematical power of the differential equations and using different methods and different assumptions instead: even if feasible, that may not provide the same global overview or the same insights.

Similarly, throwing away the mathematical power of epistemic and doxastic logic involves using different methods and different assumptions instead: again, even if feasible, it may not provide the same global overview or the same insights. Obviously, if one's aim is to study ways in which real-life agents violate the strong simplifications of epistemic logic, one cannot make those very assumptions: doing so would stipulate away one's subject matter. But if one's aim is instead to study different cognitive effects, such as perceptual limitations, then stipulating away other cognitive limitations may be a good strategy for isolating the effects under study by filtering out interference and noise.

4.12 Drawing the threads together

To see better how the pieces in this chapter fit together, we can work through an example of action explanation, building up a series of increasingly complex explanations by bringing in more pieces as we go on.

We start from the external world. H is a human, D a dog. Unusually, H has been keeping out of the garden. Someone asks: 'Why is H keeping out of the garden?' Here is an initial answer:

First Pass   D has rabies.
                 D is in the garden.

In many circumstances, First Pass would be a quite adequate explanation, by normal conversational standards. Obviously, its two conjuncts 'D has rabies' and 'D is in the garden' jointly fall well short of deductively *entailing* the explanandum 'H is keeping out of the garden', but explanations in both natural science and ordinary life are not normally required to entail the explanandum deductively. Normally, a looser connection will suffice: for example, one that holds 'for the most part', or 'other things being equal', or 'by default'. In the present case, the two conjuncts of First Pass together provide a good reason for keeping out of the garden.

Of course, the questioner may grant the two conjuncts but not know whether, if so, H would be aware of those facts. Then a more informative explanation is needed, such as:

Second Pass   H knows that D has rabies.
                H knows that D is in the garden.

In effect, First Pass relied on the open world heuristic. When that default is inhibited, we fall back on the more complex Second Pass. In such cases, people sometimes say that the knowledge ascription is 'understood'—for example, that First Pass is 'elliptical' for Second Pass. But such ad hoc metalinguistic manoeuvres are unwarranted. In First Pass, 'D has rabies' means what it says; 'H knows that' is not an unvoiced constituent. It is just that, unless the open world heuristic is inhibited, it allows us to move from First Pass to Second Pass, if we so wish.

A less informative alternative to Second Pass has 'thinks' or 'believes' in place of 'knows', for one occurrence or both. But when the open world heuristic is uninhibited, there is no need to throw away the extra information in Second Pass. We can leave the retreat from knowing to thinking for when needed, if H's alleged knowledge is cast into serious doubt. In any case, whether the attitude verb in Second Pass is 'know', 'think', or 'believe', the content to which the agent is said to have the attitude still links back to First Pass, and so to the external world, on pain of losing touch with the external action to be explained: keeping out of the garden.

Philosophers may notice that not even Second Pass excludes the possibility that it is a Frege case. 'D' is just our term for the dog; for all Second Pass says, H is in no position to use 'D' in expressing the knowledge attributed to them. For example, H might know that D has rabies only under the guise of the sentence 'That dog has rabies', where 'that dog' is a memory demonstrative—last week someone pointed out D to H as a rabid dog—while H knows that D is in the garden only under the guise of the sentence 'This dog is in the garden', where 'this dog' is a current perceptual demonstrative. The terms 'this dog' and 'that dog' here are anaphorically unrelated; H might fail to notice that it is the same dog again, and so fail to put the two pieces of knowledge together in the way required. When the open world heuristic is uninhibited, it allows the co-reference to be taken for granted, but of course something may inhibit it. In that case, if H does recognize the dog in the garden as 'that dog with rabies', then a still more informative explanation is needed, such as:

Third Pass   H knows that D has rabies under the guise 'This dog has rabies'.
H knows that D is in the garden under the guise 'This dog is in the garden'.

Here both occurrences of 'this dog' are associated with the very same state of H's visual-perceptual attention to D, and Third Pass is not a Frege case.

Just as First Pass is not elliptical for Second Pass, so Second Pass is not elliptical for Third Pass, or for any other explanation that invokes guises. Just as Second Pass invokes a new level of complexity absent from First Pass—a mental state with content—so Third Pass invokes a new level of complexity absent from Second Pass—the guise of the mental state's content. Expanding the theoretical framework with those new levels of complexity may be warranted by the need to explain subtler phenomena, but that does not mean that the extra complexity was there in the framework all along, nor even that it should have been, otherwise we should have to start with an infinitely complicated theoretical apparatus.

Even the two conjuncts of Third Pass jointly fall short of deductively entailing the explanandum, 'H is keeping out of the garden'. For example, H may not know how deadly rabies is, or H may have a death wish. But even once we have plugged such holes by attributing suitable intentional states, and specifying appropriate guises for their contents as in Third Pass, the result will *still* fall short of deductively entailing the explanandum. For H, being human, may still fail to put two and two together. Such a failure does not imply a deeply divided mind; a momentary lapse in attention or memory can have the same effect. The stereotype of the absent-minded professor is a reminder that not even a leading expert on rationality is immune to such effects. The finest brain can suffer a quantum-mechanical blip. Expanding the explanation with further conjuncts to rule out such eventualities may not yield much further insight into the action to be explained.

At least in this case, the more complex explanations do not *falsify* the simpler ones: quite the opposite. The two conjuncts of Second Pass entail the respective conjuncts of First Pass, the two conjuncts of Third Pass at least come close to entailing the respective conjuncts of Second Pass, and so on for the further elaborations. What the more complex explanations make salient are ways in which the simpler ones fall short of being strictly sufficient for the explanandum. They tighten the connection, but still without providing strict sufficiency.

Formal frameworks such as epistemic and subjective Bayesian probability theory, epistemic and doxastic logic, decision theory and game theory articulate general principles to tighten the connection further, such as various forms of logical omniscience. Applied to real agents rather than idealized rational ones, those principles are typically false: simplifying assumptions conducive to illuminating models in the scientific sense.

Heuristics for mindreading make a different sort of bridge between explanans and explanandum. They are more likely than formal models to generate inconsistency, as Kripke's puzzle about belief illustrates. That is a cost they pay for their greater flexibility and (for some of them) their sensitivity to linguistic form. Their function is not to capture universal laws, not even of an idealized type, but to act as practical problem-solvers. In good cases, they still provide local knowledge, though not as a corollary of some global principle.

Both the formal models and natural language semantics work at the level of Second Pass, using state spaces. In a historic act of pattern recognition, they have located an efficient trade-off between generality of understanding and fidelity to particular cases. The compromise is not perfectly stable, for the need to make sense of a particular case continually drags us to Third Pass or even further. But there is no equally efficient alternative trade-off in that direction, only hybrid fixes of limited though real utility—as the artificiality of the formulations in Third Pass hints. Still less should we expect to find a purely internal explanation at the limit of the endless series of passes, the El Dorado of internalism. They do not even tend in that direction, and each is intelligible only in relation to its predecessor. For mindreading heuristics, *and* the semantics of natural language, *and* theoretically sophisticated action explanations, the starting-point is still First Pass, firmly rooted in the shared external world.

5
Intensional Metametaphysics

5.1 Semantic challenges to metaphysics

This final chapter takes the approach developed in previous chapters, applying it to semantic arguments against the possibility of substantive metaphysics. Addressing these arguments will provide an opportunity to test and develop the present approach.[1]

Of all branches of philosophy, metaphysics has probably attracted the most opprobrium. It is the one most easily represented as a lazy, dogmatic, obsolete rival of natural science. It is also the most discursively abstract branch. Predictably, it is the one most often accused of being *nonsense*.[2]

When meaning is understood in epistemic terms, the charge of meaninglessness turns into the charge that metaphysics is epistemically inadequate: it lacks proper methods for achieving knowledge, or even reasonable belief, in its domain. The logical positivists gave a salient version of such a critique, wielding their verification principle as a blunt instrument. Since putative truths of metaphysics are neither analytic nor empirically verifiable, they are meaningless by logical empiricist standards. Of course, such an accusation is largely bluff without an adequate verificationist theory of meaning

---

[1] This chapter is adapted from 'Metametaphysics and semantics', *Metaphilosophy*, 53 (2022): 162–75 (Williamson 2023a). I am grateful to participants in the 2021 'New Directions in Metaphilosophy' conference at the University of Kent and a Lugano Philosophy Colloquium (both virtual), to Daniel Kodsi and Luis Rosa (in correspondence), and to two anonymous referees for *Metaphilosophy* in addition to those for this volume for helpful comments on earlier versions of this material.

[2] I use the term 'metaphysics' as it is standardly used in contemporary philosophy, with a standard view of what counts as metaphysics. The arguments of this chapter are robust to minor variations in that respect.

in the background, and the logical positivists made very little progress towards developing such a theory. Nevertheless, the logical empiricist dichotomy of all cognition into 'empirical' and 'conceptual' aspects continues to have its adherents: for example, the work of Amie Thomasson (2015, 2020) is in the tradition of Rudolf Carnap (1950), and more distantly of David Hume's dichotomy of 'relations of ideas' and 'matters of fact', though she has more interest than Carnap in non-scientific language. Between the conceptual and the empirical, no room seems left for substantive unconfused metaphysical theorizing.

Unfortunately, or perhaps fortunately, the terms 'conceptual' and 'empirical', like 'analytic' and 'synthetic', are far more problematic than they first appear. There is a crude stereotype of the conceptual, and a crude stereotype of the empirical, but the assumptions built into those stereotypes are unclear. What is clear is that both stereotypes, separately and together, are utterly inadequate for making sense of logic and mathematics, let alone of metaphysics.

For example, dialetheist logicians such as Graham Priest assert, 'The Russell set is and is not a member of itself', because they take it to be a theorem of the best theory of logic and mathematics, on broadly abductive grounds—simplicity, strength, fit with evidence, and so on. In response, classical logicians like me reject what dialetheists say as just false. We take the best theory of logic and mathematics to be classical, with no contradictions as theorems, again on broadly abductive grounds—simplicity, strength, fit with evidence, and so on. In these respects, it is just like a highly theoretical dispute in natural science. On both sides are competent speakers of English (or whatever natural language the dispute is being conducted in), using words in their current senses in the public language, and meaning what they say. In particular, 'The Russell set is and is not a member of itself' is a well-formed, meaningful sentence of English; it violates no rule of English grammar (just as $0 = 1 \wedge 0 \neq 1$ is a well-formed, meaningful sentence of a formal language for Peano arithmetic). Neither side is implicitly or explicitly proposing to change the meaning of 'and' or 'not' or any other word or construction of the language, for each side takes itself to have stated its view correctly without need of linguistic reform. Although each side may use an artificial formal language to develop its approach in more detail and with more rigour, still the underlying disagreement can be and is expressed in the shared natural language. Clearly, the dispute does not fit the stereotype of the empirical: there is no prospect of resolving it by experiment, observation, or measurement. Equally clearly, the dispute does not fit the stereotype of the conceptual: there is no prospect of resolving it by conceptual clarification either. Logicians are very familiar with the possibility that an apparent disagreement may not be what it seems, because the two sides are using the same symbols with different senses. It is insulting to suggest that, had the two sides been talking past each other, or just disputing about what to mean by the symbols, they would not have worked that out for themselves. The only charitable interpretation of the dispute, as a conversation between two parties, is as a genuine non-metalinguistic disagreement, which is how the participants treat it. More generally, there is no prospect of resolving the dispute between classical and dialetheist logicians by a *combination* of stereotypically empirical and stereotypically conceptual methods: conceptual clarification *and* experiment, observation, or measurement.

Of course, those who rely on the dichotomy of the empirical and the conceptual will insist that their understanding of it goes much deeper than the usual stereotypes. However, in my experience, their attempts to clarify the dichotomy always make it vulnerable to counterexamples by their own standards, from which it can be defended only by a retreat to the same old obscurity, perhaps disguised by new terminology. In contemporary philosophy, the contrast between 'empirical' and 'conceptual' serves—in effect, though not in intention—as an instrument of obscurantism and is best avoided. I have discussed these issues at length elsewhere and so will spare the reader the gory details here (Williamson 2007, 2021a, forthcoming-c).

This chapter addresses a different but related challenge to metaphysics. This challenge is more urgent, because its starting point is less hostile. The new challenge is semantic, like the logical empiricist critique, but unlike the latter it does not depend on an epistemic conception of semantics. Instead, one might even say, it depends on a *metaphysical* conception of semantics. But that does not make the new challenge self-defeating. For if metaphysics is already in tension with a metaphysics-friendly approach to semantics, that is bad news for metaphysics.

Uncompromising metaphysics, both ancient and modern, aspires to discover the necessary nature and structure of reality. Its primary interest is in the world, not in our thought or talk about the world—of course, our thought and talk are part of the world, but (except under extreme forms of idealism) only a very small part. Thus, a worldly approach to semantics, on which the semantic value of a linguistic expression in a context is a worldly item, looks like a good fit with metaphysics. For example, such a theory may identify the semantic value of a declarative sentence in a context with a proposition, understood as the set of possible worlds at which the sentence is true, or as a complex of the objects, properties, and relations the sentence is about (in both cases, relative to that context). In brief, such semantics correlates metaphysicians' words with the very metaphysical entities they wish to discuss (if there are such entities). That suggests a fully cooperative attitude of semantics to metaphysics. Any tension between the two is therefore all the more disturbing—as though semantics, with the best will in the world, still leaves no room for metaphysics.

The challenge to metaphysics arises in an especially stark form within just the kind of intensional framework that is mainstream in contemporary formal semantics as a branch of linguistics, and was defended in chapters 3 and 4, as section 5.2 explains.

5.2 The coarse-grained challenge to metaphysics

We first consider the challenge in the simplest framework of intensional semantics, where the only parameter of semantic evaluation is for worlds. Each sentence expresses a proposition, a total function from worlds to truth-values (truth or falsity). Thus, 'There is a god' expresses the proposition that there is a god, the function mapping each world in which there is a god to truth and each world in which there is no god to falsity.

In line with the arguments of chapter 3, semantic evaluation is compositional in the usual way. Thus, 'Not A' is true at a world w if and only if A is not true at w, 'A and B' is true at w if and only if A is true at w and B is true at w, and so on. The semantics has no truck with 'impossible worlds' in the sense of chapter 3.3. This semantic orthodoxy only makes the relevant challenge to metaphysics harder to avoid, and so for our purposes it is dialectically harmless. Some elaborations and modifications of the intensional framework will later be considered, consistent with semantic compositionality, but they turn out not to solve the problem for metaphysics.

Any standard intensional model determines a *distinguished modality*, by the condition that, for any sentence A of the object-language, 'Necessarily A' is true at a world w if and only if A is true at every world, while 'Possibly A' is true at w if and only if A is true at some world. For present purposes, the object-language is interpreted—it has an intended interpretation—so there is an intended intensional model, and a corresponding intended distinguished modality. From now on, the words 'possible' and 'necessary' will be used for that modality. In that sense, the worlds in the intended framework are all and only the *possible* worlds. Given the compositional semantics and a classical metalogic, the logical connectives behave classically at each world, so any truth of classical propositional logic is true at every world. Consequently, every theorem of the well-known modal system S5 is true at every world on this interpretation. In particular, it validates the thesis that whatever is necessary is true (the T axiom), and the more distinctive theses that whatever is necessary is necessarily necessary (the S4 axiom) and whatever is possible is necessarily possible (the S5 axiom): matters of necessity or possibility are not themselves contingent.

Since our interest is in metaphysically oriented semantic theories, we understand this distinguished modality as broadly objective rather than merely epistemic. Indeed, we may conceive it as the broadest kind of objective possibility, since it excludes no world in the model. An attractive hypothesis is that this maximal objective modality is just what is usually called 'metaphysical modality' (Williamson 2016a). But that is controversial. For example, the S4 and S5 axioms have both been denied for metaphysical modality (Salmón 1989), and the S5 axiom has been denied for the broadest modality (Bacon 2018, but see Goodsell and Yli-Vakkuri in preparation). A further complication is that, in more perspicuous frameworks for modality, worlds may be less basic than the distinction between possibility and impossibility itself, perhaps in the setting of higher-order logic (Williamson 2013a), where impossibility may even be reduced to identity with a contradiction (Bacon 2018). Still, such alternatives are compatible with versions of intensional semantics. They all face the challenge to be discussed. We can ignore the differences between them.

As an immediate corollary of this intensional approach, already noted, propositions are coarse-grained. Necessarily equivalent propositions are identical: they output the same truth-value for any given world as input, and so are the same function. In particular, there is only one necessary proposition and only one impossible proposition. If you know one necessary truth, you know them all.

For the sake of an example, read 'god' in a strong sense, on which being a god is a necessary property: whatever has it in a possible world has it in any other possible world too (it may also entail other standard attributes, such as omniscience, omnipotence, omnipresence, omnibenevolence, and eternity; for present purposes we omit ineffability, since it might cause distinctively semantic problems). So, it is either necessary or impossible that there is a god. If it is necessary, the proposition that there is a god is just the proposition that all cats are cats. If it is impossible, the proposition that there is a god is just the proposition that some cats are not cats. So, on this view, when atheists argue with theists, the two propositions in dispute are that all cats are cats and that some cats are not cats, one way round or the other. Isn't such a dispute a waste of time? The moral seems to be: insofar as metaphysics concerns the non-contingent, intensionalism *trivializes* metaphysics.

Unlike empiricist and logical positivist critiques of metaphysics, the argument from intensionalism has no epistemological premises, and its conclusion is not distinctively epistemological; the argument is just semantic. Nevertheless, it reaches a similar conclusion: there is nothing non-trivial for metaphysical claims to mean. Such arguments have had significant influence. They can be traced back to Wittgenstein's *Tractatus Logico-Philosophicus*, where ultimately every declarative sentence is to be analysed as a truth-function of atomic sentences expressing simple, mutually independent states of affairs. If it is true on every assignment of truth-values to those atomic sentences, it is merely tautologous. If it is false on every assignment, it is merely contradictory. If it is true on some assignments and false on others, it is merely contingent. This taxonomy leaves nowhere for metaphysics to hide.

A conception of impossibilities as all trivially false may explain the claim, widespread even amongst contemporary Wittgensteinians, that it is meaningless to assert an impossibility. In contemporary philosophy, Robert Stalnaker has been a leader in pressing the radical consequences of intensionalism, though with a scaffolding of possible worlds rather than simple, mutually independent states of affairs (1984, 1999).³ Such intensionalist sympathies can also be found in the works of David Lewis (1970, 1996) and, in less committed form, Saul Kripke (1979), despite their major contributions to metaphysics. More recently, Eli Hirsch (2021) has extended his nuanced semantic critique of (some) metaphysics by connecting it with the kinds of coarse-grained, worldly, semantics, including intensionalism, which at first sight look friendly to out-and-out metaphysics.

Of course, intensionalist trivialization threatens more than metaphysics. It concerns any inquiry into the non-contingent. Logic and mathematics are salient examples. They can hardly be dismissed as trivial. If the proof of Fermat's Last Theorem was just a proof that all cats are cats, why did it take centuries to find? Curiously, many philosophers find less difficulty in convincing themselves that logic and mathematics are somehow purely formal, not really concerned with *how the world is*, so not in need of non-trivial content. By contrast, traditional metaphysics stubbornly enquires into the necessary nature of the world; for it, the threat that only triviality that way lies is existential. Indeed, the question 'Is there a god?' is not easily understood as purely formal.

In what follows, the focus will be on metaphysics, not logic and mathematics as such, but the conclusions will apply to the latter too, providing a way for them to be as worldly as metaphysics, with which they indeed overlap (Williamson 2013a).

5.3 Generalizing the problem

How robust are the trivializing consequences of intensionalism? Do they survive motivated generalizations of the intensional framework?

---

[3] For an exchange on the Wittgensteinian claim about impossibility, see Marconi 2011 and Williamson 2011c. For an exchange on Stalnaker's view see Stalnaker 2011 and Williamson 2011b. For a view that combines ideas from Wittgenstein and Stalnaker, see Rayo 2013.

First indications offer metaphysics little hope. For instance, many versions of intensional semantics add a parameter for *times* to that for *worlds* in semantic evaluation, to handle tense. Then sentences express the same content if and only if they have the same truth-value at every world-time pair. But that makes no significant difference to the problem. On the operative reading of the word 'god', we may assume, the property of being a god is eternal as well as necessary: something is a god at a world and time if and only if it is a god at *every* world and time. Hence either there is a god at every world and time or there is a god at no world and time. So, as before, 'There is a god' has the same content as either 'All cats are cats' or 'Some cats are not cats'.

A more far-reaching modification of the framework is to work with *possible situations* instead of *possible worlds*, to handle the locality of much discourse (for instance, Elbourne 2005). Situations are something like world-fragments. A sentence is neither true nor false in situations which include too little to determine its truth-value. Presumably, then, sentences express the same content if and only if they have the same truth-value (if any) in every situation. But that still makes no crucial difference to the problem. For on the operative reading of the word 'god', we may assume, something is a god in a situation if and only if it is a god in *every* situation (a form of necessary omnipresence). Hence either there is a god in every situation or there is a god in no situation. If a situation s has a god in it, 'There is a god' is true in s. If s has no god in it, there must be no god, so 'There is a god' is false in s. Thus if 'All cats are cats' is true and 'Some cats are not cats' false in every situation, 'There is a god' still has the same content as either 'All cats are cats' or 'Some cats are not cats'. There is a slight complication: some versions of situation semantics may determine no truth-value for those 'cat' sentences in situations which exclude some cats. By contrast, 'There is a god' is true or false in such situations, as just explained. In that case, 'There is a god' *differs* in content from both 'All cats are cats' and 'Some cats are not cats'. But this technicality will not solve the problem. For we can introduce a logically constant sentence $\bot$ for absurdity, governed by the stipulation that $\bot$ is false, and so its negation $\neg\bot$ true, in each situation. Then 'There is a god' has the same content as either the trivially false $\bot$ or the trivially true $\neg\bot$.

These radical problems for intensional metaphysics may tempt metaphysicians to go hyperintensional. Doing so would be bad news for metaphysics, given the methodological problems discussed in chapter 3. For now, we can temporarily bracket those problems, despite their gravity, in order to see more directly how ineffective is the resort to hyperintensionality as a response to the threat of semantic trivialization.

Ignoring the warnings of chapter 3.3, one form of hyperintensional metaphysics adds impossible worlds to the semantics, understood in an ontologically harmless way as arbitrary sets of sentences of the object language. A sentence is evaluated as true at such a world if and only if it is a member of that world. To individuate content more finely in this framework, we can stipulate that sentences express the same content if and only if they are true at the same worlds, possible and impossible. Then 'There is a god' differs in content from any other sentence S, for the simple reason that 'There is a god' is true at the world {'There is a god'}, while S is not true at that world. But this strategy trivializes sameness of content by reducing it to sameness of sentence. For even if the words 'god' and 'deity' are *synonyms* by normal standards, the sentences 'There is a god' and 'There is a deity' still count as differing in content, for the reason just given (let S = 'There is a deity'). No such verbal manoeuvre will rescue the ambitions of traditional metaphysics. Of course, impossible worlds theorists may impose semantic constraints on their preferred model, for instance one requiring it to treat 'god' and 'deity' interchangeably, but that is just another case of the now familiar move of putting the desired outputs of the model into it by hand. Such ad hoc manoeuvres go nowhere towards explaining *how* metaphysical statements could express non-trivial necessary truths.

Ignoring the warnings of chapter 3.5, a more explanatory-looking move is to abandon the identification of sentential contents with (perhaps partial) functions from circumstances of evaluation to truth-values, and adopt a more structured conception instead. In particular, one might identify the content of a declarative sentence with a Russellian proposition, a complex built out of the objects, properties, and relations the sentence is about, and structured according to the structure of the sentence. For example, the proposition that there is a god might be something like <∃, divinity>, the ordered pair of the second-order property ∃ of being instantiated and the first-order property divinity, of being a god. Then a proposition p is the proposition that there is a god only if p has divinity as a constituent.

An immediate concern is that the individuation of Russellian propositions is itself hostage to the individuation of properties and relations. In particular, suppose that properties are identical if and only if they are necessarily coextensive. Then if it is in fact impossible to be a god, the property of being a god is necessarily coextensive, and so identical, with the property of being a round square; thus, the proposition <∃, divinity> is just the proposition <∃, round-squarehood>, and the threat of trivialization returns. So far, this is just an isolated case; there is no such elementary argument on the alternative hypothesis that it is possible to be a god.

However, Russellian propositions in metaphysics face a much more general threat of trivialization. We keep 'There is a god' as our sample sentence of metaphysics, but without exploiting its specific details. We introduce a new singular term 'D' by stipulating thus:

If there is a god, 'D' names 1.
If there is no god, 'D' names 0.

The stipulation is to be understood as belonging to the metasemantics of 'D', not to its semantics, in Kripkean terms, to *fix the reference* of 'D', not to *give its meaning* (Kripke 1980). Thus 'D' is not to be understood as abbreviating a definite description like 'the number *n* such that either there is a god and *n* = 1 or there is no god and *n* = 0'. Rather, 'D' is simply a name of a natural number; the stipulation specifies which number. Consequently, the Russellian proposition semantically expressed by the equation 'D = 1' has none of the complex structure of the definite description, but is simply something like <identity, <D, 1>>. Obviously, the sentences 'There is a god' and 'There is no god' have the same truth-values as the equations 'D = 1' and 'D = 0', respectively. If we want to argue about whether there is a god, we can argue about whether D = 1; it makes no dialectical difference.

Of course, whichever side is wrong about the metaphysics also has a false belief about the reference of 'D', given that they have been introduced to the name by the stipulation above. If there is a god, atheists falsely believe that 'D' names 0; if there is no god, theists falsely believe that 'D' names 1. But that does not mean that one side or the other *misunderstands* the name 'D'. It is like the name 'Jack the Ripper', introduced by the description 'whoever committed the grisly Whitechapel murders'. Some people may still falsely believe the wild theory that Edward VII committed the grisly Whitechapel murders, so that Jack the Ripper was Edward VII; familiar with the name 'Jack the Ripper' in the usual way, they falsely believe that it names Edward VII, but they do not thereby *misunderstand* the name 'Jack the Ripper'.[4]

On the Russellian view, if there is a god, the sentence 'D = 1' expresses the same proposition as the trivially true sentence '1 = 1'; if there is no god, the sentence 'D = 0' expresses the same proposition as the trivially true sentence '0 = 0'. On intensionalism, the corresponding necessary propositions are identical too.

---

[4] For relevant discussion of what counts as understanding, see Williamson 2007: 97–8 and the exchange between Stalnaker 2011 and Williamson 2011b. More generally, the discussion of analyticity in Williamson 2007 and 2021a support the arguments of this section.

The threat of trivialization has returned in completely general form. One could substitute any other sentence for 'There is a god' in the preceding argument. Nothing here depends even on the non-contingency of 'There is a god'. The argument works in the same way if one substitutes 'There is intelligent life in other galaxies' for 'There is a god':

If there is intelligent life in other galaxies, 'G' names 1.
If there is no intelligent life in other galaxies, 'G' names 0.

Everything proceeds as with 'D'. In particular, since 'G' is a proper name, it is a rigid designator, even though it is contingent whether there is intelligent life in other galaxies. Thus, if there is intelligent life in other galaxies, we use 'G' to designate 1 even with respect to counterfactual possibilities in which there is no intelligent life in other galaxies. Equally, if there is no intelligent life in other galaxies, we use 'G' to designate 0 even with respect to counterfactual possibilities in which there is intelligent life in other galaxies. Thus, we are in an epistemic position to assert both 'There is intelligent life in other galaxies if and only if G = 1' and 'Either there could have been no intelligent life on other planets while G was 1 or there could have been intelligent life on other planets while G was 0'. The biconditional is similar to proposed examples of contingent a priori truths (Kripke 1980). If we want to argue about whether there is intelligent life in other galaxies, we can argue about whether G = 1; it makes no dialectical difference. If there is intelligent life in other galaxies, the sentence 'G = 1' expresses the same Russellian proposition as the trivially true sentence '1 = 1'. If there is no intelligent life in other galaxies, the sentence 'G = 0' expresses the same Russellian proposition as the trivially true sentence '0 = 0'. Again, in both cases, the corresponding necessary propositions in the intensional framework are identical too.

Such examples cast doubt on any attempt to interpret the semantic considerations as revealing some pathology of metaphysics, for the question whether there is intelligent life in other galaxies is uncontentiously non-pathological.

Related examples occur quite naturally, with no need of artificial stipulations. Take the go-to example of synonymy from previous chapters, the natural kind terms 'furze' and 'gorse'. As we saw there, although they have the same meaning in English, by normal standards someone can understand both words without recognizing that they co-refer. On the Russellian approach (if not that of the historical Russell), the English sentence 'Furze is gorse' expresses the Russellian proposition <identity, <furze, gorse>>, which just is the obviously true Russellian proposition <identity, <furze, furze>>. Yet you could sensibly ask yourself 'Is furze gorse?' out of simple non-pathological botanical interest. A similar issue arises on a natural implementation of the intensional approach, since 'furze' and 'gorse' are rigid designators of the same genus, so 'Furze is gorse' is true at all possible worlds.[5]

The problems with 'D = 1', 'G = 1', and 'Furze is gorse' are not specific to a Russellian account of propositions. They are just as pressing for versions of truthmaker semantics (chapter 3.4) and impossible worlds semantics (chapter 3.3) that respect the key observation that competent speakers of a language can understand synonyms without appreciating their co-reference.

The evidence so far supports at least two conclusions. First, the problem of trivialization is just as hard for hyperintensionalist as for intensionalist semantics. Second, the problem is generic; it shows nothing distinctive about specific forms of enquiry. In particular, it shows nothing pathological about metaphysics. Nor does it show anything special about logic or mathematics.

---

[5] The semantics works most smoothly with the stipulation that a rigid designator for x designates x even with respect to worlds at which x is not concretely present. After all, the semantics characterizes how *we* use words, speaking in our world *about* actual and counterfactual worlds, not how those words *would have been used* in those counterfactual worlds.

5.4 The metalinguistic strategy

Some philosophers are still tempted by the idea that the ignorance or at least non-triviality displayed in the cases above is fundamentally semantic, that there are serious obstacles to knowing what the relevant words or sentences mean: for instance, it is hard to know *which* numbers the names 'D' and 'G' designate. [6] This ignorance would be of a familiar, unpuzzling kind and pose no threat to the favoured semantic framework.

Consider yet again 'furze' and 'gorse'. The obvious line for proponents of the metalinguistic strategy is to insist that anyone—such as an expert botanist—with full, non-deferential understanding of both 'furze' and 'gorse' *is* in a position to know that they co-refer. Everyone else has at most partial understanding of at least one of the two terms. Thus, the problem is fundamentally one of semantic ignorance.

Such an account may apply to this particular case, though what the 'full understanding' might be with which 'partial understanding' is implicitly contrasted is far from clear. In any case, we can vary the example. In one variant, set many centuries ago, the shrub in question is rare and grows only in remote places. It has been seen only occasionally, but never studied scientifically, and no specimens have been observed over extended periods. The term 'furze' was introduced by travellers who saw green bushes with yellow flowers, and in practice only bushes in that condition are recognized as 'furze'. Similarly, the term 'gorse' was introduced by travellers who saw brown bushes with no flowers, and in practice only bushes in that condition are recognized as 'gorse'. Not even the best botanists in our community realize that 'furze' and 'gorse'

---

[6] The leading defender of intensionalism about content is Robert Stalnaker (1984, 1999). Since I have engaged in detail with his application of intensionalism to content in philosophy elsewhere (Stalnaker 2011, Williamson 2011b), I will not do so here. In effect, his approach is a version of the metalinguistic strategy; my concern in this section is with the general strategy.

co-refer; they may regard it as an open question. Nevertheless, despite the community-wide difference between 'furze' and 'gorse' in associated recognitional capacities, there is no strictly *semantic* difference between the two words. They are both simply natural kind terms for what is in fact the very same natural kind. In that sense, they are synonyms. In these circumstances, a fully non-deferential understanding of both terms does not put one in a position to recognize their co-reference. To resolve our ignorance, our primary need is to know more botany, not more semantics.

In another variant, everything is like the original case, but without deference, since the community does not recognize the status of scientific expertise. Instead, natural kind terms are treated more as words like 'if' and 'know' are actually treated. Although some people devote themselves to studying conditionals or knowledge, they play no privileged role in the social practice of using the corresponding words, because the community has no tendency to defer to them in applying the words. Similarly, in the imagined case, even if some people devote themselves to studying shrubs, they play no privileged role in the social practice of using the words 'furze' and 'gorse', because the community has no tendency to defer to them in applying the words. At least for those who have been introduced to them ostensively, the ethos in applying them is that everyone is entitled to their own opinion. For that large, at least minimally competent group, there is no deferential partial understanding, because there is no deference to a higher level of competence. 'Furze' and 'gorse' are still treated as natural kind terms, but in an unscientific spirit. Many speakers fully competent by communal standards with both terms cannot recognize that they co-refer. Unlike the previous case, there is no community-wide difference between 'furze' and 'gorse' in associated recognitional capacities; such differences obtain only at the level of individual speakers. There is also no strictly semantic difference between the two words. They are both simply natural kind terms for what is in fact the very same natural kind. They are synonyms. In these circumstances too, a fully non-deferential understanding of both terms does not always put one in a position to recognize their co-reference. To resolve one's ignorance, one's primary need is to know more botany, not more semantics.

At first sight, the artificially introduced names 'D' and 'G' look more promising as candidates for semantic ignorance. The associated stipulation might plausibly be denied by itself to enable one to know *which* number 'D' or 'G' designates. Currently, someone familiar with the stipulation may be uncertain whether 'D' co-refers with '1' or with '0'. But that is because they are uncertain whether there is a god: the semantic ignorance seems to depend on prior metaphysical ignorance, contrary to the metalinguistic strategy. However, proponents of the strategy may respond that the relevant semantic ignorance is at the level of the *sentence*, not the singular terms: the underlying uncertainty is as to *which proposition* the sentence 'There is a god' expresses. This may seem more promising. Semantic ignorance of individual words in the sentence would be mere linguistic incompetence, which is an implausible diagnosis of the problems of metaphysics. Of course, the word 'god' is hardly straightforward, but for present purposes we may assume that it has been stipulatively defined in terms of a list of attributes. The picture is that we know the semantic values of the atomic constituents of the sentence, but cannot work out which proposition results from composing them in the relevant way.

Such an account makes more sense for intensional than for Russellian propositions. For the latter, if we know that a sentence is composed of a constituent expressing the second-order property $\exists$ predicated of a constituent expressing the first-order property of divinity, we can easily work out that the sentence as a whole expresses the Russellian proposition $\langle \exists, \text{divinity} \rangle$: there is no mystery as to which proposition that is, because the notation is already so perspicuous.[7] By contrast, if the proposition is a function from worlds to truth-values, but one is uncertain whether it maps all worlds to truth or all to falsity, one might well be counted uncertain as to which function the sentence expresses. If sentences are individuated syntactically, not semantically, it is contingent which proposition a sentence expresses, so the apparent metaphysical uncertainty has finally been traced to uncertainty about something contingent.

However, the proposal does not withstand further scrutiny. Let 'S' abbreviate whichever is false of the quotations 'There is a god' and 'There is no god', so S is the false one of those two sentences. Whatever proposition S semantically expresses is impossible. Consider a metaphysician uncertain whether S expresses a true proposition. Of course, that uncertainty is uninteresting if it results from lack of native speaker knowledge of English. We must assume our metaphysician to know what the words and modes of composition in S mean. Thus, we assume that she knows that S has semantic features F, fully characterizing the semantics of S's atomic constituents and modes of composition. Consequently, since our metaphysician is rational, she is also uncertain over the conjunction that S both has F and expresses a true proposition. But the conjunction is itself impossible, for since the semantics is compositional, a necessary consequence of the first conjunct (that S has F) is that the proposition S expresses is impossible, which is incompatible with the second conjunct. Each conjunct is possible, but they are not compossible. Thus, our metaphysician's uncertainty extends to something impossible, contrary to the metalinguistic strategy of confining the relevant uncertainty, ignorance, or error to contingent linguistic matters.

---

[7] The notation is perspicuous because <X, Y> = <X*, Y*> just when X = X* and Y = Y*, so one can individuate the whole by individuating its constituents. This justifies the ordered pair notation, though Russellian propositions need not literally *be* ordered *n*-tuples. But this fineness of grain also generates the Russell-Myhill paradox, which makes a pure Russellian account inconsistent (see chapter 3.5).

A back-up tactic for the metalinguistic strategy is to divide an agent's beliefs into separate subsystems, individually possible but jointly incompossible (Stalnaker 1984). However, in the present case, separating the metaphysician's belief that S expresses a truth from her belief that S has F misses the depth of the problem. She does not have to *ignore* her understanding of S in order to believe that it expresses a truth; she believes that S is true *in the light of* her understanding of S. Positing a cognitive wall between her belief that S expresses a truth and her belief that it has the semantics F makes no sense of the example.

Although one could develop other ways of implementing the metalinguistic strategy, they are all vulnerable to the sort of problem just explained (to my knowledge, first pointed out by Kripke in an unpublished lecture). Thus, the metalinguistic strategy fails.

5.5 Reconceiving the problem

In order to make progress, what one must take to heart is that the underlying problem is not about necessary or impossible propositions.[8] It is about necessarily equivalent propositions, whether they are contingent or not. For instance, the sentences 'There is furze in Edinburgh' and 'There is gorse in Edinburgh' express the same contingent proposition, on the worldly approach to semantics under discussion, even though a speaker who understands both sentences may be in no position to appreciate that they have the same truth-value.

Of course, this is just a variant on the problem of cognitive significance, which Frege introduced his distinction between sense and reference to solve. Some philosophers may still hope that switching to a Fregean framework would help, by building modes of presentation into the semantics. However, chapter 4 explained why the

---

[8] The approach in this section builds on the proposal in Williamson 2007: 66ff.

Fregean account, despite its initial appeal, does not get to the heart of the problem. We need not go over that ground again.

There is also a further concern about the big picture for metaphysics, if it needs to be rescued by Fregean semantics. Fregean thoughts—the senses of declarative sentences—are *perspectival* in a sense in which worldly intensional or Russellian propositions are not. A Fregean thought is a *mode of presentation* of a truth-value, presumably to a notional subject. By contrast, functions from worlds to truth-values and structured complexes of objects, properties, and relations are normally presentation- and subject-independent.[9] Thus Fregean thoughts seem less apt than such worldly propositions for being *what is objectively at stake* in an out-and-out metaphysical dispute, as traditionally conceived (in a way Kantians might describe as pre-Kantian). For thoughts can differ while the relevant non-presentational objects, properties and relations stay the same. In such cases, one might think, what is objectively at stake stays the same, while Fregean thoughts vary, so what is objectively at stake is no Fregean thought. Of course, Frege himself did not treat mathematics as lacking in objectivity; his approach was explicitly, indeed prototypically, anti-psychologistic. The commitments inherent in a Fregean semantic framework are unclear. Nevertheless, those engaged in a dispute over what they understand as a purely objective metaphysical question may be suspicious of treating what is at stake as a Fregean thought.

In any case, the moral to draw from 'furze' and 'gorse' and similar cases is not that semantic properties are Fregean. It is that cognitive significance does not supervene on semantic properties. At both the individual and the community levels, two sentences may have all the same semantic properties, yet differ in cognitive significance. Tracking cognitive significance is not just a semantic

---

[9] David Lewis (1979) turned the intensional framework perspectival by reworking it in terms of *centred* worlds, with a distinguished agent and time, although he did not build in other aspects of modes of presentation. For criticism of such hybrid approaches, see Cappelen and Dever 2013 and Magidor 2015.

exercise. Cognitive significance often depends on form as well as content. More specifically, for inquiries where the primary medium of expression is linguistic, as in logic, mathematics, and metaphysics, cognitive significance typically depends on the linguistic form in which content is semantically expressed in the given context, not just on the content itself. To track cognitive significance, we must track the words and sentences in play, not just the contents themselves. In chapter 4's terminology, we can distinguish between believing the proposition that furze is gorse under the guise of the sentence 'Furze is gorse' and believing the same proposition under the guise of the sentence 'Furze is furze'. Similarly, we can distinguish between believing the proposition that $17^2 = 289$ under the guise of the equation '$17^2 = 289$' and believing it under the guise of the equation '289 = 289' or '0 = 0', and between believing that there is a god under the guise of the sentence 'There is a god', believing it under the guise of the equation 'D = 1', and believing it under the guise of the equation '1 = 1' or '0 = 1' (depending on its truth-value).

By using linguistic guises to track cognitive significance, we liberate semantics itself from pressure to make cognitive distinctions it is ill-suited to make; we thereby avoid distorting the semantic framework. Even the quasi-syntactic structure of Russellian propositions arguably reflects such inappropriate pressure on the semantics, by contrast with a purely intensional approach (Salmón 1986 invokes linguistic guises but works within a broadly Russellian framework). Just as we should not project the difference between 'furze' and 'gorse' onto their worldly semantic values, so we should not project differences in syntactic structure between sentences onto *their* worldly semantic values.

In short, linguistic guises are not *what* we think, and not normally what we think *of*; they are what we think *with*, when we think in words. Similarly, in speech, when you make an assertion, a guise is not *what* you assert, and not normally what you assert it *of*; it is more like what you assert it *with* (though the hearer may receive it under a different guise). We must keep track of linguistic or, more generally, representational differences, without confusing them with differences at the level of reference or content.

Often, as seen in chapter 4, more than the linguistic expression type must be put into the guise to capture cognitive significance. This is clear for demonstratives: in the same context, someone may wonder 'Is that gull that gull?', where the first occurrence of 'that gull' refers to a seagull as she sees it in the distance, while the second refers to the same bird as she hears its cry. Kripke's case of someone who does not realize that the politician Paderewski and the pianist Paderewski are the same man also calls for such further differentiation of guises. Since full guises are not normally what need to be communicated, individuating them very finely carries little cost. Nor need guises always include something linguistic: the guise of a spatial thought might be more like a picture, seen or imagined.[10] As also seen in chapter 4, this separation of content from guise is not transparent to normal language-users in producing and comprehending ascriptions of propositional attitudes.

In any case, we can provisionally use the approach of ascribing acceptance or rejection of coarse-grained intensional propositions under guises to track what is going on in enquiries into non-contingent matters, such as logic, mathematics, and metaphysics. In those enquiries, propositions usually come under sentential guises, but not always: in geometry, for example, a proposition may come under a diagrammatic guise. The trap to avoid is that of taking the need for tracking sentential guises to show something distinctive about those fields—for instance, that they are somehow partly linguistic inquiries in some sense in which more 'empirical' inquiries are not.

Admittedly, fields may differ in how far we can use differences in proposition expressed as convenient proxies for cognitive differences between sentences—doing so works much better in

---

[10] What sort of Russellian proposition would correspond to an impressionist landscape painting?

history than it does in mathematics—but in principle the two levels are *never* equivalent, and in practice the inequivalence will sometimes obtrude in every field, though more frequently in some than in others. For example, in ancient history, doubt is not uncommon as to whether the same name on different tablets or inscriptions refers to one person or two. Again, there is a *practical* difference between knowing how many tiles are needed to cover the floor under the guise of the sentence '17^2 tiles are needed' and knowing it under the guise of the sentence '289 tiles are needed'; the necessity of mathematical truths is not the issue.

Another way to see that the problem is not specific to non-contingent propositions is to consider an object-language with a rigidifying modal operator, 'actually'. On the intended reading, for any declarative sentence 'P' of the object-language, 'Actually P' is true at a world *w* if and only if 'P' is true at the actual world. Thus 'P if and only if actually P' is guaranteed to be true at the actual world, so you can cheaply know the biconditional. But, if 'P' expresses a truth, whether contingent or non-contingent, 'Actually P' (as uttered in *your* world) is true at every world, so the biconditional is necessarily equivalent to 'P', so you know something necessarily equivalent to 'P'. Similarly, if 'P' expresses a falsehood, whether contingent or non-contingent, 'Actually P' (as uttered in *your* world) is false at every world, so the biconditional is necessarily equivalent to 'Not P', so you know something necessarily equivalent to 'Not P'. For an intensionalist, that is uncomfortably close to omniscience on the cheap (see Hawthorne and Yli-Vakkuri 2022 for more details).

One response is that, although you know the biconditional sentence to express a true proposition, you do not know *which* proposition it expresses (the proposition that P or the proposition that not P). However, as the previous section explained, the metalinguistic strategy does not in general provide an effective defence of intensionalism. In the present case, once you understand 'P' and the relevant logical constants, the biconditional 'P if and only if actually P' is easy to understand. In the relevant sense, knowing which proposition a given sentence expresses is not a matter of being able to enumerate the worlds at which it is true, since we are unable to do that for the simplest, most everyday true sentences. The claim that you do not know which proposition the biconditional expresses is just too unclear to be of any help.

A more effective strategy is to invoke guises and distinguish between knowing a true proposition under the guise 'P' (or under the guise 'Not P') and knowing the same true proposition under the guise 'P if and only if actually P'. Although we saw in chapter 4.10 and 4.11 some limitations of the guise-relative strategy, some cases call out for it, and the case with 'actually' was artificially designed for exactly that purpose. Just about any scientific model is vulnerable to such tricks. They reveal limitations of the model, but that is not to say that they justify its abandonment. In particular, the strategy of relativizing attitudes to linguistic guises is well-suited to describing inquiry in metaphysics, logic, and mathematics, *not* because they concern non-contingent matters but because their principal medium is a shared language, typically written, which facilitates the use of linguistic types as cognitive guises.

Naturally, the envisaged separation of semantic content from cognitive significance forms a coherent picture only if systematic connections link the two levels. Compositional semantics provides such connections. Although the semantic structure of a sentence is not even roughly similar to any structure intrinsic to the proposition it expresses, the former determines the latter in more or less principled ways, described by a compositional semantic theory for the language. Even in discourse where the only propositions are the necessary truth and its contradictory, a multitude of properties and relations are normally in play as the semantic values of predicates. Thus, a standard first-order language for arithmetic can express infinitely many distinct monadic properties (intensions) of natural numbers. The case of metaphysics is analogous. When things go well, we learn *how* the properties and relations of interest are necessarily interconnected.

One might still feel puzzled. For when we learn how those properties and relations are necessarily interconnected, *what* we learn are necessary truths, which by intensionalist lights are all one. Indeed, if metaphysical truths are all necessary, how do we learn anything in metaphysics, since presumably we already knew the trivial necessary truth before we started doing metaphysics? In response, a first point is that calling the necessarily true proposition 'trivial' already confuses the issue, because the distinction between 'trivial' and 'non-trivial', like that between 'obvious' and 'non-obvious', arises primarily at the cognitive level: the trivial is the very easily known. The necessarily true proposition is trivial under the guise of the equation '2 + 2 = 4' but highly non-trivial under the guise of a statement of Fermat's Last Theorem. Similarly, in such cases, learning and discovery must themselves be understood with respect to guises: mathematicians who already knew the necessary truth under one guise came to know it under another. The novelty was in the guise, not in the proposition known. Again, the same points apply to logic and metaphysics.

But if you know a truth under one guise, why bother to learn it under another? That would be a good question if knowledge were valued as a miser's hoard of true propositions. But not even true propositions have intrinsic value: the value is in how we are cognitively related to them. We can bear dramatically different cognitive relations to the same proposition under different guises. In learning an old truth under a new guise, we acquire a potentially valuable new cognitive relation to the old truth.

None of this involves a return to the discredited metalinguistic view. The latter makes the mistake of trying to get the content to do all the cognitive work, forgetting that even a metalinguistic content can be presented to the subject under different guises. The point is rather that *any* content is *present* to a subject at a time only in some form or other; that form is its guise. Even physical aspects of linguistic form are cognitively significant, because they facilitate or impede cognitive manipulation. Mathematicians know this well; metaphysicians would be well-advised to know it too. As Bertrand Russell observed, 'a good notation has a subtlety and suggestiveness which at times make it seem almost like a live teacher'; 'Notational irregularities are often the first sign of philosophical errors' (1922: xix). That is why definitions matter in metaphysics, even though they merely abbreviate longer forms of words: a good definition makes salient and handy a distinction which cuts at the joints. In that respect, even metaphysics is a kind of embodied cognition.

5.6 In brief

According to some philosophers, the non-contingency of metaphysics, logic, and mathematics undermines their capacity to provide substantive knowledge. That is a disastrously mistaken diagnosis of a genuine problem. The misdiagnosis results in damaging pseudo-cures. The underlying problem is not about necessary truth; it is about necessarily equivalent propositions, irrespective of their modal status. It is yet another manifestation of the non-transparency to thinkers of the contents of their thought. It arises eye-catchingly for intensionalism, but hyperintensional remedies mislocate the problem, and harm the patient in other ways. The proper cure is to make a radical cut between content and cognitive significance. It poses no threat to intensionalism.

Bibliography

Alexander, Joshua, and Jonathan Weinberg. 2014: 'The "unreliability" of epistemic intuitions', in Edouard Machery and Elizabeth O'Neill (eds.), *Current Controversies in Experimental Philosophy*. London: Routledge, 128–145.

Anderson, Alan Ross, and Nuel Belnap. 1975: *Entailment: The Logic of Relevance and Necessity*, vol. 1. Princeton, NJ: Princeton University Press.

Andjelković, Miroslava, and Timothy Williamson. 2000: 'Truth, falsity and borderline cases', *Philosophical Topics*, 28: 211–244.

Armstrong, David. 1997: *A World of States of Affairs*. Cambridge: Cambridge University Press.

Bacon, Andrew. 2018: 'The broadest necessity', *Journal of Philosophical Logic*, 47: 733–783.

Bacon, Andrew. forthcoming: 'A theory of structured propositions', *Philosophical Review*.

Bartlett, Peter, Philip Long, Gábor Lugosi, and Alexander Tsigler. 2020: 'Benign overfitting in linear regression', *PNAS*, 117: 30063–30070.

Berto, Francesco, Rohan French, Graham Priest, and Dave Ripley. 2018: 'Williamson on counterpossibles', *Journal of Philosophical Logic*, 47: 693–713.

Berto, Francesco, and Mark Jago. 2019: *Impossible Worlds*. Oxford: Oxford University Press.

Bobzien, Susanne. 2002: 'The development of *modus ponens* in antiquity: from Aristotle to the 2nd century AD', *Phronesis*, 47: 359–394.

Boghossian, Paul, and Timothy Williamson. 2020: *Debating the A Priori*. Oxford: Oxford University Press.

Branquinho, João. 1990: 'Are Salmon's guises disguised Fregean senses?', *Analysis*, 50: 19–24.

Brast-McKie, Benjamin. 2021: 'Identity and aboutness', *Journal of Philosophical Logic*, 50:1471–1503.

Braun, David. 2016: 'The objects of belief and credence', *Mind*, 125: 469–497.

Brogaard, Berit, and Joe Salerno. 2013: 'Remarks on counterpossibles', *Synthese*, 190: 639–660.

Burgess, John. 1981: 'Relevance: a fallacy?', *Notre Dame Journal of Formal Logic*, 22: 76–84.

Burnham, Kenneth, and David Anderson. 2010: *Model Selection and Multimodal Inference: A Practical Information-Theoretic Approach*, 2nd ed. New York: Springer.

Cappelen, Herman, and Josh Dever. 2013: *The Inessential Indexical: On the Philosophical Insignificance of Perspective and the First Person*. Oxford: Oxford University Press.
Cappelen, Herman, and John Hawthorne. 2009: *Relativism and Monadic Truth*. Oxford: Oxford University Press.
Carnap, Rudolf. 1947: *Meaning and Necessity: A Study in Semantics and Modal Logic*. Chicago: University of Chicago Press.
Carnap, Rudolf. 1950: 'Empiricism, semantics, and ontology', *Revue Internationale de Philosophie*, 4: 20–40.
Cassirer, Ernst. 1963: *The Individual and the Cosmos in Renaissance Philosophy*, trans. Mario Domandi. Philadelphia: University of Pennsylvania Press.
Chalmers, David. 2006: 'The foundations of two-dimensional semantics', in Manuel Garcia -Carpintero and Josep Macia (eds.), *Two-Dimensional Semantics: Foundations and Applications*. Oxford: Oxford University Press, 55–140.
Chalmers, David. 2011: 'Frege's puzzle and the objects of credence', *Mind*, 120: 587–635.
Charles, David. 2000: *Aristotle on Meaning and Essence*. Oxford: Clarendon Press.
Clark, Andy. 2016: *Surfing Uncertainty: Prediction, Action, and the Embodied Mind*. New York: Oxford University Press.
Crenshaw, Kimberlé. 1989: 'Demarginalizing the intersection of race and sex: a black feminist critique of antidiscrimination doctrine', *University of Chicago Legal Forum*, 139–167.
Crimmins, Mark. 1992: 'I falsely believe that *p*', *Analysis*, 52: 191.
Crimmins, Mark, and John Perry. 1989: 'The prince and the phone booth: reporting puzzling beliefs', *Journal of Philosophy*, 86: 685–711.
Crow, James. 1992: 'An advantage of sexual reproduction in a rapidly changing environment'. *Journal of Heredity*, 83: 169–173,
Dar, Yehuda, Vidya Muthukumar, and Richard Baraniuk. 2021: 'A farewell to the bias-variance tradeoff? An overview of overparameterized machine learning', [2109.02355] A Farewell to the Bias-Variance Tradeoff? An Overview of the Theory of Overparameterized Machine Learning (arxiv.org).
Davidson, Donald. 1970: 'Mental events', in Lawrence Foster and J. W. Swanson (eds.), *Experience and Theory*. Amherst: University of Massachusetts Press, 79–101.
Davis, Wayne. 2002: *Meaning, Expression and Thought*. Cambridge: Cambridge University Press.
Dorr, Cian. 2008: 'There are no abstract objects', in Ted Sider, John Hawthorne, and Dean Zimmerman (eds.), *Contemporary Debates in Metaphysics*. Oxford: Blackwell, 32–63.
Dorr, Cian. 2016: 'To be F is to be G', *Philosophical Perspectives*, 30, 39–134.

Dorr, Cian, John Hawthorne, and Juhani Yli-Vakkuri. 2021: *The Bounds of Possibility: Puzzles of Modal Variation*. Oxford: Oxford University Press.

Douven, Igor. 2016: *The Epistemology of Indicative Conditionals: Formal and Empirical Approaches*. Cambridge: Cambridge University Press.

Douven, Igor, and Peter Gärdenfors. 2020: 'What are natural concepts? A design perspective', *Mind and Language*, 35: 313–334.

Edgington, Dorothy. 2008: 'Counterfactuals', *Proceedings of the Aristotelian Society*, 108: 1–21.

Eklund, Matti. 2002: 'Inconsistent languages', *Philosophy and Phenomenological Research*, 64: 251–275.

Elbourne, Paul. 2005: *Situations and Individuals*. Cambridge MA: MIT Press.

Ellis, Brian. 1969: 'An epistemological concept of truth', in Robert Brown and C. D. Rollins (eds.), *Contemporary Philosophy in Australia*. London: Routledge, 52–72.

Evans, Jonathan, and David Over. 2004: *If*. Oxford: Oxford University Press.

Fagin, Ronald, Joseph Halpern, Yoram Moses, and Moshe Vardi. 1995: *Reasoning about Knowledg*. Cambridge, MA: MIT Press.

Fine, Kit. 1994: 'Essence and modality', *Philosophical Perspectives*, 8: 1–16.

Fine, Kit. 2017a: 'Truthmaker semantics', in Bob Hale, Crispin Wright, and Alexander Miller (eds.), *A Companion to the Philosophy of Language*, 2nd ed., vol. 2. Oxford: Blackwell, 556–577.

Fine, Kit. 2017b: 'A theory of truthmaker content I: conjunction, disjunction and negation', *Journal of Philosophical Logic*, 46: 625–674.

Fine, Kit. 2017c: 'A theory of truthmaker content II: subject-matter, common content, remainder and ground', *Journal of Philosophical Content*, 46: 675–702.

Fine, Kit. 2022: 'Some remarks on the role of essence in Kripke's "Naming and Necessity"', *Theoria*, 88: 403–405.

Fleming, Roland. 2012: 'Human perception: visual heuristics in the perception of glossiness', *Current Biology*, 22: R865–R866.

Fodor, Jerry. 1998: *Concepts: Where Cognitive Science Went Wrong*. Oxford: Clarendon Press.

Forbes, Graeme. 1990: 'The indispensability of *Sinn*', *Philosophical Review*, 99: 535–563.

Forster, Malcolm, and Elliott Sober. 1994: 'How to tell when simpler, more unified, or less *ad hoc* theories will provide more accurate predictions', *British Journal for the Philosophy of Science*, 45: 1–34.

Fritz, Peter. 2022: 'Ground and grain', *Philosophy and Phenomenological Research*, 105: 299–330.

Gärdenfors, Peter. 2000: *Conceptual Spaces: The Geometry of Thought*. Cambridge, MA: MIT Press.

Gettier, Edmund. 1963: 'Is justified true belief knowledge?', *Analysis*, 23: 121–123.

Gigerenzer Gerd. 2021: 'Embodied heuristics', *Frontiers in Psychology*, 12:711289. doi: 10.3389/fpsyg.2021.711289.
Gigerenzer, Gerd, and Daniel Goldstein. 1996: 'Reasoning the fast and frugal way: models of bounded rationality', *Psychological Review*, *103*: 650–669.
Gigerenzer, Gerd, Ralph Hertwig, and Thorsten Pachur (eds.). 2011: *Heuristics: The Foundations of Adaptive Behavior*. New York: Oxford University Press.
Goodman, Jeremy. 2017: 'Reality is not structured', *Analysis*, 77: 43–53.
Goodman, Jeremy, and Harvey Lederman. 2021: 'Perspectivism', *Noûs*, 55: 623–648.
Goodsell, Thea. 2013: 'Mental files and their identity conditions', *Disputatio*, 5: 177–190.
Goodsell, Zachary, and Juhani Yli-Vakkuri. In preparation: *Logical Foundations*.
Gordon, Robert. 2000: 'Sellars's Ryleans revisited', *Protosociology*, 14: 102–114.
Gordon, Robert. 2021: 'Simulation, predictive coding, and the shared world', in Michael Gilead and Kevin Ochsner (eds.), *The Neural Basis of Mentalizing*, 237–256. Cham: Springer.
Gordon, Robert. forthcoming: 'How the brain makes knowledge first', in Arturs Logins and Jacques Vollet (eds.), *Putting Knowledge to Work: New Directions for Knowledge—First Epistemology*. Oxford: Oxford University Press, forthcoming.
Grice, Paul. 1989: *Studies in the Way of Words*. Cambridge, MA: Harvard University Press.
Haslanger, Sally. 2000: 'Gender and race: (what) are they? (what) do we want them to be?' *Noûs*, 34: 31–55.
Hawthorne, John, and Ofra Magidor. 2009: 'Assertion, context, and epistemic accessibility', *Mind*, 118: 377–397.
Hawthorne, John, and Ofra Magidor. 2010: 'Assertion and epistemic opacity', *Mind*, 119: 1087–1105.
Hawthorne, John, and Ofra Magidor. 2018: 'Reflections on the ideology of reasons', in Daniel Star (ed.), *The Oxford Handbook of Reasons and Normativity*. Oxford: Oxford University Press, 113–140.
Hawthorne, John, Daniel Rothschild, and Levi Spectre. 2016: 'Belief is weak', *Philosophical Studies*, 173: 1393–1404.
Hawthorne, John, and Juhani Yli-Vakkuri. 2022: 'Intensionalism and propositional attitudes', *Oxford Studies in Philosophy of Mind*, 2: 114–174.
Hintikka, Jaakko. 1962: *Knowledge and Belief*. Ithaca, NY: Cornell University Press.
Hintikka, Jaakko. 1975: 'Impossible worlds vindicated', *Journal of Philosophical Logic*, 4: 475–484.
Hirsch, Eli. 2021: 'Ontology by stipulation', in J. T. M. Miller (ed.), *The Language of Ontology*. Oxford: Oxford University Press, 7–22.

Hodes, Harold. 2015: 'Why ramify?', *Notre Dame Journal of Formal Logic*, 56: 379–415.
Holguín, Ben. 2022: 'Thinking, guessing, and believing', *Philosophers' Imprint*, 22: 1–34.
Holliday, Wesley, and Matthew Mandelkern. 2023: 'The orthologic of epistemic modals', https://arxiv.org/abs/2203.02872.
Horschler, Daniel, Laurie Santos, and Evan MacLean. 2019: 'Do non-human primates really represent others' ignorance? A test of the awareness relations hypothesis', *Cognition*, 190: 72–80.
Jackson, Frank. 1998: *From Metaphysics to Ethics: A Defence of Conceptual Analysis*. Oxford: Clarendon Press.
Jeffrey, Richard. 1964: 'If' (abstract), *Journal of Philosophy*, 61: 702–703.
Kagan, Shelly. 1988: 'The additive fallacy', *Ethics*, 99: 5–31.
Kahneman, Daniel, Paul Slovic, and Amos Tversky (eds.). 1982: *Judgment under Uncertainty: Heuristics and Biases*. Cambridge: Cambridge University Press.
Kaplan, David. 1989: 'Demonstratives: an essay on the semantics, logic, metaphysics, and epistemology of demonstratives and other indexicals', in Joseph Almog, John Perry, and Howard Wettstein (eds.), *Themes from Kaplan*. New York: Oxford University Press, 481–563.
Kaup, Barbara, Rolf Zwaan, and Jana Lüdtke. 2007: 'The experiential view of language comprehension: how is negation represented?', in Franz Schmalhofer and Charles Perfetti (eds.), *Higher Level Language Processes in the Brain: Inference and Comprehension Processes*. Mahwah, NJ: Lawrence Erlbaum Associates, 255–288.
Kim, Jaegwon. 1984: 'Concepts of supervenience', *Philosophy and Phenomenological Research*, 45: 153–176.
Kitcher, Philip. 2023: *What's the Use of Philosophy?* New York: Oxford University Press.
Kment, Boris. 2022: 'Russell-Myhill and grounding', *Analysis*, 82: 49–60.
Knobe, Joshua. 2021: 'Philosophical intuitions are surprisingly robust across both demographic groups and situations', *Filozofia Nauki*, 29: 11–76.
Kornblith, Hilary. 2002: *Knowledge and Its Place in Nature*. Oxford: Oxford University Press.
Kornblith, Hilary. 2012: *On Reflection*. Oxford: Oxford University Press.
Kratzer, Angelika. 1977: 'What "must" and "can" must and can mean', *Linguistics and Philosophy*, 1: 337–355.
Kripke, Saul. 1965: 'Semantical analysis of modal logic II: non-normal modal propositional calculi', in John Addison, Leon Henkin, and Alfred Tarski (eds.), *The Theory of Models*. Amsterdam: North Holland, 206–220.
Kripke, Saul. 1972: 'Naming and necessity', in Donald Davidson and Gilbert Harman (eds.), *Semantics of Natural Language*. Dordrecht: Reidel, 235–355, 763–769.

Kripke, Saul. 1979: 'A puzzle about belief', in Avishai Margalit (ed.), *Meaning and Use*. Dordrecht: Reidel, 239–283.

Kripke, Saul. 1980: *Naming and Necessity*. Oxford: Blackwell.

Kripke, Saul. 1988: 'A puzzle about belief', in Nathan Salmon and Scott Soames (eds.), *Propositions and Attitudes*. Oxford: Oxford University Press, 1988, 102–148 (reprint of Kripke 1979).

Kuhn, Thomas. 1962: *The Structure of Scientific Revolutions*. Chicago: University of Chicago Press.

Lakatos, Imre. 1970: 'Falsification and the methodology of scientific research programmes', in Imre Lakatos and Alan Musgrove (eds.), *Criticism and the Growth of Knowledge*. Cambridge: Cambridge University Press, 91–196.

Langford, Cooper. 1942: 'The notion of analysis in Moore's philosophy', in Paul Schilpp (ed.), *The Philosophy of G. E. Moore*. Evanston: Northwestern University, 319–342.

Lasersohn, Peter. 2005: 'Context dependence, disagreement, and predicates of personal taste', *Linguistics and Philosophy*. 6: 643–686.

Lederman, Harvey. 2018a: 'Uncommon knowledge', *Mind*, 127: 1069–1105.

Lederman, Harvey. 2018b: 'Two paradoxes of common knowledge: coordinated attack and electronic mail', *Noûs*, 52: 921–945.

Lewis, David. 1968: 'Counterpart theory and quantified modal logic', *Journal of Philosophy*, 65: 113–126.

Lewis, David. 1970: 'General semantics', *Synthese*, 22: 18–67.

Lewis, David. 1973: *Counterfactuals*. Oxford: Blackwell.

Lewis, David. 1974: 'Tensions', in Milton Munitz and Peter Unger (eds.), *Semantics and Philosophy*. New York: New York University Press, 49–61.

Lewis, David. 1976: 'Probabilities of conditionals and conditional probabilities', *Philosophical Review*, 95: 581–589.

Lewis, David. 1979: 'Attitudes *de dicto* and *de se*', *Philosophical Review*, 88: 513–543.

Lewis, David. 1996: 'Elusive knowledge', *Australasian Journal of Philosophy*, 74: 549–567.

Lipton, Peter. 1991. *Inference to the Best Explanation*. 2nd ed., 2004, London: Routledge.

Lombrozo, Tania. 2007: 'Simplicity and probability in causal explanation', *Cognitive Psychology*, 55: 232–257.

Lombrozo, Tania. 2016: 'Explanatory preferences shape learning and inference', *Trends in Cognitive Science*, 20: 748–759.

Lord, Errol, and Barry Maguire (eds.). 2016: *Weighing Reasons*. Oxford: Oxford University Press.

MacFarlane, John. 2014: *Assessment Sensitivity: Relative Truth and Its Applications*. Oxford: Oxford University Press.

Machery, Edouard, Stephen Stich, David Rose, Amita Chatterjee, Kaori Karasawa, Noel Struchiner, Smita Sirker, Naoki Usui, and Takaaki Hashimoto. 2017: 'Gettier across cultures', *Noûs*, 51: 645–664.
Magidor, Ofra. 2015: 'The myth of the de se', *Philosophical Perspectives*, 29: 249–283.
Mahtani, Anna. 2017: 'The *ex ante* Pareto Principle', *Journal of Philosophy*, 114: 303–323.
Mahtani, Anna. 2021: 'Frege's Puzzle and the *ex ante* Pareto Principle', *Philosophical Studies*, 178: 2077–2100.
Mahtani, Anna. 2023: *The Objects of Credence*. Oxford: Oxford University Press.
Marconi, Diego. 2011: 'Wittgenstein and Williamson on Conceptual Analysis', in Richard Davies (ed.), *Analisi: Annuario e Bollettino della Società Italiana Analitica (SIFA) 2011*. Milan: Mimesis, 91–102.
Mares, Edwin. 2004: *Relevant Logic: A Philosophical Interpretation*. Cambridge: Cambridge University Press.
Mates, Benson. 1949: 'Diodorean implication', *Philosophical Review*, 58: 234–242.
Menzel, Christopher. 2024: 'Pure logic and higher-order metaphysics', in Peter Fritz and Nicholas Jones, *Higher-Order Metaphysics*. Oxford: Oxford University Press, 421–459.
Merleau-Ponty, Maurice. 1945: *Phénoménologie de la Perception*. Paris: Gallimard.
Mortensen, Kaija, and Jennifer Nagel. 2016: 'Armchair-friendly experimental philosophy', in
Justin Sytsma and Wesley Buckwalter (eds.), *A Companion to Experimental Philosophy*. Oxford: Wiley-Blackwell, 53–76.
Myhill, John. 1958: 'Problems arising in the formalization of intensional logic', *Logique et Analyse*, 1: 78–83.
Nagel, Jennifer. 2012. 'Intuitions and experiments: a defense of the case method in epistemology', *Philosophy and Phenomenological Research*, 85: 495–527.
Nagel, Jennifer. 2013: 'Knowledge as a mental state', *Oxford Studies in Epistemology*, 4: 273–306.
Nagel, Jennifer. 2014: *Knowledge: A Very Short Introduction*. Oxford: Oxford University Press.
Nagel, Jennifer. 2017: 'Factive and nonfactive mental state attribution', *Mind and Language*, 32: 525–544.
Nagel, Jennifer. In preparation: *Recognizing Knowledge: Intuitive and Reflective Epistemology*. Oxford: Oxford University Press.
Nair, Shyam. 2021: '"Adding up" reasons: lessons for reductive and nonreductive approaches', *Ethics*, 132: 38–88.
Nolan, Daniel. 1997: 'Impossible worlds: a modest approach', *Notre Dame Journal for Formal Logic*, 38: 535–572.

Nolan, Daniel. 2014: 'Hyperintensional metaphysics', *Philosophical Studies*, 171: 149–160.

Nouwen, Rick, Adrian Brasoveanu, Jan van Eijck, and Albert Visser. Fall 2022 edition: 'Dynamic semantics', *Stanford Encyclopedia of Philosophy*, Edward N. Zalta and Uri Nodelman (eds.). https://plato.stanford.edu/archives/fall2022/entries/dynamic-semantics/.

Paul, L. A., and Ned Hall. 2013: *Causation: A User's Guide*. Oxford: Oxford University Press.

Perner, Josef. 1993: *Understanding the Representational Mind*. Cambridge, MA: MIT Press.

Phillips, Jonathan, Wesley Buckwalter, Fiery Cushman, Ori Friedman, Alia Martin, John Turri, Laurie Santos, and Joshua Knobe. 2020: 'Knowledge before belief', *Behavioral and Brain Sciences*, 44: e140.

Pratt, Vaughan. 1976: 'Semantical considerations on Floyd-Hoare logic', *Proceedings of the 17th IEEE Symposium on Foundations of Computer Science*, Los Alamitos, CA: IEEE Computer Society, 109–121.

Priest, Graham. 1985: 'Inconsistencies in motion', *American Philosophical Quarterly*, 22: 339–346.

Putnam, Hilary. 1969: 'Is logic empirical?', *Boston Studies in the Philosophy of Science*, 5: 216–241.

Putnam, Hilary. 1975: *Mind, Language and Reality: Philosophical Papers*, vol. 2. Cambridge: Cambridge University Press.

Putnam, Hilary. 2012: 'The curious story of quantum logic', in Mario De Caro and David Macarthur (eds.), *Philosophy in an Age of Science: Physics, Mathematics, and Skepticism*. Cambridge, MA: Harvard University Press, 162–177.

Quine, Willard Van Orman. 1951: 'Two dogmas of empiricism', *Philosophical Review*, 60: 20–43.

Radford, Colin. 1969: 'Knowing and telling', *Philosophical Review*, 78: 326–336.

Rakoczy, Hannes, Delia Bergfeld, Ina Schwarz, and Ella Fizke. 2015: 'Explicit theory of mind is even more unified than previously assumed: belief ascription and understanding aspectuality emerge together in development', *Child Development*, 86: 486–502.

Ramsey, Frank. 1929: 'General propositions and causality'. MS. Reprinted in Hugh Mellor (ed.), *Foundations: Essays in Philosophy, Logic, Mathematics, and Economics*, to which page numbers refer. London: Routledge and Kegan Paul, 133–151

Rantala, Veikko.1982: 'Impossible world semantics and logical omniscience', *Acta Philosophica Fennica*, 35: 106–115.

Rayo, Agustín. 2013: *The Construction of Logical Space*. Oxford: Oxford University Press.

Recanati, François. 2012: *Mental Files*. Oxford: Oxford University Press.

Ripley, David. 2016: 'Experimental philosophical logic', in Justin Sytsma and Wesley Buckwalter (eds.), *A Companion to Experimental Philosophy*. Oxford: Wiley-Blackwell, 523–534.

Rothschild, Daniel. 2020: 'What it takes to believe', *Philosophical Studies*, 177: 1345–1362.

Rothschild, Daniel: 2023: 'Living in a material world: a critical notice of *Suppose and Tell: The Semantics and Heuristics of Conditionals* by Timothy Williamson', *Mind*, 132: 208–233.

Rubinstein, Ariel. 1989: 'The electronic mail game: strategic behaviour under "almost common knowledge"', *American Economic Review*, 79: 385–391.

Russell, Bertrand. 1903: *The Principles of Mathematics*. London: George Allen and Unwin.

Russell, Bertrand. 1910-11: 'Knowledge by acquaintance and knowledge by description', *Proceedings of the Aristotelian Society*, 11: 108–128.

Russell, Bertrand. 1918/1919: 'The philosophy of logical atomism', *The Monist*, 28: 495–527, 29: 32–63, 190–222, 345–380.

Russell, Bertrand. 1922: 'Introduction', in Ludwig Wittgenstein, *Tractatus Logico-Philosophicus* (trans. C. K. Ogden), ix–xxv. London: Routledge and Kegan Paul.

Russell, Gillian. 2018: 'Logical nihilism: Could there be no logic?', *Philosophical Issues*, 28: 308–324.

Salmón, Nathan. 1984: 'Impossible worlds', *Analysis*, 44: 114–117.

Salmón, Nathan. 1986: *Frege's Puzzle*. Cambridge, MA: MIT Press.

Salmón, Nathan. 1987/88: 'How to measure the standard metre', *Proceedings of the Aristotelian Society*, 88: 193–217.

Salmón, Nathan. 1989: 'The logic of what might have been', *Philosophical Review*, 98: 3–34.

Salmón, Nathan. 1993: 'This side of paradox', *Philosophical Topics*, 21: 187–197.

Saul, Jennifer. 1997: 'Substitution and simple sentences', *Analysis*, 57: 102–108.

Saul, Jennifer. 2010: *Simple Sentences, Substitution, and Intuitions*. Oxford: Oxford University Press.

Schnieder, Benjamin. 2011: 'A logic for "because"', *Review of Symbolic Logic*, 4: 445–465.

Schroeder, Mark. 2008: *Slaves of the Passions*. Oxford: Oxford University Press.

Schroeder, Mark. 2021: *Reasons First*. Oxford: Oxford University Press.

Shope, Robert. 1983: *The Analysis of Knowing: A Decade of Research*. Princeton, NJ: Princeton University Press.

Sider, Ted. 2016: 'On Williamson and simplicity in modal logic', *Canadian Journal of Philosophy*, 46: 683–698. Reprinted in Mark McCullagh and Juhani Yli-Vakkuri, (eds.). 2017: *Williamson on Modality*. London: Routledge, 231–246.

Sober, Elliott 1982: 'Why logically equivalent predicates may pick out different properties', *American Philosophical Quarterly*, 19: 183–189.

Stalnaker, Robert. 1968: 'A theory of conditionals', *American Philosophical Quarterly Monographs*, 2: 98–112.
Stalnaker, Robert. 1970: 'Probability and conditionals', *Philosophy of Science*, 37: 64–80.
Stalnaker, Robert. 1984: *Inquiry*. Cambridge, MA: MIT Press.
Stalnaker, Robert. 1999: *Context and Content*. Oxford: Oxford University Press.
Stalnaker, Robert. 2011: 'The metaphysical conception of analyticity', *Philosophy and Phenomenological Research*, 82: 507–514.
Strawson, Peter. 1971: *Logico-linguistic Papers*. London: Methuen.
Strawson, Peter. 1974: *Subject and Predicate in Logic and Grammar*. London: Methuen.
Szabó, Zoltán Gendler. 2000: *Problems of Compositionality*. New York: Garland.
Thomasson, Amie. 2015: *Ontology Made Easy*. New York: Oxford University Press.
Thomasson, Amie. 2020: *Norms and Necessity*. Oxford: Oxford University Press.
Titelbaum, Michael 2019: 'Reasons without reasons for', *Oxford Studies in Metaethics*, 13: 189–215.
Troquard, Nicolas, and Philippe Balbiani. Summer 2022 Edition: 'Propositional Dynamic Logic'. *Stanford Encyclopedia of Philosophy*, Edward N. Zalta (ed.). https://plato.stanford.edu/archives/sum2022/entries/logic-dynamic/.
Undorf, Monika, Sofia Navarro-Báez, and Malte Zimdahl. 2022: 'Metacognitive illusions', in Rüdiger Pohl (ed.), *Cognitive Illusions*, 3rd ed. London: Routledge, 307–323.
Vetter, Barbara. 2016: 'Williamsonian modal epistemology, possibility based', *Canadian Journal of Philosophy*, 46: 766–795, and in Mark McCullagh and Juhani Yli-Vakkuri, (eds.). 2017: *Williamson on Modality*. London: Routledge, 314–343.
Weatherson, Brian 2003: 'What good are counterexamples?', *Philosophical Studies*, 115: 1–31.
Weinberg, Jonathan, Shaun Nichols, and Stephen Stich. 2001: 'Normativity and epistemic intuitions', *Philosophical Topics*, 29: 429–460.
Weisberg, Michael. 2013: *Simulation and Similarity: Using Models to Understand the World*. Oxford: Oxford University Press.
Williamson, Timothy. 1990: *Identity and Discrimination*. Oxford: Blackwell. 2nd ed., Oxford: Wiley-Blackwell, 2013.
Williamson, Timothy. 1994: *Vagueness*. London: Routledge.
Williamson, Timothy. 1998: 'Indefinite extensibility', *Grazer Philosophische Studien*, 55: 1–24. Reprinted in Johannes Brandl and Peter Sullivan (eds.). 1999: *New Essays on the Philosophy of Michael Dummett*. Amsterdam: Rodopi, 1–24.

Williamson, Timothy. 2000: *Knowledge and Its Limits*. Oxford: Oxford University Press.

Williamson, Timothy. 2005: 'Contextualism, subject-sensitive invariantism and knowledge of knowledge', *Philosophical Quarterly*, 55: 213–235.

Williamson, Timothy. 2007: *The Philosophy of Philosophy*. Oxford: Wiley-Blackwell.

Williamson, Timothy. 2011a: 'Philosophical expertise and the burden of proof', *Metaphilosophy*, 42: 215–229. Reprinted in Timothy Williamson. 2021a: *The Philosophy of Philosophy*, 2nd ed. Oxford: Wiley -Blackwell, 413–430.

Williamson, Timothy. 2011b: 'Reply to Stalnaker', *Philosophy and Phenomenological Research*, 82: 515–523. Reprinted in Timothy Williamson. 2021a: *The Philosophy of Philosophy*, 2nd ed. Oxford: Wiley-Blackwell, 471–480.

Williamson, Timothy. 2011c: 'Three Wittgensteinians and a naturalist on *The Philosophy of Philosophy*', in R. Davies (ed.), *Analisi: Annuario e Bollettino della Società Italiana Analitica (SIFA) 2011*, 127–137. Milan: Mimesis. Reprinted in Timothy Williamson. 2021a: *The Philosophy of Philosophy*, 2nd ed. Oxford: Wiley-Blackwell, 481–483, 553–562.

Williamson, Timothy. 2013a: *Modal Logic as Metaphysics*. Oxford: Oxford University Press.

Williamson, Timothy. 2013b: 'Gettier cases in epistemic logic', *Inquiry*, 56: 1–14.

Williamson, Timothy. 2014a: 'Logic, metalogic and neutrality', *Erkenntnis*, 79: 211–231.

Williamson, Timothy. 2014b: 'Very improbable knowing', *Erkenntnis*, 79: 971–999.

Williamson, Timothy. 2014c: 'How did we get here from there? The transformation of analytic philosophy', *Belgrade Philosophical Annual*, 27: 7–37. Reprinted in Timothy Williamson. 2021a: *The Philosophy of Philosoph*, 2nd ed. Oxford: Wiley-Blackwell, 313–350.

Williamson, Timothy. 2015: 'A note on Gettier cases in epistemic logic', *Philosophical Studies*, 172: 129–140.

Williamson, Timothy. 2016a: 'Modal science', *Canadian Journal of Philosophy*, 46: 453–492. Reprinted in Mark McCullagh and Juhani Yli-Vakkuri, (eds.). 2017: *Williamson on Modality*. London: Routledge, 1–40.

Williamson, Timothy. 2016b: 'Reply to Sider', *Canadian Journal of Philosophy*, 46: 699–708. Reprinted in Mark McCullagh and Juhani Yli-Vakkuri, (eds.). 2017: *Williamson on Modality*. London: Routledge, 247–256.

Williamson, Timothy. 2016c: 'Abductive philosophy', *Philosophical Forum*, 47: 263–280. Reprinted in Timothy Williamson. 2021a: *The Philosophy of Philosophy*, 2nd ed. Oxford: Wiley-Blackwell, 351–371.

Williamson, Timothy. 2016d: 'Philosophical criticisms of experimental philosophy', in Justin Sytsma and Wesley Buckwalter (eds.), *A Companion to*

Experimental Philosophy. Oxford: Wiley-Blackwell, 22–36. Reprinted in Timothy Williamson. 2021a: *The Philosophy of Philosophy*, 2nd ed. Oxford: Wiley-Blackwell, 440–463.

Williamson, Timothy. 2016e: 'Knowing by imagining', in Amy Kind and Peter Kung (eds.), *Knowledge through Imagination*, 113–123. Oxford: Oxford University Press. Reprinted in Paul Boghossian and Timothy Williamson. 2020: *Debating the A Priori*. Oxford: Oxford University Press, 175–185.

Williamson, Timothy. 2017a: 'Model-building in philosophy', in Russell Blackford and Damien Broderick (eds.), *Philosophy's Future: The Problem of Philosophical Progress*, 159–173. Oxford: Blackwell-Wiley. Reprinted in Timothy Williamson. 2021a: *The Philosophy of Philosophy*, 2nd ed. Oxford: Wiley-Blackwell, 372–385.

Williamson, Timothy. 2017b: 'Semantic paradoxes and abductive methodology', in Bradley Armour-Garb (ed.), *The Relevance of the Liar*. Oxford: Oxford University Press, 325–346.

Williamson, Timothy. 2017c: 'Counterpossibles in semantics and metaphysics', *Argumenta*, 4. https://www.argumenta.org/wp-content/uploads/2017/06/2-Argumenta-22-Timothy-Williamson-Counterpossibles-in-Semantics-and-Metaphysics.pdf.

Williamson, Timothy. 2018a: 'Alternative logics and applied mathematics', *Philosophical Issues*, 28: 399–424.

Williamson, Timothy. 2018b: 'Counterpossibles', *Topoi*, 37: 357–368.

Williamson, Timothy. 2020: *Suppose and Tell: The Semantics and Heuristics of Conditionals*. Oxford: Oxford University Press.

Williamson, Timothy. 2021a: *The Philosophy of Philosophy*, 2nd ed. Oxford: Wiley-Blackwell.

Williamson, Timothy. 2021b: 'Epistemological consequences of Frege puzzles', *Philosophical Topics*, 49: 287–319.

Williamson, Timothy. 2021c: 'Degrees of freedom: is good philosophy bad science?', *Disputatio*, 13: 73–94.

Williamson, Timothy. 2021d: 'The KK principle and rotational symmetry', *Analytic Philosophy*, 62: 107–124.

Williamson, Timothy. 2022: 'Metametaphysics and semantics', *Metaphilosophy*, 53: 162–175.

Williamson, Timothy. 2023a: 'Moral Anti-Exceptionalism', in Paul Bloomfield and David Copp (eds.), *The Oxford Handbook of Moral Realism*. Oxford: Oxford University Press, 554–576.

Williamson, Timothy. 2023b: 'Higher-order metaphysics and small differences', *Analysis Reviews*, 83: 213–224.

Williamson, Timothy. 2024: 'Menzel on pure logic and higher-order metaphysics' in Peter Fritz and Nicholas Jones. 2023: *Higher-Order Metaphysics*. Oxford: Oxford University Press, 460–471.

Williamson, Timothy. Forthcoming-a: 'Justifications, excuses, and sceptical scenarios', in Fabian Dorsch and Julien Dutant (eds.), *The New Evil Demon: New Essays on Knowledge, Justification, and Rationality*. Oxford: Oxford University Press.

Williamson, Timothy. Forthcoming-b: 'Where did it come from? Where will it go?', in Arturs Logins and Jacques Vollet (eds.), *Putting Knowledge to Work: New Directions for Knowledge-First Epistemology*. Oxford: Oxford University Press.

Williamson, Timothy. Forthcoming-c: 'Disagreement in Metaphysics', in Maria Baghramian, J. Adam Carter, and Richard Rowland (eds.): *Routledge Handbook of the Philosophy of Disagreement*. London: Routledge.

Williamson, Timothy. Forthcoming-d: 'Is Logic about Validity?', in Elke Brendel, Massimiliano Carrara, Filippo Ferrari, Ole Hjortland, Gil Sagi, Gila Sher, and Florian Steinberger (eds.), *The Oxford Handbook of the Philosophy of Logic*. Oxford: Oxford University Press.

Williamson, Timothy. Forthcoming-e: 'Knowledge, credence, and strength of belief', in A. K. Flowerree and Baron Reed (eds.), *Expansive Epistemology: Norms, Action, and the Social World*, London: Routledge.

Wright, Crispin. 1976: 'Language-mastery and the sorites paradox', in Gareth Evans and John McDowell (eds.), *Truth and Meaning: Essays in Semantics*. Oxford: Clarendon Press, 223–247.

Yablo, Stephen. 2014: *Aboutness*. Princeton, NJ: Princeton University Press.

Yli-Vakkuri, Juhani, and John Hawthorne. 2018: *Narrow Content*. Oxford: Oxford University Press.

https://plato.stanford.edu/archives/fall2022/entries
https://plato.stanford.edu/archives/sum2022/entries/logic-dynamic/.

Index

For the benefit of digital users, indexed terms that span two pages (e.g., 52–53) may, on occasion, appear on only one of those pages.

a posteriori, 64, 71–72, 177–78, 179, 180, 181
a priori, xx, 64–65, 71–72, 177–79, 180, 181, 242
abduction, ix–xi, xxiii, 91, 93–94, 104, 231–32
  see also inference to the best explanation
Alexander, J., 51–52
analysis, paradox of, 64–65
analysis, philosophical, ix, 63–73, 82, 97–98, 195, 236
analyticity, xviii–xix, 1, 5, 15, 46–47, 66–67, 85, 184, 230–31, 233
  see also conceptual connections; conceptual possibility; conceptual truth
Anderson, A.R., 89
Andjelković, M., 38
animals, 2, 3–4, 10, 33, 69–70, 97–98, 169, 186–87, 192–94
Aristotle, 29, 155–56
Armstrong, D.M., 129–30
artificial intelligence, 2, 10, 62, 97–98

Bacon, A., 144–45, 235
Barcan Marcus, R., 117–18
Bayesianism, 98, 159–60, 219, 222, 228–29
belief, 6, 11, 12, 32–34, 39, 43, 45–47, 48, 99–100, 114, 159, 160, 161, 163–64, 168–69, 171–72, 174–76, 182–88, 189–91, 192–95, 197–99, 200, 202, 203, 205, 206, 211, 213, 219–20, 223–24, 226–27, 230–31, 248, 249–50
belief ascription, heuristics for, 185–88, 189–90, 211–12
  see also DP, SDP, non-reticence heuristic; sincerity heuristic; mindreading
belief ascription, paradoxes of, 34, 174–75, 182–84
Belnap, N., 89
Berto, F., 118–19, 124, 128–29
betting heuristic, 211–12, 213–14, 221–22
bivalent semantics, CPP12 15, 88, 132
Bobzien, S., 87
Boghossian, P., 181
Branquinho, J., 168–69
Brast-McKie, B., 153
Braun, D., 213
Brogaard, B., 128–29
Burgess, J., 89

Callimachus, 22
Cantor, G., 61, 136, 137
Cappelen, H., 82, 165, 249
Carnap, R., 75–77, 79, 143, 230–31
Cassirer, E., 91–92
ceteris paribus laws, 96
Chalmers, D., 180–81, 213

Charles, D., 155–56
charity in interpretation, 1, 17, 49, 69, 151, 171, 191, 231–32
children, 33, 42, 69–70, 126–27, 186–87, 192, 193, 194, 195–96, 199, 200
Clark, A., 10
cognitive difference, 160, 251–52
cognitive significance, xxi–xxii, 113–14, 116–17, 118–19, 248–50, 251, 253, 255
common belief, 223, 224
common knowledge, 102–3, 201–2, 219–20, 222, 223, 224
communication, xvii, 24, 165–66, 174, 177, 190, 191–92, 195–96, 200, 251
see also testimony
composition of operators, 139–40
compositionality, semantic, 73, 74–75, 76–77, 80–81, 106–7, 110–11, 113–14, 121–25, 130, 132, 133, 157–58, 165, 167–69, 174–75, 234–35, 247, 253
computational constraints, 6–7, 65, 82–83, 94–96, 97, 99–100, 117–18, 198, 216, 222
conceptual connections, xviii–xix, 5, 15, 34, 46–47, 63, 64–65, 66–68, 230–33
conceptual possibility, 67–68
conceptual truth, xii, 1, 12
see also analyticity
conditional proof, 21, 22–23
conditionals, xii, 16–27, 43, 47–48, 53, 54–55, 84, 119–20, 121, 122–23, 126–27, 137, 245–46
see also counterfactuals; counterpossibles; modus ponens
conspiracy theories, 61
content, narrow, 180, 195
context, xviii, 24, 26–27, 28, 29, 30, 32–33, 35, 36, 37, 38, 48–50, 53, 66–67, 79–81, 82, 83–84, 120, 133, 134, 146–47, 149–50, 154, 156–57, 161–62, 164–65, 166, 167, 168–71, 173, 179, 183–84, 185, 191–92, 202–3, 233, 249–50, 251
conversational implicature, 158, 169–71, 186
convexity, 47–48
counterfactuals, xii, 11, 28, 53, 63, 68, 97–98, 119–21, 123, 124–26, 128–29, 134, 145, 242, 243
counterpart theory, 112–13
counterpossibles, xiii–xv, 119–20, 125–29, 145–46
credence, 198, 211–12, 213–14, 216, 217, 218–22
see also subjective probability
Crenshaw, K., 10
Crimmins, M., 168–69, 190–91

data, x–xii, xviii, 1–2, 9–10, 49, 50, 52, 54–57, 58–60, 61–62, 63, 74, 81–82, 84–87, 91–94, 96–97, 103–4, 111, 118, 125–26, 145, 158, 159, 171, 185–86, 191, 202–3
see also evidence
Davidson, D., xix–xx, 115–16
Davis, W., 63
decision theory, 4–5, 39–40, 98, 218–19, 222, 228–29
deference, semantic, 171–72, 244–46
definition, ix, 5–6, 46, 71–72, 137–41, 144, 179, 184, 212–13, 217, 254–55
degenerating research programmes, ix–x, 64
degrees of freedom, x–xi, xviii, 58–59, 60–62, 67, 72–74, 77, 79, 81, 94–95, 100–2, 103, 111, 123–24, 126, 132, 134, 158, 165, 216
demonstratives, 9, 11, 49–50, 79–80, 186–87, 195–96, 207–8, 227, 251

Descartes, R., 165
Dever, J., 165, 249
dialetheist logic, 91–92, 231–32
direct reference, 116, 162–63, 178–79, 180, 209–10
disquotational heuristics, xix, 28, 31, 32, 34, 36, 37–39, 45–46, 54–55, 165, 181–82, 185–86
Dorr, C., 14, 128–29, 136, 141, 144–45, 152
doubt, 16, 91–92, 161, 176, 197, 204–5, 207, 226–27, 251–52
Douven, I., 17, 47–48
doxastic logic, xxi–xxii, 71–72, 98, 99–100, 114, 118–19, 159–60, 222, 223–24, 225, 228–29
DP (principle of belief ascription), 181–83, 184–88, 189–90, 211–12
Duhem, P., 52
Dummett, M., ix–x, xix–xx
dynamic logic, 78–79
dynamic semantics, 83–84

economics, 61, 78–79, 117–18, 201, 212, 217, 218–19, 220–21, 222
  see also welfare economics
Edgington, D., 119–20
efficiency, 199
Eklund, M., 15
Elbourne, P., 238–39
Ellis, B., 20
empiricism, 66, 91–92, 230–31, 233, 236
epicycles, 64
epistemic logic, xxi–xxii, 98, 99–100, 101, 102–3, 114, 118–19, 159–60, 201–2, 222–24, 225, 228–29
epistemic modality, 86, 101, 102–3, 119–20, 166, 179–80, 181, 209–10, 211, 212–15, 223–24, 235

epistemic probability, 166, 211, 212–15, 222
  see also probability
error theory, 171
error-fragility, 51–52, 53, 55–57
Escher, M.C., xix
essences, xx–xxi, 106–7, 114, 117, 155–56
Evans, J., 17
evidence, x, 12, 34, 45, 55, 56, 61, 85–87, 145, 203–10, 211, 231–32
  see also data
excluded middle, law of, 86–87, 90–91
experimental philosophy, xii–xiii, xvii, 43–44, 54, 160–61
explanation, ix–x, xiii–xv, xx–xxii, 39, 61, 69, 87, 97–98, 104, 108, 110, 111, 123–24, 126, 145–50, 151–56, 158, 169, 177, 192–93, 214–15, 216, 221, 222, 225–26, 227, 228, 229, 240
extensionality, xxiii, 74–76, 105–6, 109, 110–14, 141, 154–55
externalism, 192

falsificationism, 1–4, 6
falsity, principles of, xix, 6–7, 29–30, 34, 35–37, 38, 43, 48, 54–55, 88, 129–30, 134, 238–39
Fine, K., xx–xxi, 105, 106, 117–18, 129–30, 131–32, 133–34, 152, 153, 155–56
Fodor, J., 66–67
Forbes, G., 207–8
Forster, M., x–xi, 59, 60–61
four-valued logic, 88
freedom, see degrees of freedom
Frege, G., 32–33, 105, 113–14, 161–62, 174, 248–49
Fregean semantics, xxi–xxii, 32–33, 113–14, 116, 135, 161–66, 168–69, 173–76, 177, 180–81, 207–8, 211–12, 213–14, 248–50

French, R., 128–29
Fritz, P., 137

game theory, 98, 201, 219–20, 222, 223, 224, 228–29
Gärdenfors, P., 47–48
generics, 16, 19
geometry, 251
Gettier cases, 68–69, 71–72, 193
Gigerenzer, G., 3–5
Goodman, J., 136, 168–69, 171
Goodsell, T., 208
Goodsell, Z., 235
Gordon, R., 198–99
Grice, H.P., 63, 158, 169–70
grounding, 105, 115–16, 137, 158
grounding, paradoxes of, 137
guises, xxi–xxii, xxiv, 32–33, 48, 168–69, 186–87, 191–92, 200, 203–4, 205, 206, 207, 208–10, 211, 213–14, 217–19, 220–22, 223–25, 227–28, 249–52, 253, 254–55
see also modes of presentation

Hall, N., 63
Hawthorne, J., 14, 42, 82, 144–45, 181, 201, 208, 252
Heap, paradox, 14, 133
see also sorites paradoxes
Hegel, G., 91
Heraclitus, 53–54
heuristics, ix, 1–7, 11–16, 17–27, 28, 30–34, 36, 38–39, 41–48, 49–50, 54–55, 56–57, 61–62, 66–67, 68–69, 84, 92, 104, 111, 125–29, 145, 150, 151, 152, 153–54, 158, 159, 160–61, 185–92, 193–94, 202–3, 211–12, 219–20, 221–22, 226–27, 229
see also belief ascription, heuristics for; betting heuristic; disquotational heuristics; 'Just ask' heuristic; language-sensitive heuristics; non-reticence heuristic; open world heuristic; persistence heuristic; shared world default; sincerity heuristic; suppositional heuristic; take-the-best heuristic; weighing heuristic; 'Why' heuristic
Hintikka, J., 99–100, 118–19, 222
Hirsch, E., 236–37
Hodes, H., 137
Holguín, B., 185–86
Holliday, W., 86
Hume, D., 63, 230–31
hyperintensionality, xx–xxii, xxiii, 105–58, 159–61, 239, 243, 255

idealism, 114, 233
illusions, metacognitive, 150, 152, 153–54, 156, 159
illusions, perceptual, xix, 3–4, 6, 24, 44–45
imagination, xvii, 12, 14, 18, 26–27, 190–91, 251
impossible worlds semantics, xiii–xiv, xxiii, 56–57, 105–6, 109–10, 111–12, 118–20, 121–26, 128–29, 130, 134–35, 159, 216, 239, 243
indiscriminability, 14, 223–24
inference to the best explanation, ix–x, 87
see also abduction
intensional structures, 143–44
intensionality, xxi–xxii, xxiii, 74, 76–77, 79, 80–81, 105–14, 115–19, 120, 121, 125–26, 128–29, 131, 134, 144–45, 151, 152, 158, 159–60, 215–16, 233–39, 241, 242, 243–44, 246–47, 249, 250, 251, 252–53, 254, 255
intentionality, 159, 219–20, 221–22, 228
internalism, 45, 69–71, 195, 229

INDEX 275

intersectionality, 42
introspection, negative, 102–3
introspection, positive, 101–3
intuitionistic logic, 87–88, 89–90, 91–92

Jackson, F., 66–67
Jago, M., 118–19, 124
Jeffrey, R., 20
'Just ask' heuristic, 188, 189–90
justified true belief account of knowledge (JTB), 53, 68–72, 87–88, 97–98

Kagan, S., 40
Kahneman, D., 3, 4–5
Kant, I., 249
Kaplan, D., 80–81, 117–18, 162–63, 180, 207
Kim, J., 115–16
Kitcher, P., 158
Kment, B., 137
Knobe, J., 54, 192–93
knowledge ascription, 34, 68–70, 160, 161, 188, 190–91, 192–202, 219–20, 223–24, 226–27
 see also open world heuristic; shared world default; mindreading
Kornblith, H., 4–5, 69–70
Kratzer, A., 79
Kripke, S., xix–xx, xxiii–xxiv, 32–33, 71–72, 74–75, 76–79, 80–81, 87–88, 89–90, 105, 106, 109–10, 111–12, 117–19, 162–63, 166–67, 177–80, 181–82, 183–86, 188, 190, 207, 209–10, 211–12, 229, 236–37, 240–41, 242, 248, 251
Kuhn, T., 52, 81

Lakatos, I., ix–x, 64
Langford, C., 64–65

language-sensitive heuristics, 188–89, 190–91, 211–12
Lasersohn, P., 82
Lederman, H., 168–69, 171, 201
Leibniz, G., 75–76, 112–13
Leibniz's law, 29, 128–29
Lewis, D., xvii, 20–21, 53, 63, 112–13, 117–18, 120, 121, 143, 236–37, 249
Liar paradox, xix, 34, 88, 133
 see also semantic paradoxes
linguistic turn, 15, 118
Lipton, P., ix–x
logic, ix–x, xxiii, 15, 22, 23, 29, 30, 35, 36, 38–39, 43, 52–53, 74–75, 79, 84–94, 98, 110, 125, 129, 134, 216, 231–32, 234–35, 237, 243, 249–50, 251, 253, 254, 255
 see also dialetheist logic; doxastic logic; dynamic logic; epistemic logic; four-valued logic; intuitionistic logic; many-valued logic; modal logic; paraconsistent logic; politeness logic; quantum logic; relevance logic; three-valued logic; excluded middle, law of
logical empiricism, 230–31, 233
logical form, 73–74, 135, 192
logical positivism, 75–76, 118, 230–31, 236
logical omniscience, see omniscience, logical
logical truth, 74–75, 91
Lombrozo, T., 148

MacFarlane, J., 82
Magidor, O., 42, 165, 201, 249
Mahtani, A., 212–13, 216–17, 220–21
Mandelkern, M., 86
many-valued logic, 88, 89–90
maps, see mental maps
Marconi, D., 236–37

Mares, E., 89
material implication, paradoxes of, xviii, 22
Mates, B., 22
mathematics, ix, 23–24, 25, 52–53, 90–91, 96, 112–13, 121–22, 231–32, 237, 243, 249–50, 251–52, 253, 255
memory, 8–9, 10–11, 24, 42, 48–50, 177, 189–90, 197, 199, 227, 228
mental files, 207–8, 210
mental maps, 34, 198–99
Menzel, C., 144
mereology, 98, 130, 131
Merleau-Ponty, M., 199
metalinguistic negation, 171
metaphysics, xix–xxi, xxiv, 11–12, 61, 67–68, 77–78, 79, 91, 98, 105–7, 110, 112–13, 114–20, 128–29, 133, 140, 142, 145–46, 149, 153–54, 158, 159, 169, 230–31, 233–41, 242–43, 246–48, 249–50, 251, 253–55
metaphysical modality, xiii, 14, 67–68, 106, 111–12, 119, 127–28, 209–10, 235
metasemantics, 14, 46–48, 90–91, 240–41
mindreading, 33, 184–85, 188, 192, 195, 198–99, 200, 219–20, 229
see also belief ascription, heuristics for; knowledge ascription
modal logic, xiii–xiv, xix–xx, 74, 75, 76–79, 87, 112–13, 117–18
modal realism, 112–13
model-building, xxiii, 10, 40–41, 42, 49, 58–59, 60–62, 71–74, 79, 94–103, 123–24, 126, 132, 159–60, 196–97, 209–10, 214–15, 216, 224–25, 228–29, 239, 253
modes of presentation, 32–33, 163–64, 165–66, 212–13, 248–49
see also guises

modus ponens, 21, 22–23
Moore paradoxes, 190–91
Mortensen, K., 54
Myhill, J., 136
see also Russell-Myhill paradox

Nagel, J., 43–44, 54, 69–70, 188, 192–93, 194
Nair, S., 40
negative facts, 133
Nichols, S., 43–44
Nolan, D., 105, 128–29
non-reticence heuristic, 30–31, 32, 33, 185–86

objective modality, 235
objective probability, 45–46, 217
see also probability
offline/online processing, xvii, 12, 17–18, 190
omniscience, logical, 99–100, 101–2, 114, 118–19, 215–16, 222, 223–25, 228–29, 235–36, 252
open world heuristic, 226–27
ordinary language, 63, 105, 118
Over, D., 17
overfitting, ix, 59–61, 62, 64, 66–68, 69, 72–73, 74, 81–85, 87, 91–95, 96–97, 100–1, 103, 104, 111, 118, 125–26, 134, 144–45, 158, 159, 191, 216–24

paraconsistent logic, 110
paradoxes, xix, 6, 23
see also analysis, paradox of; belief ascription, paradoxes of; grounding, paradoxes of; Heap paradox; Liar paradox; material implication, paradoxes of; Moore paradoxes; Russell-Myhill paradox; Russell's paradox; semantic paradoxes; sorites paradoxes

past-tense updating, 9, 10
Paul, L., 63
Perner, J., 192
Perry, J., 168–69
perception, xv, 6, 10, 11, 12, 42, 44, 45, 51, 70–71, 101–2, 195–96, 197, 198, 199, 207–8, 221–22, 225, 227
see also illusions, perceptual, *and* seeing
persistence heuristic, 11–16, 22, 28, 47–48, 54–55, 193–94
Plantinga, A., 117–18
Plato, ix, 29
politeness logic, 89
Popper, K., ix–x, 1, 51
possible worlds semantics, xiii, 74, 75–78, 100, 105–6, 112–13, 122–23, 126–27, 208–9, 215–16, 222, 233, 234–37, 243
Pratt, V., 78–79
predictive processing, 10
present-tense updating, 9–11
Priest, Graham, 91, 119–20, 128–29, 231–32
probability, xvii, 20, 21–22, 24, 25–27, 33, 40–42, 95, 126–27, 211, 212–17, 219–20, 222, 228–29
see also epistemic probability; objective probability; subjective probability
proof, 22–24, 90–91, 93–94
properties, xx–xxii, 108–9, 115–16, 129–30, 135, 137, 142, 153, 154–55, 163–64, 213, 233, 240, 246–47, 249–50, 253–54
propositional attitudes, xxi–xxii, xxiii–xxiv, 32–33, 54–55, 58, 60–61, 69, 160–62, 165, 182, 188, 191, 196, 207, 251
propositions, xxi–xxii, xxiii, 14, 26–27, 37, 48, 56, 66, 71–72, 80–81, 91, 107–8, 116–17, 129–30, 132, 133–37, 138, 139–40, 141–46, 147–48, 153–54, 159, 161–64, 168–70, 188, 191–92, 203–5, 206, 207, 208–9, 213–14, 215–16, 220–21, 223–24, 233, 234, 235–36, 240–41, 242, 243, 246–47, 248, 249–50, 251–55
prospect, personal, 212, 217–18
PT, *see* translation, principle of
Putnam, H., 85

quantum logic, 85, 86–87
Quine, W.V., 66–67, 77–78, 105, 112–13

Ramsey, F., xvii, 16
Rantala, V., 100, 118–19
rationalism, 91–92
rationality, 3, 24, 100, 114, 182–83, 188, 201, 203, 211, 213–14, 215, 216, 218–19, 222, 223–24, 228–29, 247
Rayo, A., 236–37
reasons, 39–42, 48
Recanati, F., 207–8
recognitional capacities, 169, 171–72, 176, 244–46
relations, xx, 115–16, 118, 135, 137, 233, 240, 249, 253–54
relativism, 82
relevance logic, 89, 93–94
reliability, xii–xiii, xv, 3, 4–7, 14, 43–44, 45–46, 47–48, 49–50, 55, 56–57, 61–62, 70–71, 92, 111, 125–26, 127–28, 150, 151, 160–61, 176, 181, 185, 187, 188, 189–90, 191, 202–3
representations, xxi–xxii, 114, 145, 149–50, 159, 198, 218–19, 250–51
Ripley, D., 87, 128–29
Rothschild, D., 4–5, 24, 186–87
Rubinstein, A., 201

Russell, B., 66, 133, 135, 137, 254–55
Russell, G., 91
Russell-Myhill paradox, xxi–xxii, 136–37, 141, 144–45, 246–47
Russell's paradox, xv, 133, 137, 231–32
Russellian propositions, xxi–xxii, xxiii, 116–17, 135, 136, 144–45, 240–43, 246–47, 249, 250, 251

safety from error, 44, 125–26, 201–2
Salerno, J., 128–29
Salmón, N.,C1P46, 116, 118–19, 168–70, 179, 205, 235, 250
Saul, J., 171
scepticism, xii–xiii, xxii, 2, 9–10, 44, 66–67, 69, 82–83, 85, 101–2, 160, 195–96
Schnieder, B., 107, 151–52
Schroeder, M., 39, 40
SDP (principle of belief ascription), 182, 183, 184–87, 188, 189–90, 211–12
seeing, 11, 186–87, 189–90, 193–94, 195–97, 198, 199, 200, 208–9
semantic paradoxes, xix, 34, 35, 36, 37, 38–39, 86–87, 88, 133
semantics, ix–x, xiii–xiv, xvii, 6–49, 53, 54–55, 66–67, 73–74, 76–78, 79–84, 86–88, 89–91, 94, 96–97, 98, 105–7, 108, 109–14, 117–25, 126, 128–33, 134–35, 136, 142, 151, 152, 157–58, 159, 160–63, 164–66, 167–70, 171–72, 174–75, 177, 178, 179, 180, 185, 191, 202–3, 209–10, 214–15, 216, 222, 229, 230, 233–37, 238–39, 240–41, 242–50, 253
    see also bivalent semantics; dynamic semantics; Fregean semantics; impossible worlds semantics; possible worlds semantics; situation semantics; truthmaker semantics; two-dimensional semantics; direct reference; metasemantics
shared world default, 199–201, 219–20
Shope, R., 63
Sider, T., 61
simplicity, x, 6, 20–21, 50, 53, 60–62, 68–69, 75–77, 82–83, 84, 86, 93–94, 97–98, 103, 104, 123–24, 132, 144–45, 148, 151–52, 153, 159–60, 169–70, 185–86, 191, 202, 220, 231–32, 234, 236–37
simplification, 71–72, 94–95, 98–100, 101, 210, 214–15, 225, 228–29
sincerity heuristic, 30–32, 33, 37–38, 185–86
situation semantics, 238–39
Sober, E., x–xi, xx, 59, 60–61, 108–9, 115, 154
sorites paradoxes, xviii–xix, 14–15, 47–48, 54–55, 88, 133
Spectre, L., 185–86
Stalnaker, R., xxi–xxii, 20, 53, 100, 117–18, 120, 121, 236–37, 241, 244, 248
Stich, S., 43–44
Strawson, P.F., 207–8
strength, x, 86, 91, 93–94, 103, 104, 132, 163, 231–32
subject-matter, 131, 134, 153
subjective probability, 166, 211, 212–13, 214–16, 217–19, 222, 228–29
    see also credence; probability
supervenience, xx, 46–47, 110, 115–16, 249–50
suppositional heuristic, xvii, 16–20, 22–24, 25, 26–27, 47–48, 49, 54–55, 84, 125–27, 128–29, 145

symmetry-breaking, 101–2
Szabó, Z., 122

take-the-best heuristic, 4–5
testimony, 12, 24, 40, 41–42, 48, 49–50, 91–92, 177
　see also communication
Thomasson, A., 230–31
thought experiments, 53–57, 62, 72, 74
three-valued logic, 88
Titelbaum, M., 40
tolerance principles, xviii–xix, 14–15, 49
translation, principle of, 182, 183–84
transparency, epistemic, xviii, 24, 203–5, 206, 207, 208, 209, 210, 211, 218, 251, 255
truth, principles of, xix, 29, 34, 37, 43, 45–46, 48, 54–55, 88, 107–8, 129–30, 134, 145–46, 182
truthmaker semantics, xxiii, 105–6, 109–10, 129–35, 152, 243

Tversky, A., 3, 4–5
two-dimensional semantics, 180

vagueness, ix–x, xviii–xix, 9, 13–15, 43, 48, 54–55, 86–87, 88, 90–91, 92
　see also Heap paradox; sorites paradoxes; tolerance principles
Vetter, B., 119–20

Weatherson, B., 68–69
weighing heuristic, 39–42
Weinberg, J., 43–44, 51–52
Weisberg, M., 94, 96, 97
welfare economics, 212–13, 214–15, 217–19, 220–21, 222
　see also economics
'Why' heuristic, 146–51, 152–56, 158
Wittgenstein, L., 236–37
Wright, C., 14

Yablo, S., 133
Yli-Vakkuri, J., 40–41, 144–45, 181, 208, 235, 252

www.ingramcontent.com/pod-product-compliance
Ingram Content Group UK Ltd.
Pitfield, Milton Keynes, MK11 3LW, UK
UKHW022120060226
467760UK00005B/21